PRINCIPLES OF PUBLIC POLICY PRACTICE

ABOUT THE AUTHOR

Professor Lok Sang Ho, Director of the Center for Public Policy Studies and Professor of Economics, Lingnan University, has a long-standing interest in public policy. With a doctorate in economics from the University of Toronto, he started his career of policy research in the Ontario Ministry of Treasury and Economics as Economist and then as Research Officer at the Ontario Economic Council. Prior to his appointment at Lingnan University in 1995, Professor Ho was Senior Lecturer at the Chinese University of Hong Kong. Professor Ho remains affiliated with the Chinese University as an Honorary Research Fellow.

He has sat in a number of government and public advisory bodies. The list includes the Central Policy Unit of the Hong Kong Special Administrative Region Government, the Pacific Economic Cooperation Council Hong Kong Committee, the Trade Policy Forum, and the committee of advisors for the Hong Kong Institute of Monetary Research of the Hong Kong Monetary Authority. Professor Ho has been President of Hong Kong Economic Council since 1999 and Managing Editor of the Pacific Economic Review since 1996.

PRINCIPLES OF PUBLIC POLICY PRACTICE

by

Lok Sang Ho

Center for Public Policy Studies
Lingnan University, Hong Kong

Foreword by Yew-Kwang Ng

SPRINGER SCIENCE+BUSINESS MEDIA, LLC

Library of Congress Cataloging-in-Publication Data
Ho, Lok-sang.
Principles of public policy practice / by Lok Sang Ho; foreword by Yew-Kwang Ng.
p.cm.
Includes bibliographical references (p.) and index.
ISBN 978-1-4613-5622-6 ISBN 978-1-4615-1575-3 (eBook)
DOI 10.1007/978-1-4615-1575-3
1. Public adminstrataion--Philosophy. 2. Economic Policy--Philosophy. 3. Risk management.

JF1351.H59 2001
320'.6'01--dc21 00-048692

Originally published by Kluwer Academic Publishers in 2001
Softcover reprint of the hardcover 1st edition 2001

Printed on acid-free paper.

To Alvin, Emily, and Irene

Would I be wise;
Would the World learn.

CONTENTS

Foreword		ix
Preface		xv
Acknowledgments		xvii
Chapter 1	Introduction	1
Part 1	The Theory of Public Policy Design	7
Chapter 2	What Makes Good Public Policy	9
Chapter 3	Human Nature and Public Policy	19
Chapter 4	Institutional Foundations for a Just Society	37
Part 2	Microeconomic Risk Management	57
Chapter 5	Health Care Delivery and Financing: In Search of an Ideal Model	59
Chapter 6	Legal Aid and Justice	71
Chapter 7	Bank Deposit Insurance	77
Chapter 8	Towards an Optimal Public Pension Scheme	87
Part 3	Macroeconomic Risk Management	99
Chapter 9	The Risks of Monetary Crises: Inflation	101
Chapter 10	The Risks of Monetary Crises: Currency Crises and Interest Rate Gyrations	109
Chapter 11	Savings Instruments, Bubbles, and Financial Crises	117
Chapter 12	Transparency	129
Part 4	Resource Allocation and Redistribution	133
Chapter 13	Optimal Size of the Government	135
Chapter 14	Education Policy	143
Chapter 15	Housing (with a Digression on Transportation Pricing)	153
Chapter 16	Social Safety Net and Redistribution	163
Part 5	Public Policy and Economic Ecology	171
Chapter 17	Economic Ecology: The Case of the Great Depression of the Nineteen Thirties	173
Chapter 18	Economic Ecology: The Case of Hong Kong	183

Epilogue 199
Chapter 19 Public Policy in the New Millennium 201

References 211
Index 219

FOREWORD

It is a pleasure to read this well-written book and an honor to write the foreword.

The breadth of coverage of this book is phenomenal. Apart from the general principles of public policy design discussed in Part I, it covers the microeconomic problems like education, health care, housing, legal aid, and social security as well as the macroeconomic problems like inflation, exchange rates, and financial crises. It also ranges from the efficiency issues to the distributive issues. I admire Professor Ho's ability to tackle such a wide range of issues. Also, I am more confident dealing with the ultimate principles for public policy in general. Practical issues are more diverse and involve many aspects with conflicting considerations. Thus, we have the joke about the government's dislike for economists with two hands. This consideration makes me admire even more the ability and courage of Ho. Moreover, while I expect few readers to have complete agreement with Ho on all issues discussed in this book, I am confident that most readers will find, as I have, many enlightening discussions and thought-provoking ideas. Thus, I have no hesitation in recommending this book to readers.

I find some of the proposals courageous, even provocative, and perhaps outrageous to some. For example, many readers may find the suggestion of corporal punishment of criminals (Ch. 4) barbaric. I strongly suggest that such readers should carefully consider the arguments put forth by Ho. Personally, I sympathize with such readers. The very mental image of corporal punishment may be disgusting. It would be much better if more 'civilized' methods like imprisonment may achieve the same purpose without even more undesirable effects. Corporal punishment may also be counter-productive in cases. However, on balance, I am convinced by Ho's argument that imprisonment is worse than corporal punishment. I prefer the use of fines as far as possible. If either corporal punishment or imprisonment is needed, I will side with Ho in opting for the former. In particular, imprisonment imposes higher costs on innocent people, particularly the family members of the convicts. If a person is convicted of a crime, why should the innocent spouse, children, and possibly parents suffer the very serious damage of long separation? They may be dependent on the convict for financial and personal care and love. In many cases, it is these innocent people who suffer more from the imprisonment than the convict himself.

While corporal punishment may also impose damage on family members, the magnitude is certainly smaller than that of imprisonment in most cases. By concentrating damage on the convict, corporal punishment is much fairer than imprisonment. Moreover, as Ho convincingly argues, imprisonment is likely to cause much more differences in damages on different persons even from the viewpoint of the convicts themselves. The dislike of corporal punishment is usually based more on the very superficial emotion triggered by the vivid mental image than on the cool analysis of justice. Ho's proposal deserves serious attention. (His proposals on education policy in Chapter 14 also merit close examination.)

Another provocative proposal is that of a 100% inheritance tax, which he recommended as socially desirable and just when the government is in the position to support the education and the basic living expenses of children (Ch. 4). An economist is likely to disagree with the desirability of such a drastic measure, believing that the inefficiency of discouraging savings and distorting choices may be too high. While such inefficiencies have to be taken into account, economists tend to ignore another type of inefficiency – rich parents tend to give too much inheritance to children to their *disadvantage* in terms of happiness if not in terms of money. Having too much money to start with is usually corrosive of one's characters and bad for self-reliance and personal development. Also, the prevalence of relative-income effects (on which Frank, 1999, is a highly recommended reading) may mean that most of us are over-working from the viewpoint of social optimality, and some discouragement through a 100% inheritance tax may really be desirable. Perhaps a compromise that provides a basic exemption and a sliding scale of tax-rates fast approaching 100% may be desirable. Also, it may be desirable to combine with Meade's (1964) suggestion that the rate of tax should not be a function of the size of the estate of the deceased but a function of the size of the total assets inclusive of the bequeathed amount of the recipient.

On health care (Chapter 5), Ho proposed an annual spending limit of about 6% of the mean household income for a household of average size, over which society will reimburse all the medical expenditures. I suggest an improvement upon this proposal by replacing the single limit separating full self-payment with full reimbursement with at least two limits separating full self-payment, part self-payment (i.e. part reimbursement), and full reimbursement to increase the range where individuals still have some incentives to economize on medical expenditures.

In his discussion of financial crises in Chapter 11, Ho proposes the issue of bonds denominated in the 'World Currency Unit' (defined by a composite output consisting of the US, Euro, Japanese, Canadian, and Australian GDPs in some base year). Such bonds are argued to be effective in avoiding financial crises as savers who need an inflation hedge can buy these bonds rather than properties and stocks, creating bubbles in these markets. To have a more complete discussion, Ho should go on to discuss what happen to the funds the issuers of these bonds obtain from investors. Might they use them to buy properties and stocks, especially in a climate when the general investors would have found it attractive to buy properties and stocks?

When first reading through Chapters 2 and 3, my first reaction was that many of the propositions may be debatable or insufficiently justified. However, I found it difficult to fault most propositions after further thoughts. For example, under Proposition 1 in Chapter 3, Ho says that 'all human beings have the same true utility (happiness) function.' I first inclined to disagree. Then I realized that if all factors explaining personal differences are put as elements in the function, then we may at least in principle make it the same function.

I do have differences with Ho. In his discussion of human nature in Chapter 3, Ho makes the distinction that 'happiness is the state of total well-being whereas utilitarian utility is the summation of the balance of pleasures over pains.' I regard my happiness (or welfare) as, by definition, the same as my total well-being and is measured by the summation (or integration) of the balance of pleasures over pains, taking a wide definition to include both the sensuous, the spiritual, etc. I use utility to represent preference which may differ from happiness due to ignorance, a concern for the welfare of others, and irrationality.

To justify his distinction, Ho gives an example of a person of high summation of the balance of pleasures over pains but of low total well-being. 'A person who has never had any experience of pain in any form will not be able to communicate with other fellow men and may not be able to experience or appreciate such human experiences and qualities as love, courage, and will power. Such a person would be the loneliest person on earth.' I quite agree that the experience of pain may have some positive effects like the training of will power. However, Ho's example fails to make me see his distinction. If the person has low total well-being because of loneliness and lack of communication, then his summation of the balance of pleasures over pains must also be low, since these pleasures and pains should include the effects of loneliness and failure to appreciate love, etc.

Ho also explains (in Proposition 7 of Chapter 3) that 'Spiritual happiness is derived from going through and reflecting upon the ups and downs in life. Spiritual happiness is based on a sensitivity to the joys and sorrows of other human beings and an inner harmony achieved through the resolution of inner conflicts.' I also allow the happiness of others to affect one's happiness and allow one to choose to increase the happiness of others, even at a cost of lowering one's own happiness. (See Ng 2000, Ch.4.) However, I see no need to distinguish total well-being from the balance of pleasures over pains. (For a compelling axiomatic argument that happiness or total well-being is properly measured by the integration of the balance of pleasures and pains, see Kahneman, et al. 1997.)

Ho is strongly in favor of the Harsanyi-Rawls construct of the veil of ignorance which I also find ingenious. However, while Harsanyi convincingly deduces the utilitarian social welfare function (maximizing the equally weighted sum of individual welfares) from this construct, Rawls mysteriously obtains an almost opposite conclusion of maximizing the welfare of the worst-off person. Ho has not discussed this obvious contrast between Harsanyi and Rawls. In my view, at least at the fundamental level of ultimate social objective, Harsanyi is obviously right. (Recent queries on the validity of Harsanyi's arguments have been answered in Ng 1999.) Some people use risk aversion to explain Rawls' conclusion. However, while it is rational to be risk averse with respect to income due to diminishing marginal utility of income, it is not rational to be risk averse with respect to utility/welfare, as one cannot have diminishing marginal utility of utility (Ng 1984). Moreover, even accepting the rationality of being risk averse with respect to utility/welfare, one still need an infinite degree of risk aversion to have Rawls' extreme result. I do not believe that an infinite degree of risk aversion is rationally possible.

On a more specific point, both the expected utility hypothesis (Proposition 12 in Chapter 3) and my 1984 argument on the rationality of expected subjective utility maximization (middle of Chapter 3) are criticized as ignoring the *ex ante* disutility of fear and uncertainty of risky prospects. In the presence of such 'mental bads,' we have to construct more complicated choice alternatives. However, the ultimate rationality of expected subjective utility maximization is not affected.

In conclusion, I reaffirm that I have benefited from reading this book and believe that many of his courageous proposals are thought-provoking and merit close attention.

Yew-Kwang Ng
Dept. of Economics, Monash University

REFERENCES

Frank, Robert H. (1999) *Luxury Fever: Why Money Fails to Satisfy in an Era of Excess*, New York: The Free Press.

Kahneman, Daniel, Peter P. Wakker, and Rakesh Sarin (1997) "Back to Bentham? Explorations of Experienced Utility", *Quarterly Journal of Economics*, 112:2, May, 375-405.

Meade, James E. (1964) *Efficiency, Equality, and the Ownership of Property*, London: Allen & Unwin.

Ng, Yew-Kwang (1984) "Expected Subjective Utility: Is the Neumann-Morgenstern Utility the Same as the Neoclassical's?" *Social Choice and Welfare*, 177-186; reprinted in Ng (1990).

Ng, Yew-Kwang (1990) *Social Welfare and Economic Policy*, Hemel Hempstead, Hertfordshire, U.K.: Harvester Wheatsheaf.

Ng, Yew-Kwang (1999) "Utility, Informed Preference, or Happiness?", *Social Choice and Welfare*, 16:2, 197-216.

Ng, Yew-Kwang (2000) *Efficiency, Equality, and Public Policy: With a Case for Higher Public Spending*, Basingstoke, Hampshire: Macmillan.

PREFACE

This book is written for those who are interested in the practice of public policy. Two main themes pervade the entire book. The first is that the foremost task facing policy makers is to anticipate the problems that may arise and to set up the elements of policy which will deal with or avoid those problems in a way that will serve the interest of the "the representative individual" best. In technical parlance, we say that public policy is designed to maximize the *ex ante* welfare of the representative individual.

This is not quite the same as maximizing "expected utility" or expected welfare. In a world with different possible states of the world that can occur, expected utility may be defined as the mathematical expectation of the various utility levels that would be realized under different states of the world, the probabilities of occurrence of which being assumed to be known.

The distinction is best illustrated by a society made up of individuals all of whom want to subscribe to an insurance plan to protect them from a risk which is expected to hit one of them randomly in the upcoming period. Because everyone prefers having the insurance plan to not having one, the insurance plan, by definition, enhances *ex ante* welfare for everyone. *Ex post*, the one hit with misfortune, receiving compensation, becomes better off than otherwise, while all others, who contribute to the insurance plan but get nothing back, become worse off than otherwise.

In speaking for "the representative individual," this book implores that policy makers try to forget about their own identities and those of others. Their job is to work out a policy that they feel most comfortable with, imagining that they could fall into the shoes of any of the real persons who constitute the society.

It is the belief of the author that social scientists have spent too much time working on conflict resolution and finding out whether "social welfare" is higher or lower when there are both losers and gainers. Clearly conflict resolution is a real and important subject. In practice, however, conflict resolution is sorted out through the political process—regardless of what social scientists think. Although consensus has seldom been the hallmark of public policy, now is the time to ponder an alternative to the often thankless task of conflict resolution. Considering the welfare of the representative individual—assuming that everyone has an equal chance to be everyone else while designing public policy—will allow us to look for a new consensus, and will contribute to a more stable, happier society.

The second theme of the book is the importance of the "systems perspective" in the design and consideration of public policy. The human being is a bio-psychological and economic system, with complicated input-output and production-consumption relationships. The socio-economic system is an ecological "general equilibrium" system, with each component related and dependent on other components in ways which we do not fully understand. The systems perspective will help us avoid terrible policy mistakes and enhance the chances of success.

Understanding human nature, working with human nature, and meeting the needs of human nature should then be the preoccupation of policy makers. To do this effectively, policy makers must also understand the socio-economic system, its dynamics, and its ecological relationships. It is hoped that this book has provided a good starting point in illuminating what may be called the principles of public policy practice, which must be grounded on such understanding.

Lok Sang Ho
Lingnan University
September 2000

ACKNOWLEDGMENTS

I would like to thank, in particular, Prof. Yew-Kwang Ng of Monash University and Prof. David Weimer of the University of Wisconsin, Madison, for carefully reading through the manuscript and valuable suggestions. I benefited much from the intellectual stimulation that Prof. Ng offered and from Prof. Weimer's meticulous guidance and encouragement from the initiation of the project through its completion. Prof. Barton Starr of Lingnan University kindly read Chapter 17 and made valuable suggestions. Naturally remaining errors are entirely my own.

Gary Wong and Wilson Tang have contributed valuable research assistance during the course of the project. Dorothy Kok offered excellent help in typesetting and reorganizing the manuscript.

Financial support from Lingnan University is gratefully acknowledged.

I would also like to express thanks to the Hong Kong Institute of Bankers, JAI Press/North Holland, the Western Economic Association, Kluwer Academic Publishers, the MCB Press, the Hong Kong Economic Association, and Blackwell Publishers for using materials previously published, sometimes extensively. Thanks are also due to Allard Winterink of Kluwer Academic Publishers for facilitating the publication process in the most efficient manner.

Chapter 1

INTRODUCTION

1. DEMOCRATIC INSTITUTIONS, "SUBSTANTIVE DEMOCRACY," AND POLICY

Governments affect human welfare in at least four ways. They do so by providing more or less of the goods and services that are complementary to private production and consumption. They may obstruct or tax private sector production and consumption. They may limit the freedom to access the goods and services that are otherwise available in the market. They may redistribute income and wealth.

Governments can serve "the public interest," however interpreted. Governments can, however, also inadvertently hurt the public interest. They can even be "predatory" in nature—that is, they can tax the private sector for the benefit of the powerful people in the government, as discussed in Young and Marcouiller (1995). This book, however, assumes that governments serve the people and the public interest. Based on this assumption, I shall demonstrate some principles of public policy practice that should be useful to policy makers as well as all those who are concerned with the quality of public policy.

While governments are supposed to serve the public interest, government bureaucrats are not saints. Given the opportunity and the inducements, some individuals are susceptible to corruption. They need to be prevented by certain institutional constraints from taking advantage of the power that they wield at the expense of the public. Institutional arrangements that protect the private sector from harassment by government officials are favorable to economic development. A free press, an independent ombudsman installed with authority, a "commissioner for administrative complaints," an "independent commission against corruption," etc., are part of an institutional framework that can serve this purpose. Democratic institutions, in particular a representative government, may also serve the purpose. In practice, however, formal democratic institutions *per se*—electoral politics and party politics—do not have a better performance record than the other mechanisms mentioned above to combat predatory behaviour by the state. They are neither a necessary nor a sufficient condition for what I call "substantive democracy"—governments which are truly responsive to and meet the needs of the public.

"Non-predatory" governments—governments that set out to serve rather than to extract from the people—may contribute more or less to welfare. That depends on whether it is efficient and whether it adopts the right policies.

There are two kinds of things that governments do. The first kind has to do with the welfare of the entire society. The second kind has to do with redistribution. Government activities that improve the social capital or infrastructure and thus help expand production and consumption and reduce risks and uncertainty belong to the first kind. Government activities that cater to the welfare of selected target groups belong to the second kind.

It is my contention that an "economically friendly" constitution, enshrined by popular support and protected by a free press, an independent judiciary and legal process, and a bureaucracy accountable to the people, are the best means to ensure that governments do the right things to promote the social good—certainly a far better guarantee than democratic institutions narrowly interpreted as universal suffrage and an elected government.

The main contribution of democratic institutions to economic development is to provide smooth transfer of leadership, so that society is not destabilised by a scramble for power, which had been the single most destabilizing force to China's economic development since the inauguration of the Peoples' Republic of China on October 1 1949. Political upheavals in China had cost tens of millions of lives, had disrupted productive activities, and had driven hundreds of thousands out of the country as illegal emigrants. Only when China found a strong leader, namely Deng Xiao-ping, who put economic development and stability ahead of everything else, was China spared of more power struggles from 1979 to 1989. The Tiananmen incident of 1989, however, showed once again the potential horrors of power struggle in the absence of a democratic process for transfer of power.

Democratic institutions are, however, neither a necessary nor a sufficient condition to protect property rights, to enforce contracts, to provide adequate infrastructure, or to provide a stable macroeconomic environment. All of these functions are necessary regardless of who is in power, if the economy is to flourish. There is no room for a democratically elected government to alter this basic mission. On the other hand, any government that is effective in delivering these public goods is like a producer that responds to consumers' needs and abides by "the consumers' sovereignty."[1] We can describe such a government as "substantively democratic" even though it may not be "formally democratic."

My second contention is that the modern day democratic process is more often than not used by various sectarian or partisan interests for redistribution purposes. The democratic process has been the avenue through which various business, labor, and social groups further their narrow interests. The pursuit of private, conflicting, interests through the political process is often disruptive to economic development. It should be minimized and restrained.

While an effective, "economically friendly" constitution (written or implicit) and a bureaucracy disciplined to support such a constitution are a boon to economic development, they are generally not considered to be the substance of democracy. During the colonial days Hong Kong (since 1972) had an Independent Commission Against Corruption and a Commissioner for Administrative Complaints, and the Public Accounts Committee of the Legislative Council was charged with the responsibility of examining and reporting on reports prepared by the Director of Audit. But Hong Kong was certainly not a democracy in the formal sense. In China, steps have been taken to make the bureaucracy accountable to the people, but the PRC does not tolerate an effective political opposition. None of its leaders derived his mandate from the popular vote. It is clearly undemocratic. In Korea when the military took over the government in 1961 it revamped the bureaucracy to support President Park Chung Hee's economic program ("the economically friendly constitution") that sought to provide the institutional and physical infrastructure for development. The economic development that unfolded, both in China and in Korea, is testimony that the lack of democratic institutions does not in itself inhibit economic progress.

India has practised democracy for quite some time, but for years its market institutions had been underdeveloped. Only recently has it liberalised its policy for foreign investment and embarked on bolder economic reform.

Political scientists are also well aware of the danger posed by "the tyranny of the majority" and seek to protect minority interest with a constitution. Economists are also well aware of the possibility of "the tyranny of the minority." It is recognized in the economics profession that disperse interest groups are often under-represented in the democratic process, because costs are concentrated among the activities while the benefits are dispersed. In contrast, narrow interest groups stand to capture most of the gains achieved by their political activities. Consequently the silent majority often suffer. Over the years, their interest has been eroded by various tax concessions granted at different times to pacify the narrow interest groups. Protectionism is the most glaring example whereby consumers at large suffer while much smaller groups gain.

These sentiments of mine are shared by Robert Barro. Barro found the US insistence on promoting democracy—sometimes ignoring the sacrifice in terms of the rule of law—dubious. "China was continually attacked for its lack of democracy, although it had made major strides in enhancing the rule of law, whereas Russia was applauded for its free elections despite its difficulties in maintaining law and order." (Barro, 2000, p.8) Commenting on US efforts to promote democracy among developing countries, Barro concluded: "If there is a limited amount of energy that can be used to accomplish institutional reforms, then it is much better spent in a poor country by attempting to implement the rule of law—or more generally, property rights and free markets. These institutional features are the ones that matter most for economic growth, and these features are not the same thing as (formal) democracy." (p.9)

The economic success of the four little dragons or "tigers": Korea, Taiwan, Hong Kong, and Singapore in the past thirty years, has not been predicated on the existence of democracy. The spectacular take-off of the Chinese economy since 1979 is, likewise, not based on the existence of a democratic government. Yet common to all of these success stories are the prevalence or the emergence of the market system, the existence or the emergence of the rule of law so that contracts are enforceable and property rights are respected, a government that is intent to supply adequate infrastructure and educate and train its labor force, and relative social and political stability.

Concomitantly, if we cast our eyes on the economic stagnant economies such as those found in Africa, we find that they often lack basic market institutions, are marked by social and political instability, poor infrastructure, and the absence of the rule of law caused by rampant corruption. Some of these countries are formal democracies. The existence of democratic process, then, is insufficient to result in an effective government that can provide the crucial government services that are complementary to private sector activity.

In typical democratic states, various factions in society try to use the political process to gain an edge over others. This happened in the United States, Germany, France, among others in the league of industrial nations, and in India and various African states among the less developed countries. Depending on the extent of strife, these political manoeuvring can have potentially damaging economic consequences. Higher taxes may be needed to fund expenditures that benefit special groups. Protectionist regulations and special tax favors benefit one industry at the expense of others. Barriers to trade damage economic efficiency.

Elected or otherwise, governments have to do two kinds of things: first to promote the common good and second to balance the interests of diverse groups. Before the advent of modern day economics people may not know what are the ingredients of good government, and they may either place their bets on a dictator or on the arbitrary outcome of the democratic process. Nowadays we know the ingredients of good government: provision of adequate infrastructure, upholding the rule of law and fair play in the market place, ensuring public order and social stability, providing a stable macroeconomic environment. No matter which party takes power, it has to work in these areas, and the bureaucracy—not political parties—should be relied upon to deliver these needed governmental services. Different parties, of course, may balance the interests of diverse groups in somewhat different ways, but minor balancing acts should not have a material effect on economic development as long as the common good is put on the top of the agenda ahead of the minor balancing. The public should be educated to hold their governments responsible for the delivery of the key government services.

2. THE CENTRAL FOCUS OF THIS BOOK

This book is about public policy. There are currently tens of dozens of books on public policy. However, the focus of this book is on the practical principles of public policy. The theory of public policy will be discussed only in so far as it is of help to policy makers and the public in arriving at more intelligent policy decisions. It is important that practices of public policy are sound. This means that they must have a solid theoretical basis. Misguided policy, those that bring misfortune to many people, are usually based on misunderstandings about human nature, about how the different components of the economy hang together, and about the dynamics of collective behavior. It is the knowledge that misguided policy has ruined the lives of many people that motivated the current book. Numerous examples drawn from different countries will be used to illustrate this fundamental point.

Public policy practice is always about choice. It is the role of policy analysts to work out alternative choices about policy design, and it is the role of policy analysts to spell out the implications of alternative choices, so that decision makers can do so in an informed manner. Policy analysts also need to work out the mechanisms whereby the aspirations of the public can translate into decisions and eventually translate into desirable policy outcomes.

Only theories having to do with decision making and public choice are relevant. There are several kinds of such theories. First is theories about human nature. We need to understand human nature in order to work out policy designs and make the right choice. Second is theories about policy designs. Different policy designs have different distributional consequences, different consequences on peoples' incentives and behavior, and different implications about risk. Third is theories about public choice mechanisms. Making the assumption that human beings share many similar aspirations—aspirations to be free, to be protected from major disasters, and to realize one's own life potential, I propose to see public choice mechanisms NOT as a balancing act about different people's gains and losses. The public choice problem is not to be resolved by adopting the Hicksian criterion, which says that a change is desirable as long as the losers cannot bribe the gainers into forfeiting the change. It is also not to be resolved by adopting the Kaldorian criterion, which says that a change is desirable if the gainers can compensate the losers. The public choice problem is, rather, to be seen as one of trying to find out what will maximize *ex ante* welfare for *everybody*, when no one knows in whose shoes one will fall. Rather than saying A should be a slave to serve B because A's loss is smaller than B's gain (or vice versa), we will argue it is far better not to make anyone a slave. Both A and B will feel better off if they feel assured that none of them will ever be made a slave. These ideas will be further explored in the rest of this book.

I intend that this book will be of practical value to policy makers and to citizens interested in shaping the course of public policy making. I shall use plenty of real life examples to illustrate my points. The subjects covered will be broad. They include macroeconomic policy, international monetary economics, labor market policy, health policy, housing, transportation, social security, crime and punishment, education, and banking and finance. While the areas look diverse, readers should find the arguments intelligible and should find that the same themes about policy design and decision making mechanisms recur again and again.

NOTES

1 Consumers' sovereignty refers to the operation of market force that directs producers of goods and services to produce to meet the demands of consumers.

Part 1

THE THEORY OF PUBLIC POLICY DESIGN

Public policy should further the public interest. "The public interest," however, must not be divorced from the private interest of you and me. Indeed it is the private interest of you and me and her/him that constitute the public interest. While the private interests of different individuals may and do conflict, policy makers should try to be impartial—should try to maximize the *ex ante* welfare of "the representative individual," who is the embodiment of you and me and her/him—with the aspirations and concerns that are common to all of us.

Public policy should be designed with a keen awareness of human nature, particularly the common concerns and worries of those served by the policy. If possible we should spell out the key policy parameters that affect peoples' lives and confront the public with the consequences of the alternative options. We should solicit public participation in the choice of such parameters.

As Chapter 2 argues, public policy should take cognizance of the hierarchy of policy goals and should take human nature as a constraint.

One central aspect of human nature is aversion to extreme risks. Another aspect is that human beings make choices on the basis of their perceptions. Chapter 3 notes that these perceptions are imperfect and are subject to change. Public policy design should be keenly aware of the dynamics of perception changes and should alleviate the worries about extreme risks.

The subject of risks and how to handle them will be taken up further in Chapter 4. We will explore the institutional foundations of a just society. We will use various examples to show how policy can improve or reduce human welfare depending on the way it handles risks.

Chapter 2

WHAT MAKES GOOD PUBLIC POLICY

The design of public policy must take full consideration of human nature. Understanding the propensities, fears, and worries of the human mind allows us to know how we should order policy objectives. It also allows us to design our policies in a way that anticipates response, so we will have a better idea of their effects.

Once human nature is seen in the proper light and the multiple needs of society are recognized, it is not difficult to see the logic of a hierarchy of policy objectives with some being treated as constraints and others as objectives to be pursued as far as possible. Optimal public policy making would treat basic policy objectives as given constraints in the short term but the constraints themselves are also subject to revision over the longer term. Public policy analysts will have done a great service if they can lay bare the trade-off among conflicting policy goals and the relationship between policy choice parameters and policy target variables.

1. INTRODUCTION

Policies are designed and implemented for specific purposes, but they are always made in the context of human societies, subject to the constraints of human nature, values prevailing in society, and the political reality. In democratic societies policies are often introduced as a response to political pressures, although sometimes they may represent a conscious attempt at problem solving or as a means to achieve specific ends.

The fact that public policies are subject to political pressures is not a problem. Indeed, the political process is needed to translate the aspirations and needs of the community into actual policy choices, otherwise policy choices would be made in a vacuum. However, it is of vital importance that people taking part in the political process should know what they are doing, particularly the implications of various policy decisions on the society at large. To facilitate the process of *informed public choice* policy analysts must spell out, as accurately and as explicitly as possible, the constraints that the community faces and the trade-off implicit in various policy decisions.

It is highly desirable that the alternative policy designs provide key choice parameters so that by adjusting these parameters different outcomes can result, because the public debate then can focus on the suitable value of these parameters.

The next section will discuss the constraint of human nature. This will be followed by a discussion on the range of policy objectives. There is a hierarchy of policy goals and it is important to assign some policy goals as *constraints* (i.e., they are so basic that they cannot be compromised) and others as *objects for maximization* (i.e., they are to be achieved as far as possible). We will then make the case that the concept of optimality is generally applicable to all kinds of policies and that costs and benefits are also very general concepts that can cover economic, social, as well as political, and moral as well as non-moral aspects. Finally, the concluding section will explore the various dimensions of optimality.

2. THE CONSTRAINT OF HUMAN NATURE

Policies interact with human beings living in a social context to produce different results. The design of policy must therefore take full recognition of the inherent propensities and weaknesses of human nature.

Economists assume that human beings try to maximize "utility." Regardless of what is meant by utility, it is in the nature of human beings that they respond to incentives. They assess the situation, weigh the various options, and attempt to make choices that they believe they will lead to the most favorable results from their standpoints. They may of course make mistakes, but they will learn. An important aspect about human nature is that people share similar aspirations and fears.

Policy makers must recognize that the public will learn. The famous "Lucas critique," which says essentially that macroeconomic policies that do not take account of the behavioral response of people are ill-founded (Lucas, 1976), is a direct application and illustration of this concept. There are also plenty of examples from the realm of social policy which equally forcefully demonstrate the same principle. Thus, in the U.S., it was found that policies intended to help single parent families financially turned out to create single parent families.[1] Policy makers have now also learnt that unemployment insurance always increases unemployment. In order to design policies that fully take into account the behavioral response of the affected groups we need to know more about human nature. Thus a good knowledge of human nature is really fundamental to the design of effective policies. Chapter 3 will be devoted to a discussion of human nature.

Proposition 1

The design of policies should take full account of the interaction between behavior and the policies, and must recognize the fact that individuals will respond to incentives.

Policies always produce a myriad of different effects, and there are always multiple policy goals. It is very often the case that the policy goals conflict among themselves. Economists sometimes simplify the problem confronting policy makers with a conceptual framework called the *social welfare function*. Once the social welfare function is defined, the policy problem can then be described simply as choosing the policy instrument and the values of policy parameters so as to maximize the social welfare function. In practice, unfortunately, the social welfare function does not exist objectively and there is no scientific way to gauge neither the form nor the parameters of the social welfare function. The neatness of the social welfare function belies and stands in sharp contrast with the complexity of real world policy problems.

For policy makers and for the public who want a direction or guidance in coming up with better policy choices discussions about the social welfare function go no where. Instead, what we need are mechanisms and considerations that can allow us to translate *the similar-aspirations of the different segments of the society into policy choices*. This process should involve some form of public participation, but the participation should not be a "rent-seeking"[2] process or based on self-aggrandizement. Society needs to know what choice parameters are open and how different choices of these parameters impact on the various policy goals (Ho, 1997a). In the end no social scientist should make decisions for society, which must make the policy decisions collectively. We know that there will never be a consensus over the details of the final choice to be made and we should not attempt to reach such a consensus. But as Chapter 4 argues, there exist principles that are universally accepted. Following these principles will go a long way towards establishing a consensus in principle and a just society.

Proposition 2

An important role of policy studies is to illuminate the choice parameters of society, how they relate to indicators that bear on the public interest, and how different policy goals conflict and "trade off" among themselves, so the public can participate in the discussion over the choice of the policy parameters.

3. THE HIERARCHY OF POLICY GOALS

Traditionally, economists regard achieving economic efficiency and promoting economic growth as important policy goals. However, sustainable development has become, in recent years, an even more basic policy goal (Tisdell, 1995). Still more basic, and one that is almost fundamental to the aspirations of all cultures, is preservation of the principle of basic justice.[3] On top of these more long term objectives, there are other, more specific, policy objectives, which emerge under specific contexts, and which may conflict with these general objectives.

Thus, public opinion in Hong Kong during the several years leading to the transfer of sovereignty in 1997 had put much pressure on the government to curb the inflation of housing prices, to increase the housing supply, and to increase home ownership. The Hong Kong Government decided to intervene, with short-lived "success" in 1994 and then with remarkable and certainly excessive "success" in 1997.[4] Even though many of the intervention initiatives were widely understood to compromise economic efficiency, policy analysts cannot and should not simply dismiss the objectives of increasing home ownership and raising housing supply as incorrect or inappropriate. Similarly, the aspirations for instituting a minimum wage or a level of income for each household have to be recognized, even though an alternative mechanism may meet those aspirations at a lower cost. Equalizing regional disparity is a common concern in large countries such as Canada and China. Protecting young people against sexual abuse, drugs, and crimes is yet another important goal. Most of these policy goals are defined at a specific time and at a specific place by the dynamics of social and political actions. Rather than dismissing them off-hand we should ask:- at what cost is the policy implemented? Do the benefits justify the cost?

We can see, therefore, that there is a hierarchy of policy goals. In general, policies that come into being as a response to public demand can be regarded as having specific, "second order" goals. Underlying these policy goals, there are other, more long-standing, more fundamental social goals. As alluded to earlier, economic efficiency, economic growth, particularly sustainable development, are longer term and more general goals. More fundamental still, the preservation of freedoms and social justice in the sense of minimizing arbitrary welfare redistribution (Ho, 1997b) are extremely important. They are important because there is evidence of widespread support approximating a consensus in many cultures and through history.

In contrast to these longer term objectives, other objectives are much more specific to the political context and can be described as second order goals. In the face of the specific short-term goals it is convenient to treat longer term objectives as constraints. Thus a policy aimed at providing housing for the elderly must not excessively compromise economic efficiency. Policies aimed at promoting economic growth must be consistent with sustainable development and should not unduly disturb the ecological balance in the living world. A policy aimed at curbing excessive speculation in the property market must not contravene society's sense of justice and must not punish investors to the detriment of entrepreneurship and thriftiness.

The distinction between variables designated as constraints and variables designated as objects for maximization is akin to that between fixed costs and variable costs in the theory of the firm. In the theory of the firm, fixed costs refer to costs which are fixed in the short term, i.e., which are not subject to choice in the short term. Over the longer term, however, they are also variable. Operationally, we cannot work out the optimal values of all variables simultaneously and instantaneously, particularly when the socioeconomic and the political environments are changing all the time. Over the longer term, when the values of the society have undergone a fundamental change, it will be necessary to revise the values of the variables chosen as constraints. This is similar to revising the "fixed" factors of production when relative factor prices have settled down to a permanently different set of values.

Proposition 3

More general, more basic, and longer term policy objectives should be treated as constraints while more specific, less basic, and shorter term policy objectives should be treated as objects for maximization. As the system of values in society changes and as we gain more knowledge, policy objectives designated as constraints may change.

4. COSTS, BENEFITS, AND OPTIMALITY

The concept of optimality, developed in economics and mathematical programming, is useful in public policy studies. Contrary to what is often believed, the cost-benefit calculus that is implicit in the concept of optimality need not relate to economic efficiency at all. The cost-benefit calculus is a method of policy analysis, and is not restricted to the economic dimension. In a discussion of crime and punishment, for example, we can talk about the cost and benefit to society of the size of a jury. Suppose unanimity is required for a conviction. Increasing the size of a jury will reduce the chance of wrongly convicting an innocent, which is a benefit. It will, however, increase the chance of acquitting a culprit, which is a cost. We cannot avoid considering costs and benefits in deliberating on such matters. It is only when all the costs, direct and indirect, present and future, economic and social, moral and non-moral, are considered that we can hope that policies, over the long run, will do more good than harm.

Proposition 4

Intelligent decision making about policies should consider the full range of costs and benefits, direct and indirect, present and future, economic and social, moral and non-moral. Over all optimality means the maximization of net benefits. This requires an optimal choice of policy, including the values of policy parameters, and implies the optimal trade-off between conflicting policy objectives.

Take the example of the mandatory private provident fund (MPPF) which began in Hong Kong in 2000. This is a plan similar to the Central Provident Fund (CPF) in Singapore and Malaysia in being a forced savings scheme but it is decentralised and operated by private fund managers. Each policy parameter within the scheme has an optimal level:[5] the percentage of employer and employee contribution out of the salary, the level of income below which employees are exempt from the need to make contributions, the normal age at which an employee can collect benefits, the age at which early withdrawal is allowed and the conditions. Too large a percentage of contribution would excessively burden enterprises and reduce disposable income and hurt the quality of life prior to retirement. Too small a percentage would lead to an accumulation of savings that will be too small for retirement needs and would defeat the purpose of the exercise, and would not worth the administrative cost that will be required to service the scheme. In general, by making reference to certain stylized facts that apply to large cross sections of the population it is not difficult to come up with a good initial guess. Through an iterative process the initial values can be adjusted to reflect the aspirations of the population.

The mandatory private provident fund scheme at its best—i.e., when all its parameters are set optimally—must also be considered against other alternative schemes. Introducing the MPPF may imply that other viable schemes cannot be introduced, or may be introduced at a greatly reduced scale. If the MPPF fails to deliver a benefit at least as large as the net benefit of the best alternative scheme it should be scrapped. Any policy designed for a specific purpose must be considered along with its competing alternatives.

While some of the costs and benefits may be very difficult to estimate accurately, "practical optimality"—a feasible state of affairs that is highly desirable in its own right—does not require accurate estimation of costs and benefits. Indeed, sometimes the expected benefit from a full-fledged benefit-cost analysis may not be large enough to justify the benefit-cost analysis itself. However, policy makers and the public should both be alerted to all the dimensions and the nature of the consequences, so that decisions over policy instruments and policy parameters are made with an awareness of the full range of consequences. In this regard social scientists, particularly economists, have an important role to play.

It is a pity that some areas of public policy have been compartmentalized and policy makers in those areas have been given the mandate to focus on a single dimension of performance. This underscores the importance of the "systems perspective." For example, it is still often held that central banks only need to achieve stable prices. One tragedy of the eighties and the nineties is that a number of central bankers have single-mindedly pursued price stability to the complete neglect of economic growth, employment, and social justice. The deep recession of 1980-81 in the U.S., which was associated with very high real interest rates aimed at "squeezing inflation out of the system," was engineered by the U.S. central bank and personified by Paul Volcker, the then Chairman of the Federal Reserve. It succeeded in sharply bringing down inflation but left a legacy of large fiscal deficits and high unemployment.[6] The same mistake was repeated by John Crow at the Bank of Canada during the eighties. Although Alan Greenspan has taken a much more flexible and pragmatic approach towards monetary policy the lingering fear that a rise in real wages would bring uncontrolled inflation resulted in a monetary policy that was effectively anti-labor. As a result, notwithstanding years of good economic growth during the eighties, workers in America had been intimidated by rising interest rates and the threat of rising unemployment whenever there was some sign of an increase in real wages. To wit, private sector hourly earnings in 1982 dollars (according to the Bureau of Labor Statistics) showed that the 1989 figure was $7.63, down from $8.17 in 1979. Only during Greenspan's reign, when a broad range of macroeconomic indicators were looked at to determine if there was overheating in the economy, did real wages rise slightly, reaching $7.86 by 1999, still lower than what they were twenty years ago.

Proposition 5

Policy studies should follow a systems approach so that students of public policy are made aware of the different needs of society and the full range of costs and benefits of policies.

Social scientists will have done a great service if they succeed in laying bare the constraints and trade-offs faced by society. This requires that they illuminate the relationship between key policy parameters and key target variables. This way policy decisions will not be made by default and will be made as a conscious search for the optimal choice.

5. CONCLUSIONS

Policy makers work with policy parameters and deal with people. To conclude this chapter we should remind ourselves of the need to distinguish between basic policy objectives and less basic ones, and the general applicability of the concept of optimality. While there are many dimensions of optimality and policies cannot please everybody, pursuing the more universal, general principles will go a long way towards maximizing *ex ante* welfare for society.

The Dimensions of Optimality

The example of health policy provides an excellent illustration of the multiple dimensions of optimality. Do we have the optimal configuration and quantities of medical infrastructure? Do we have the optimal balance between resources devoted to prevention, and those devoted to diagnosis and to treatment? Do we have the optimal structure of incentives, in the form of fees, charges, and other forms of compensation for services rendered as applied to the suppliers and consumers of medical services for them to demand and supply the optimal amount and kinds of medical services? Do we provide the optimal level and kinds of social medical insurance to supplement private medical insurance?

In the case of education, do we have the right balance for resources devoted to primary, secondary, tertiary education, and vocational training? Do we give students the optimal amount of drills, tests, and assignments for them to derive the greatest net benefit from such exercises? Do we administer the optimal number of public examinations with the optimal coverage or syllabus? Do we give would-be teachers the optimal amount of training and in-service teachers the optimal amount of continuous training? Do we have the optimal balance between autonomy for teachers and directives from the Education Department?

Evidently, all of these dimensions of public policy cannot be attended to by bureaucrats operating from the Central Government Offices. There has to be an optimal degree of decentralization, and again there are different dimensions of decentralization. Some decisions may be best centralized while others may be best left to local decision makers. For example, bureaucrats cannot possibly know enough about the students in a school to know whether they will benefit from more tests, or from a particular style of instruction. Officials in the Central Government Offices are not in the position to judge how a local hospital should spend its equipment budget, or whether the Police Department should spend more on its network of informants or on rank and file police officers. On the other hand, the central government should dictate the decision of "going metric" so as to facilitate communication.

The *Ex Ante* Welfare Maximization Paradigm

Although the public consists of heterogeous people, and clearly no policy will benefit different people equally, the design of most policies should not be controversial if we assume that despite the differences people are essentially the same—in the sense that if something is undesirable to A, it would be undesirable to B too, provided that B was in the same boat as A. As the next chapter argues, human beings share similar inclinations and fears. If we make the assumption that what happens to somebody could happen to anybody, and that it is the role of public policy to protect everybody from big risks, then we are much more likely to come up with consensus policies that aim at maximizing "*ex ante* welfare" for the representative individual. If a policy is good for the representative individual, it is good for society.

NOTES

1 Mickey Kaus (1992) coined the term "the Law of Unintended Consequences," which is just another name for the Lucas' Critique. He observed that each extension of welfare created new problems, which in turn could seemingly be solved only by extending welfare still further. "If the problem was that unemployed fathers were deserting their families, then (liberals argued) you should offer welfare to poor families with unemployed fathers who hadn't deserted. But that created an incentive for fathers to

become unemployed. To eliminate that incentive, you had to extend aid to families who were unemployed, but nevertheless poor, which created another perveerse incentive for the family to split up if the husband began earning enough to move out of poverty." (p.112)

2 Rent seeking is an activity that is not productive for society and is pursued to capture the benefits which otherwise may accrue to someone else.

3 See Chapter 4.

4 Housing prices declined more than 50 per cent producing negative asset values for a large segment of otherwise economically vibrant households in the year after the transfer of sovereignty.

5 Professor David Weimer offers the reminder that the first best optimum requires that the policy parameters be optimized simultaneously rather than independently from one another.

6 As the economy went into recession government revenue fell and the fiscal deficit grew. Notwithstanding the argument made herein, even to date there are many commentators who believe that central banks' role is to single-mindedly maintain stable prices. Our argument is simple: fighting inflation should be the goal as long as the benefit justifies the cost. So we have to remember there is a cost in every policy act.

Chapter 3

HUMAN NATURE AND PUBLIC POLICY

Human nature is a vast subject. For the purpose of policy analysis and policy design, however, what we need to know is the common concerns and worries that human beings share. Human beings all pursue happiness by engaging in various activities that are presumed to bring satisfaction and joy. Such activities require the consumption of market goods and services, but individuals' ability to transform such market goods and services into the "substantive goods" that bring "utility" varies from person to person. Moreover, the limited life experience of an individual constrains his perception of his constraints and opportunities. As a result, individual maximization behavior is based on preconceived notions of what matters and what does not in generating happiness (perceived utility function) and preconceived notions of what activities will generate what sensory stimuli (perceived household production function).

> *"How selfish soever man may be supposed, there are evidently some principles in his nature, which interest him in the fortune of others, and render their happiness necessary to him, though he derives nothing from it, except the pleasure of seeing it... That we often derive sorrow from the sorrow of others, is a matter of fact too obvious to require any instances to prove it."*
>
> *Adam Smith:* The Theory of Moral Sentiments, *p.9*

1. INTRODUCTION

Rationality is a traditional assumption in economics. Formally by this is meant that a person has a stable objective function to maximize, implying that his behavior is consistent and predictable. Economists see the economic problem as maximization, at the individual or societal level, of some objective function subject to constraints.

Yet rationality in household theory is taken to imply something more than this. The objective function is called the *utility function* and has normative connotations. Achieving a higher value of the objective function is treated identically as achieving a higher level of welfare. Individuals are depicted as entirely motivated by self-interest and thus selfish. Someone who sacrifices his life for someone else will, according to this logic, be regarded as selfish as he is considered to be merely pursuing his own utility. This has invited criticism (Kohn, 1986) and is, as argued in this chapter, both inaccurate and potentially misleading.

Altruistic behavior has attracted the attention of economists (Hirschleifer, 1977; Oswald, 1983; Stark, 1989; Chami and Fischer, 1996) and is typically modeled by including the utility function of others into one's own utility function.[1]

This traditional approach has some important drawbacks. In its unattenuated form, it assumes perfect knowledge—knowledge both of the utility function (including the utility function of others in the case of altruistic behavior) and of the constraints. The formulation does not allow learning about the utility function—that of the individual, or that of others. It is apparent that in the case of the altruistic model, how one's loved ones fare in reality may not count as much as how one sees how one's loved ones fare. Clearly, even if the son has attained a high level of utility it would certainly not affect the father's overall utility unless it comes to his knowledge. For the same reason, fathers often dictate a lifestyle for the sons' benefit against their will in the belief that this is good for them—whether or not that turns out to be true. Rather than formulating the objective function in terms of two lower-level utility functions, a logically superior approach is to assume that an altruistic father has a perceived utility function for a larger projected self that includes his son in a way Fromm described in his *Art of Loving* (1957, p.24). However, we know from experience that fathers do not, even with the best of intentions, always maximize the true happiness of that larger self because there is often a gap between perception and reality.

In this Chapter it is argued that perceptions are fundamental to behavior. We shall introduce a general model that will accommodate revisions of perceptions which can be described as learning and personal development. Decisions are based on an *ex ante* perceived utility function (as distinct from a true utility or "happiness") function. The perceived utility function is actually only a strategy or decision function for the purposes of making decisions. The individual, moreover, faces perceived constraints rather than known objective constraints.

Similar in spirit to the approach taken here, De Palma *et.al.* (1994) distinguished between the perceived utility function and the true utility function. However, De Palma *et. al.* assumed that both the perceived utility function and the true utility function are based on market goods, ignoring problems arising from household production. They proposed an iterative process in which an individual searches for the most effective or efficient consumption bundle in terms of generating the attributes that contribute to happiness (p.423). In contrast, we argue that because of limited life experience and because life is short, individuals may never get to know about certain attributes. As the realization of attributes requires time and effort, the search for greater happiness is not a simple matter of spending on alternative consumption bundles. A comparison of incremental utilities based on marginal spending may not be possible or relevant. So a convergent iterative process may not exist.

2. A MODEL OF HUMAN NATURE

People in real life display different preferences. This may be explained in either of two ways. First is that they have fundamentally different utility functions. Second is that even though they have fundamentally the same utility functions, they show different preferences because of their different capabilities[2] of realizing the "substantive goods" or fulfillment attributes that affect utility.

There are at least two problems with the first approach. It could imply that communication among human beings about feelings and emotions is impossible. It also takes differences in "tastes" as given. The second approach, on the other hand, has both the advantage that it allows such communication, and the advantage that it offers an intuitively appealing explanation behind differences in tastes. Even more important, it implies that interpersonal comparison of utility is meaningful even if difficult.

To appreciate the intuitive appeal of the second approach, consider the case of a blind person who will not appreciate what is visually beautiful because he cannot. It is certainly inaccurate to say that he lacks a taste for it. His problem is only that he cannot realize this attribute in his life. Thus, *realizing* an attribute requires a *personal* "household production" process that requires various inputs.

Proposition 1: The Personal Nature of Fulfillment Attributes

Fulfillment attributes must be personally produced and realized.

While all human beings have the same true utility (happiness) function in fulfillment attributes, people have different household production functions,[3] both because of their different endowments and because of different specialization and increasing returns to specialization efforts.[4]

Moreover, even though they share the same true happiness function they typically have different and changing perceptions about it.[5] Bertrand Russell described this learning process thus:

> In adolescence, I hated life and was continually on the verge of suicide, from which, however, I was restrained by the desire to know more mathematics. Now, on the contrary, I enjoy life... This is due partly to having discovered what were the things that I most desired, and having gradually acquired many of these things. Partly it is due to having successfully dismissed certain objects of desire.... as essentially unattainable. But very largely it is due to a diminishing preoccupation with myself.... (Russell, 1968, p.6)

Proposition 2: Diversity of Perceptions

Different individuals are in different stages of learning about the true utility function and have different perceptions of what is desirable and what is not.

Axiom: The Universal Nature of Human Nature[6]

Human nature is universal. What contributes to happiness is essentially the same for all human beings. Formally, there is an objective "true utility (happiness) function" that relates the state of fulfillment to various "fulfillment attributes"[7] *and it is common to all human beings.*[8]

Traditionally, utilitarians have adopted the dictum that maximizing happiness is the same as maximizing the balance of pleasures over pains, while maximizing the greatest happiness of the greatest number is the same as maximizing the total of individual happinesses thus calculated. They assume, therefore, that utilities are both internally and socially additive.[9]

I distinguish between happiness (*true utility*) and *utilitarian utility* as follows. Happiness is the state of total well-being whereas utilitarian utility is the summation of the balance of pleasures over pains. However, in reality, pain and pleasure are both part of the life experience and may both contribute to a fuller life and greater happiness. A person who has never had any experience of pain in any form will not be able to communicate with other fellow men and may not be able to experience or appreciate such human experiences and qualities as love, courage, and will power. Such a person would be the loneliest person on earth.

Definition: Happiness vs. Utilitarian Utility

Happiness is the state of total well-being whereas utilitarian utility is the summation of the balance of pleasures over pains.

We assume that the overall state of well-being for any representative individual depends on four kinds of attributes that he realizes over his life: health attributes, sensory attributes, mental attributes, and spiritual or transcendental attributes.

Because of the limited life experience of each person, it is generally not possible to know about all the attributes that affect happiness sufficiently to produce an accurate ranking among them. Still, individuals are confronted with choices all the time, and they are forced to make decisions. They are forced to make decisions by virtue of the movement of two kinds of cycles. First is what I call an *attribute/satiation fluctuation cycle.* Second is what I call a *perceived opportunity cycle.*

The attribute/satiation fluctuation cycle may be biochemically driven. Thus hunger, thirst, or sex drive seeks to be satisfied and may resurface after some time (satiation fluctuation).[10] Different dimensions of the health condition may deteriorate and recover (attribute fluctuation). Fluctuations in some perceived attributes, particularly mental attributes, may have some unknown origin. For example, a sense of loneliness may strike from time to time. The state of one's well being therefore typically rises and falls. An individual will be triggered into action by virtue of the ups and downs of perceived attributes. These cycles are exogenous to the person in the short run but tend to become endogenous over the longer run. For example, the taking of addictive drugs will bring about an attribute fluctuation cycle which otherwise may not have existed before.

The perceived opportunity cycle refers to the coming and going of perceived opportunities for the production of attributes. These opportunity cycles may be internally driven, as one's capabilities of realizing attributes will fluctuate, or externally driven, as the external opportunities come and go. The opportunities presented to the individual in the short run are given, but opportunities open to him in the long run may be affected by his decisions.

Proposition 3: Context of Decision Making

Movements of the attribute/satiation fluctuation cycle and the perceived opportunity cycle drive individuals to make choices.

Because of the inherent impossibility of making decisions ahead of time for one's entire life individuals do not maximize a known life-time utility/happiness function subject to a known life-time opportunity set. Instead, an individual at any one time maximizes an *ex ante perceived utility function* or, more appropriately, the *life strategy function, over a self-defined time horizon.* Compared to true marginal utilities derived from the true utility function U, the marginal perceived utilities of some of the relevant attributes (which may be positive or negative) are exaggerated, while others are assumed to be zero.

Definition: Life Skills

The ability to undergo various household activities to produce fulfillment attributes and the ability to approximate the true utility function are summarized by the term "life skills."

Among the constraints that an individual faces, a key constraint is the *perceived household production functions*, i.e., the set of activity opportunities for transforming inputs of market goods and services, his effort, and time into *perceived fulfillment attributes.* In addition, the individual may also derive satisfaction or disutility from work and from training.

For someone with an opportunity to earn more by working for longer hours (suppose, for example, he is paid by the hour at a uniform wage rate), the perceived marginal utility of work is negative in equilibrium, since the perceived marginal benefit of work in terms of higher income must exactly equal the perceived marginal disutility of work. The efforts on improving work skills and life skills, over the long run, can push out the constraints that condition the maximization process.

Other constraints include a *budget constraint* that says that the individual's total expenditures plus his savings cannot exceed his income, an *employment opportunities constraint* given his skills, and a *time constraint* that says that the time allocated to various activities cannot exceed the time that is available. In addition, the individual is subject to his own limitations that can be described as a *mental capital constraint.* "Mental capital" describes the degree of mastery of life skills at the time an individual faces the choices of life. The accumulation of mental capital can be depicted as a process of *learning*, the effectiveness of which depends on an ability to free oneself from and reflect upon the constraint of the perceived utility function and that of the perceived production function.

Proposition 4: Maximization of Perceived Utility

Within the self-defined time horizon, the individual tries to maximize perceived utility subject to perceived constraints (some of which may coincide with true constraints). This he does by pursuing various activities. In pursuance of these activities he will need to consume market goods and services. The "household production functions" transform market goods and services, time, and other inputs into various "substantive goods," otherwise known as "characteristics," or "fulfillment attributes" that contribute to true utility.

Just as there is a true utility function along the perceived utility function, so there is a true household production function along the perceived household production function. It is, however, the perceived utility function and the perceived household production function that determine the individual's behavior. The individual is frustrated when an activity is undertaken but it fails to generate the intended fulfillment attributes.

As the individual makes his decisions, he will in time see the results of those decisions. Perceived attribute outcomes are compared with actual outcomes, and perceived utility is compared with realized utility. The individual attempts to find the causes of the success or failure of his actions. This crucial process of interpretation will modify his behavior and his perceptions through an adjustment in the perceived utility function and the perceived constraints, leading to a change in his personal outlook and his life strategy.

Proposition 5: Revision of Perceptions and Decisions

The individual compares realized outcomes with ex ante perceived outcomes, realized utility with ex ante perceived utility, then modifies his perceptions and behavior.

Definition: Personal Development

Personal development is a process of interpreting life experiences and learning about the true utility function and true constraints.

Just as one can increase one's work skills by investing in human capital and thus increase the ability to earn a higher income, so one can increase one's life skills by a process of reflection. As one makes a greater effort in improving life skills, the perceived utility function will change—to approximate the actual utility function better. The time horizon will change so that he may become more forward-looking. Learning, however, requires effort to break away from old habits. Moreover, some unhappy experience may make him more risk-averse and reduce his time horizon, while some pleasurable experience may make him overlook the opportunities for satisfaction offered by other dimensions of the life experience.

Definition: Life Entrepreneurship

Life entrepreneurship is an ability to reflect upon one's life experience and to capitalize on the opportunities jointly presented to one by one's true utility function and the household production possibility set.

Proposition 6: Human Weaknesses

Given the limited life experience of each individual and the lack of knowledge about the possibilities of life, each individual is liable to overlook some dimensions of the life experience. The individual is also liable to be inhibited by habits acquired over the years and the fear about change, both of which may prevent learning.

The formulation of the true utility function with happiness being dependent on attributes may suggest that each attribute has an independent effect on happiness. Actually, the experience of both pleasurable and painful attributes, when considered in the right light, may enrich the life of a person, build up his strength, make him more sensitive to the joy and pain of other human beings, and thus increase his satisfaction as a living human being far beyond the "net happiness" calculated as the excess of pleasures over pains according to the traditional utilitarian calculus. This kind of happiness is "spiritual" in nature and is based on the "total life experience," in contrast to the traditional utilitarian utility calculus which assumes that pain and discomfort are always bad, while pleasure and comfort are always good. Another aspect of spiritual happiness is derived from a feeling of mastering and being at ease with oneself. It is a feeling of inner harmony, the opposite of which is so aptly described by Ainslie, a psychologist, when he coined the term "picoeconomics":

> behavioral economics does not necessarily deal with the case in which one part of an individual seems to undermine the efforts of another part.... Earlier I had proposed, with tongue in cheek, that the discipline that studies this case could be called 'picoeconomics,' that is, micro-micro-economics.... Just as classical economics describes negotiation for limited resources among institutions, and microeconomics describes such negotiation among individuals, so picoeconomics describes

> interactions that resemble negotiation among parts that can be defined within the individual for control of that individual's finite behavioral capacity (Ainslie,1992, p.viii).

Proposition 7: Spiritual Happiness

Spiritual happiness is derived from going through and reflecting upon the ups and downs in life. Spiritual happiness is based on a sensitivity to the joys and sorrows of other human beings and an inner harmony achieved through the resolution of inner conflicts.

One may find some inconsistency in this framework which incorporates both utilitarian utility and spiritual happiness in one true utility function. If both pains and pleasures contribute to spiritual happiness what is the net effect of, say, a pleasurable experience on true utility? In general, spiritual growth is a gradual process. Before the full development of the spiritual personality, the individual attempts to maximize a temporal perceived utility function over a self-chosen time horizon.[11] The temporal perceived utility function is traditional utilitarian in nature. As the spiritual personality gradually develops, utilitarian utility will count less and less, while spiritual or total happiness will count more and more. The spiritually developed person will be not be affected by the ups and downs in life to the extent that a spiritually less developed person will.

3. DISCUSSION AND IMPLICATIONS

The Nature of Fulfillment Attributes (Substantive Goods)

The fulfillment attributes that I discuss in this chapter are similar to the "substantive goods" that Scanlon (1991) and Harsanyi (1997) referred to. Harsanyi's view of substantive goods closely parallels the discussion in this chapter in that he noted that a person's own experience and disposition is very much behind a substantive good's being desirable. This chapter goes further and argues that a fulfillment attribute has to be personally produced and realized to be meaningful.

Among the *health attributes* are the full range of physical faculties of the body, including sensory, mobility, and thinking faculties. As well freedom from pain and discomfort are included. Market goods and services are often needed to produce and maintain the level of these attributes.

Among *the sensory attributes* are various stimuli received by the body's faculties including sight, hearing, smell, taste, touch, and ideas and mental pictures created through various media.

Among *mental attributes* are the sense of security versus fear, the sense of recognition versus exclusion from one's identified social group, the sense of superiority versus inferiority, the sense of relative fulfillment vs. deprivation,[12] the sense of self-esteem and self-realization versus the loss of such self-esteem and self-realization, and the sense of autonomy and freedom. Different individuals are assumed to value these mental attributes the same but they produce these mental attributes in different ways and with varying degrees of efficiency.

Mental attributes are often produced and destroyed through various household activities interacting with one another. Jealousy is a mental "bad" due to a feeling of relative deprivation as others are observed to possess something desirable. Fear is a mental "bad" that can be caused by observing a large influx of immigrants who bring new values and behavior to the society. The resulting racist behavior may cause more fear as a result of backlash prompted by racist behavior. However, self-dignity and self-fulfillment may substitute for relative fulfillment, while confidence can overcome fear.

Reference to mental goods and bads allows us to explain things that seem to run counter to rationality. For example, Ng (1984), using what he described as compelling axioms, proved that maximizing expected utility as von Neumann-Morgenstern suggested is rational, implying risk neutrality with respect to the dispersion of utility outcomes. However, he only considered the realized utilities of alternative risky outcomes as being relevant in decision making in his set of axioms. He did not consider the *ex ante* disutility of the *mental bad* in the form of fear and uncertainty arising from having to face risky outcomes. Once this mental bad is accorded negative utility, it is not at all clear that maximizing the mathematical expected value of realized utilities is rational, while choosing a less uncertain prospect involving a somewhat lower expected utility is irrational.

Proposition 8: *Mental Goods and Bads*

Mental goods and mental bads, often experienced ahead of the realization of the outcomes, which are thought to have direct impact on utility, affect the true utility of individuals.

The Perceived Utility Function, the Perceived Household Production Function, and the Perceived Constraints

In contrast to the true utility function that determines how happy one really is, the *ex ante* perceived utility function is only a "strategy function." To see the nature of this strategy function consider someone going to a new restaurant and having to choose from an unknown menu. Although a "preference" may be registered it is not a true preference. The fact is with a limited life one cannot have a full range of experience to enable one to tell what is best for oneself. Living is a process of redefining the perceived utility function and discovering what is good and what is bad. At any given time, maximization is based on one's limited perception and prejudices. Information is generated and reinterpreted. *Ex ante* perceived utility functions and perceived constraints are redefined. Behavior is modified.

The *ex ante* perceived utility function is the "utility function" actually estimated in empirical studies. It is the basis on which households make their decisions regarding what to buy in the market place and what household activities to engage in. To the extent that information is imperfect and households have to operate in an uncertain environment they often look at one another in revising their strategy functions. Pingle (1995) showed that people often modify their behavior and decisions by a process of imitation. Sah (1991) introduced the idea of "social osmosis" and suggested that individuals form subjective probabilities about apprehension, conviction, and punishment for criminal activities (which is one form of "household production") under influence from their social groups.

Just as the *ex ante* perceived utility function will change from time to time, the perceived household production function will also change. Thus when an individual is in a rat race trying to keep up with the Joneses there is no presumption that he becomes better off with greater and greater consumption of market goods. This is because the mental goods are being destroyed even as more and more material goods are consumed.

Differences in the household production functions among different individuals are fundamental to the difficulty of interpersonal comparison of utilities. Some people may have very efficient household production functions and can realize self-recognition (a mental good) with very little resource input. Other people may have inefficient household production functions. Because the attributes that count in the true utility functions must be personally produced and realized, inferences of welfare based on differences in physical resource consumption are generally not meaningful.

Proposition 9: Interpersonal Comparison of Utility

Because of differences in household production functions, interpersonal comparison of utility based on differences in physical consumption is not meaningful. Interpersonal comparison of utility based on fulfillment attributes, on the other hand, is both possible and meaningful.

Many of the constraints that households face are actually *perceived constraints* rather than actual constraints. Life is not only a process of discovering one's true utility function, but it is also a process of discovering one's potential by ever pushing back perceived constraints.

The tragedy of life is that very often individuals ignore true constraints while creating imaginary constraints.[13] The life experience involves learning about the true constraints. As it turns out, some people engage in a process of virtuous circle of positive learning and development, while others fall into a vicious circle of negative learning and "immiserising development."

Some people fail to invest in work skills and life skills not because of inherent irrationality, but because their limited outlook of life make them project a large cost in terms of the marginal effort needed to achieve skills and a relatively small return in terms of the benefits that will accrue from them in the future.

Our model has important implications for benefit-cost analysis. In general, most benefit-cost analyses as practiced today are based on compensated variations calculated with estimated utility functions. If the estimated utility functions are only perceived utility functions and they are subject to misperceptions, then the compensated variations derived can be quite misleading in terms of welfare implications of policies.

In particular, it is common among economists to estimate the value of human lives by surveying respondents' willingness to pay in order to obtain marginal reductions in life risks. These exercises may be quite misleading if the respondents have wrong perceptions to begin with. For example, if we ask a teenager suffering from a depression how much he values his life, the value reported may be negative and he may indeed behave as if life had negative value. But this may be because he is obsessed with his temporary set-back, and he may have completely overlooked the range of life experience that he may yet explore.

Proposition 10: Benefit-Cost Analysis

Benefit-cost analysis based on empirically estimated utility functions and the contingent valuation method may be misleading if households' perceptions deviate significantly from reality or are limited by experience.

Discount Rates and Risks

According to our model, there are two reasons behind the appearance of a rate of time preference. First, the individual constantly redefines his time horizon as his perception of his constraints changes. A poorer person living in a highly dangerous place with a short expected lifespan will, according to the model, have a high rate of discount because he does not look forward to living very long. An elderly person is also expected to have a high rate of discount. These different discount rates are not truly rates of time preference. Only because they perceive their constraints differently, they form different strategy functions.

The second reason behind the appearance of a rate of time preference relates to the satiation/attribute fluctuation cycle and possible changes in the household production function. Depending on the ups and downs of the satiation/attribute cycle, something that is useful now may not be useful in the future. Depending on changes in the household production function, an attribute that can be realized today may not be realized in the future. One's biochemistry may not give one the desire or the ability to produce a specific attribute.

Proposition 11: Rate of Discount

It is rational to have a pro-present rate of time preference for specific consumption which is subject to the satiation/attribute cycle and the perceived opportunity fluctuation cycle. The rate of discount should be smaller for generalized purchasing power than for specific goods, and there should be no discount for future utility.

A number of studies have borne out the implications of this theory. Lawrence (1991) is one of them. Poorer people are found to have higher rates of time preference, suggesting that time preference may not have anything to do with preference *per se* but with differences in perceived opportunities. The implication that older people have a higher rate of discount apparently is contradicted by Chaloupka (1991) who, in his study of cigarette smoking and addictive behavior, discovered that older people apparently do not discount the future at all. This result was inferred from the fact that the coefficient for consumption of cigarettes in the "future period" is not much different from that for consumption of cigarettes in the "current period." Actually, in the empirical study, reported current consumption is taken as "future period consumption" while the reported lagged consumption is taken as "current period consumption." The empirical study also required statistics on "consumption in the previous period." This was taken as zero for those who started smoking within the past two years, had stopped smoking more than two years before the interview, or had never smoked before. For others maximum consumption was used as a proxy for lagged consumption. To conclude that the elderly had a zero or low discount rate on the basis of such statistical results is erroneous. But the results do indicate a positive time preference for specific consumption, and suggest that observed "time preference" is related to the risk of non-survival. While realized "future" consumption is not discounted, the observed low demand elasticity with respect to price for the elderly (pp.739-740) suggests a *high* discount rate. A low demand elasticity implies that cutting back current consumption in response to a price increase to increase future consumption is not valued highly by the elderly.

Mental Bad and *Ex Ante* Perceived Utility

In an uncertain environment, traditional economics takes rationality to imply the maximization of the (mathematical) expected value of the objective function. If two alternative states of the world are possible, each with a known probability, the individual is assumed to maximize the probability-weighted average of the values of the utility function under the two alternative states of the world. This is the Bernoulli-Morgenstern-von Neumann theory, but this has been questioned as being inconsistent with some observations.[14]

Our distinction between *ex ante perceived utility* and *realized utility*, and our reference to the *perceived ex ante disutility* of an uncertain prospect mean that people may be risk-averse independently of the effect of the shape of the utility function defined over outcomes. According to the von Neumann framework, consumers are assumed to maximize the *expected* value of *realized* utility outcomes. Within our framework, persons may maximize a *perceived, ex ante,* utility function whose value may well vary with the variance of the utility even when the expected utility is the same. In particular, given the fact that a person has a limited time horizon and repeated trials for an extended period is often infeasible or irrelevant, he may well be averse to a prospect involving a small risk of a large welfare loss but a large chance of a relatively small welfare gain, even if the prospect implies an expected *ex post* utility gain. One cannot deny the fact that *ex ante* and at the time of decision making, 50 utils guaranteed is different from the prospect of an equal chance for 0 and 100 utils. Once again in terms of our framework, perceived insecurity due to the variance of the realized utility is a mental bad independently of the utility derived from outcomes and may tip the balance of attraction in favor of the guaranteed 50 utils.

Proposition 12: Expected Utility Framework vs Ex Ante *Utility*

The von Neumann-Morgenstern Expected Utility framework ignored the ex ante mental bad arising from the distribution of ex post utilities. Once this is taken into account, it is not always rational to maximize the mathematical expectation of ex post utilities. At the time of decision making, given uncertainty, people maximize perceived ex ante *utility.*

Racism, Parochial Nationalism, and the Productivity of Education

Racist and nationalistic behavior stems from household production that creates "mental outputs" that are positive for some but negative for others. They stem from the perceived good feeling of being more secure from threat by aliens and being superior over others. Clearly, the perception of threat is enforced every time a member of one's own race is attacked or unfairly treated. An economic downturn that throws people out of jobs may also increase perceived threat and thus create a "mental bad." On the other hand an economic recovery may reduce such perceived threat and thus create a "mental good." Any racist behavior, unfortunately, is inherently counter-productive because it engenders ill will and destroys valued mental goods. On the other hand, a sense of security is promoted by a sense of equality, respect for one another, and protection under the law.

Welfare maximization is not achieved just by maximizing physical output. Larger physical output relaxes only one of the many constraints for welfare maximization. Equally, if not more, important is the pushing out of mental constraints. Resources can and should be devoted to pushing out our mental constraints. Individuals should be educated in life skills. With better mastery of the reality, an individual is better positioned to take advantage of the opportunities of life. However, to master these life skills requires a strong desire and an open mind to learn to interpret life experiences positively—i.e., in a direction that will enhance realized utility. The community should work to produce mental goods such as a sense of security, equality, and self-respect and should learn to steer away from mental good destruction activities such as intolerance and racist jibe. Education that causes a change in attitude by exposing an individual to more dimensions of life directly modifies the efficiency in the production of certain mental attributes and thus may have productivity far beyond the imagination of those concerned only with the development of job skills or with education as a consumption good.

Proposition 13: Life-Skill Enhancing Education

Life-skill enhancing education is highly productive. It allows people to realize more fulfillment attributes with less resources.

4. CONCLUSIONS

One basic premise of this book is that public policy must work with human nature and must not work against human nature. This chapter argues that despite the appearance of diversity, there is a universal human nature. The apparent diversity arises largely because of differences in the abilities of households to produce the substantive goods which they all value and because of differences in the stage of personal development and the ability to learn. Behind the veil of diversity, it is part of human nature to abhor big risks, to value autonomy and freedom, to enjoy being accepted as part of a social group and recognized and respected as an individual, and to respond to material and psychological incentives.

The subject of human nature has been an ongoing theme of great interest to economists.[15] Veblen (1934), however, objected to the rationality assumption made almost universally by economists. In his view, human action is instinctive rather than rational, and is based on impulsive desires rather than maximizing calculations. To be sure, people often do act impulsively. Yet, behind most instincts there is rationality. The instinctive withdrawal of a hand from a flame is part of nature's plan to preserve his life. Sexual drives and instincts are part of nature's plan to preserve the species. An instinctive "time preference" reflects the working of the attribute/satiation cycle and life risks. Quite apart from these considerations, it is argued in this chapter that individuals' perceptions are limited by their experiences and by their mental constraints, and this conditions maximization.

In recent years, the role of changes in perception in household choice has attracted increasing attention among economists. Pingle (1995) suggested that individuals may make choices on the basis of imitation when "comparing alternatives is relatively costly." (p.281) Dietz and Stern (1995) introduced the concept of "socially embedded preference." They again assumed that this was a departure from the rational choice paradigm. But to say that a decision strategy is not rational because it is based on cost considerations seems to be a contradiction in terms. This chapter suggests that household behavior is based on maximizing a perceived utility function subject to perceived constraints. The perceived utility function is by nature a strategy function that is only an instrument for maximizing true utility. It changes with experience and with information collected from the social and physical environment. Likewise, perceived constraints as well as actual constraints change over time. Personal development is a process of learning about one's true utility function and learning about and realizing one's true capabilities. Public policy development is a process of learning about human nature and finding policy designs that best fit in with the aspirations of human nature. This process can be called *ex ante* welfare maximization.

NOTES

1 Thus an individual may have a utility function written as follows:

$$U(c1, u2(c2))$$

where c_1 is his own consumption and u2(c2) is the utility of his family. It is also common to model U as comprising two lower level utility functions (e.g., Stark, 1989). Thus:

$$U = w_1.u_1(c_1) + w_2.u_2(c_2)$$

where w_1 and w_2 are weights of the lower-level utility functions u_1 for himself and u_2 for his family.

2 c.f. Sen (1985).

3 This approach is strikingly similar to Stigler and Becker (1977), which was succinctly interpreted by Muellbauer (1987). The similarity was pointed to me by Prof. K.Y.Tsui of the Chinese University of Hong Kong.

4 Yang and Ng (1993) discussed specialisation in the production of goods. Here we note that household production in the production of *direct objects of consumption* or attributes is also subject to specialisation. One thus needs to learn to enjoy (realize the attributes associated with) classical music. Learning to enjoy classical music may prevent one from learning to enjoy watching sports games.

5 This line of reasoning remarkably parallels that of Harsanyi (1997), who distinguished between “informed preferences” and “actual preferences.” (p.140-141)

6 An axiom is a statement assumed to be true but one that cannot be verified empirically or logically. However, the universal nature of human nature is consistent with the similar way people of different cultures respond to incentives and objects of fear so there is such a thing as behavioral science.

7 This approach is borrowed from Lancaster (1966) but Lancaster has in mind objective attributes, unlike what is referred to here, which are the attributes that a person himself realizes through household production.

8 c.f. Stigler and Becker (1977) and Harsanyi (1997), p.141.

9 Internally additive utilities need not imply zero cross derivatives, as the Total Marginal Utility of X may comprise the partial derivative of U with respect to X plus the cross derivative of U for Y with respect to X.

10 This can be described as a readiness or a capacity to realize certain attributes.

11 Readers may be interested to find that this framework is consistent with Maslow's self-actualization framework (Maslow, 1965).

12 The rat race has attracted the attention of economists including Galbraith (1969) and Ng (1997)

13 c.f. Russell (1968), p. 6, previously cited.

14 See Fishburn (1988).

15 See Freeman (1993) for a historical review .

Chapter 4

INSTITUTIONAL FOUNDATIONS FOR A JUST SOCIETY

This chapter distinguishes between fundamental justice and incremental justice and argues that the Harsanyian/Rawlsian, ex ante, concept of justice is the only concept of justice relevant to the design and evaluation of institutions. Unlike incremental justice for which a concensus as to what constitutes justice is generally not possible the conditions that satisfy the Harsanyian/Rawlsian concept of justice are derived from the assumptions of rationality and aversion to large risks, and the postulate of fairness. A concensus occurs not fortuitously but inevitably. The chapter develops eight principles of institutional design that contribute towards a just society and that follow logically from these assumptions and postulates. The chapter argues that these principles are by and large needed for social welfare maximization, so that justice is generally consistent with efficiency. The chapter applies the theory to the concept of exploitation, crime and punishment, as well as labor market and social security, to illustrate the working of the principles developed.

"...justice, a thing more precious than much gold..."

"Injustice is never more profitable than justice."

Plato, The Republic

1. INTRODUCTION: TOWARDS A DEFINITION OF A JUST SOCIETY

In the view of Socrates, as related by Plato, justice is profitable and enhances the quality of life. Notwithstanding the common belief that Plato held the view that justice and moral conduct should be valued for their own sake, throughout much of the discourse in *The Republic* Socrates promotes the cause of justice on the ground that justice is ultimately conducive to happiness. In asserting that speaking the truth and paying back a debt one may have contracted would not be just if such actions were badly timed and reduced happiness, he comes close to *defining* justice as a mode of conduct that brings greater happiness or the social good.[1] "Everyone would surely agree that if a friend has deposited weapons with you when he was sane, and he asks for them when he is out of his mind, you should not return them." (Plato, pp. 5-6)

In important ways John Rawls' *Theory of Justice* (1971) corresponds to Plato's views. According to Rawls, the concept of a just society is based on some notion of "fairness" that should be universal. What constitutes a just action should therefore be capable of being reasoned and therefore not controversial. He maintains that principles of justice should be those that "free and rational persons concerned to further their own interests would accept in an initial position of equality as defining the fundamental terms of their association." (p. 11) In saying this Rawls follows the Platonic assumption that justice is consistent with one's expected self-interest. Perhaps the most celebrated element of Rawls' theory is the proposition that principles of justice should be chosen "behind a veil of ignorance" about what initial position each individual would find himself, so that "no one is able to design principles to favor his particular condition." (p.12) While Rawls is usually associated with this hypothetical procedure, the hypothetical procedure can be traced much earlier to Harsanyi (1953, 1955).[2] The principle of impartiality in social welfare judgments and analysis was also emphasized by Mill, whose utilitarian notion of justice requires agents to be strictly impartial between their own happiness and the happiness of others when they make judgments (Mill, 1969, Vol. X, Chapter IV).

It should be noted that the notion of fairness and the requirement of acceptability to free and rational persons without predetermined interest would imply *non-arbitrariness*. That is, the rules about distribution of welfare must be agreed upon *ex ante* rather than on an *ad hoc* basis after a distributive process. This would imply *equal distribution of the initial resource endowment and subsequent distribution of incomes according to merit or other allocation mechanism elected through social consent.*

The Harsanyian/Rawlsian approach defines what I call *fundamental justice*, which looks at basic rules of justice while ignoring the question of whether a specific change from the status quo is more just or less just. The actual distribution of incomes and wealth at any given time is the result of the working of many factors, including the working of the principle of merit, historical and cultural forces, as well as random factors. Redistributing *actual* incomes and wealth is *incremental* and not the essence of Rawlsian justice. On the other hand while the assumption of everyone being behind a veil of ignorance is hypothetical it gives us a framework to evaluate alternative institutions. Thus we can conclude, for example, that a random redistribution of incomes or wealth that is imposed on members of the society involuntarily would be arbitrary and hence unjust. On the contrary, voluntarily assumed risks from lottery-like arrangements are consistent with justice because they are not arbitrarily imposed (Friedman and Savage, 1947; Ng, 1965).

To illustrate the concept of *incremental justice* consider the case of a very poor man stealing from a very rich man, the case of Robin Hood stealing goods from the rich and giving them to the poor, the case of a government taxing the rich heavily and transferring to the poor, and affirmative action programs in favor of minorities. In such cases a concensus view about justice is impossible, because a person's ethical position about the matter is likely to be colored by his background and interest. In a communication with the author, Gordon Tullock finds the notion of "veil of ignorance" problematic. As he says, "behind the veil of ignorance, you know what nation you belong to. ... [I]f we divided our income evenly with the Indians and the Chinese [Rawls] would never have been able to get his book published." Tullock's point is well taken and relevant with respect to incremental justice but not with respect to fundamental justice. As we shall see, we would have come a long way in illuminating what constitutes just and unjust institutions, if only we used the uncontroversial concept of fundamental justice alone. It should be added that, notwithstanding what has been said earlier about the desirability of equal wealth distribution *in the initial position,* the Rawlsian principle does *not* imply that it is just to equalise *actual* incomes and wealth. Before we proceed further, let us recall our assumptions about human nature as discussed in the last chapter:

We will state the following definitions:

Human beings are assumed to be rational utility maximizers and characterized by an aversion to pain and an affinity to pleasure. They are also assumed to be averse to risks which are sufficiently large.[3] *Human beings are also assumed to value freedom and autonomy.*

Definition of Arbitrariness

Any redistribution of welfare, incomes, or wealth or any decision rule that has an impact upon someone's welfare, incomes, or wealth that does not follow principles agreed upon by free and rational individuals acting behind a veil of ignorance is arbitrary.

Definition of Just Society

A just society is defined as one such that its institutional arrangements, particularly those governing the distribution of the initial endowments and the accrual of incomes and welfare, are acceptable to free and rational persons who have no predetermined interests.

Definition of the Degree of Justness

It is postulated that free and rational persons with no predetermined interest have common and consistent ordering among alternative institutional arrangements which differ only *in their implications on risk and the degree of arbitrariness. A set of institutional arrangements A that is characterized by less arbitrariness than B is by definition "more just" and will be preferred,* other things being equal.

2. A UTILITARIAN APPROACH TO INSTITUTIONAL CHOICE

The foregoing suggests to us that other things being equal, we should opt for institutions which are more just. That is, we should try to minimize arbitrariness or maximize "justness," *unless the greater justness is gained at the expense of other socially desired objectives.* In practice, reducing arbitrariness carries a cost, so that there exists "an optimal degree of justness." We can formulate the following maximization problem:

Lemma: Social Welfare Maximization

Social welfare is ex ante *maximized (with respect to institutional choice) when the most preferred institutional arrangements among all alternatives available is implemented.*[4]

This approach to social welfare maximization is clearly utilitarian. Institutions are chosen not because of their inherent qualities but because of their implications for social welfare. However, while the father of utilitarianism, Jeremy Bentham, implored us to maximize "the greatest happiness of the greatest number," many people are not prepared to accept adding 100 "utils" for one person is equivalent to adding one "util' for 100 people. In contrast, the *ex ante* social welfare maximization approach absolves us from this difficulty. Assuming we are all behind a veil of ignorance, we are all identical for the purposes of contributing to a collective decision: we have the same chance to take up any particular utility function, and the same chance to enjoy the abundance or the lack of the "capability to convert primary goods to substantive freedom" (Sen, 1992). We would not know if we are black or white, clever or handicapped, fat or thin, beautiful or unsightly. Because we are all identical *ex ante* there is no need to sum up the *realized* welfares of different people and no need for distributional weights. Summing up *realized* welfares and comparing the "total happiness" under one state with that under another state would be tantamount to evaluating incremental changes, in contrast to the proposed *ex ante* approach.

By definition, the *ex ante* preferred set of institutions is *efficient* because it maximizes expected welfare. Note that to make an intelligent choice about our institutions we only need to assume (i) that we are all rational utility maximizers and that we share a common utility function defined over "substantive goods," (ii) that we share an aversion to pain and an affinity to pleasure, (iii) that we share an aversion to large risks, and finally (iv) that we value freedom and autonomy.

3. HARSANYI/RAWLS VS ARROW

While Harsanyi and Rawls are implicitly interested in *ex ante* welfare maximization and have defined justice in the *ex ante,* fundamental sense, justice may also be defined in the *ex post,* incremental sense.[5] This approach appears to be implicit in Arrow (1950).

Arrow's analysis started with the social welfare function, which is an indicator of social welfare based on the welfare of the individuals constituting the society. There are some basic properties which a social welfare function should have. One basic property is consistency. Given the individual orderings for alternative social states (one ordering for each individual), there has to be a corresponding and consistent social ordering of the alternative social states (Arrow, 1950). Arrow made the distinction between *tastes* and *values*. The former reflects orderings of social states based on the direct consumption and hence welfare of the individuals while the latter reflects also the general standards of equity of various individuals. A just society should reflect the preferences of all individuals rather than those of one individual (*nondictatorial*). A just society should also allow the freedom to choose among the alternative social states available even as their values change.

Using such an *ex post* approach and making some general and reasonable assumptions, Arrow derived the famous "Possibility Theorem": *if we exclude the possibility of interpersonal comparisons of utility, then the only methods of passing from individual tastes to social preferences which will be satisfactory and which will be defined for a wide range of sets of individual orderings are either imposed or dictatorial (Arrow, 1950, p. 24).*

Arrow's apparent misgiving about the inevitability of the imposed or dictatorial rule suggests that in his mind justice should imply giving due weight to each individual in a social choice decision. This "due weight" may involve recognizing the (realized) utilities of individuals in the social welfare function or recognizing the role of individuals in the design of social choice decision rules. This misgiving about the result that he derived so elegantly which has subsequently been referred to as Arrow's Possibility Theorem is apparent from the following passage:

> To the extent that individuals are really individual, each an autonomous end in himself, to that extent they must be somewhat mysterious and inaccessible to one another. There cannot be any rule that is completely acceptable to all. There must be, or so it now seems to me, the possibility of unadjudicable conflict, which may show itself logically as paradoxes in the process of social decision making (Arrow, 1973, p.263).

The inherent difficulties of social decision making can be illustrated using the following example. Consider a society with two individuals A and B. Under the *ex post* approach, we would be interested in the configuration of realized welfare of the two persons. Suppose three alternative social states are possible so that in the first state, $U_A = 100$, and $U_B = 20$; in the second state, $U_A = 50$, and $U_B = 50$; while in the third state $U_A = 20$, and $U_B = 100$. Arrow could not find a mechanism to determine the social ordering among the three social states that is most acceptable. The difficulties involved are obviously inherent in the lack of an objective set of criteria to adjudicate between the conflicting interests of A and B.[6]

The *ex ante* approach offered by the Rawlsian/Harsanyian framework allows us to consider the problem of social choice from another perspective. Under this approach we would not be interested in any of the three outcomes at all. Instead, we ask A and B to forget about their identities and instead look at alternative institutional arrangements under which they would live. We would look for those arrangements that are most acceptable to both A and B if they have no idea which welfare or social position they would assume. According to Rawls, under this assumption a universal concept of justice exists. We argue that this alternative approach has important applications beyond the adjudication of day-to-day conflicts among individuals, namely in the realm of institutional design.

The contention that most practical decisions are in fact made incrementally in a historical context by real people with different backgrounds is well taken. However, if we are looking for the set of *institutions* that is consistent with the concept of justice it seems that the *ex ante* approach, which assumes impartiality, rather than the incremental, *ex post,* approach, which assumes existing interests as given, is both more appropriate and less controversial. Judgments about "*incremental justice,*" which relates to changes in the social state from the status quo, are bound to be controversial and "unadjudicable."

4. OPTIMAL INSTITUTIONAL ARRANGEMENTS

We can instil further, more specific meanings behind Harsanyian-Rawlsian, *ex ante* fundamental justice. Let us consider a hypothetical world in which a mechanism for randomly picking one member to serve as a slave for the rest is instituted. To the extent that everyone has equal chance to be picked as the slave the mechanism can be said to be "fair." Yet we would not call this a just society because someone is victimized *arbitrarily* against his consent.

For the same reasons, if a mechanism is instituted such that everyone has the same chance to be picked to have all of his wealth redistributed among the rest of the population, the society cannot be said to be a just society. Take a still less extreme example—the case of everyone being subjected to the same chance of being picked to have one per cent of his wealth redistributed among the rest of the population. We still would not call it a just society, unless the mechanism was agreeable to everyone.

Note that in each of these examples, one person loses while other people gain in the random process. In the traditional sense of the Pareto principle, we cannot say that the random mechanism is Pareto-deteriorating. However, in the *ex ante* sense, to the extent that everyone abhors the mechanism, introducing the mechanism is obviously Pareto-deteriorating. Eliminating such a mechanism when it exists is not only just but also Pareto-improving (*efficient*[7]). It should be noted that in the above examples the risks are not borne voluntarily.

Definition of Residual Risks

Risks that are thrust upon individuals and cannot be avoided are called residual risks.

Proposition 1

The Principle of Residual Risk Reduction is a necessary condition to a just society. In order to maximize expected social welfare a society must reduce "residual" or unwanted risk that causes arbitrary welfare redistribution among its members as long as the marginal benefit of the residual risk reduction achieved is higher than the cost of reducing such risks.

The concept of justice, then, stands in opposition to arbitrariness. Apart from being imposed institutionally, "arbitrariness" may also come about as a result of the randomness of natural processes ("acts of God"). Such randomness may occur to a person before birth through genetic differences or after birth through all kinds of "accidents," both favorable and unfavorable.[8] If we are all put behind a "veil of ignorance," and if we all want to maximize our expected welfare, we would seek a mechanism whereby the risks imposed by the natural random process can be minimized. The *Principle of Insurance* provides exactly such a mechanism. Through such a mechanism the effects of unhappy events are diffused so that the sufferings of individuals who are hit by misfortunes are reduced. In the real world insurance is often available in the market place. When, however, private insurance will not cover certain individuals, mandatory or state-provided insurance may be necessary.

Proposition 2

When the arbitrariness inherent in residual risks cannot be avoided through social action or reducing residual risks is too costly, insurance mechanisms that reduce the impact of arbitrary welfare assignment that occurs as acts of God (such as an earthquake) or acts of men (such as armed robbery) through a mechanism of insurance make the society more just. Mandatory social insurance makes the society more just and possibly though not necessarily more efficient. Voluntary private insurance, other things being equal (in particular in the absence of social insurance), makes the society both more just and more efficient.

Apart from residual risks, unequal opportunities are also arbitrary and are therefore unjust. Unequal opportunities prevent people from competing on an equal basis. In the job market this results in less competent people getting the jobs at the expense of more competent people. In the engineering works market this results in weaker contenders getting the contracts at the expense of stronger contenders. This is clearly inefficient.

The *Principle of Equal Opportunities*, which is obviously fundamental to justice, once again is consistent with efficiency.

Proposition 3

A just society abides by the Principle of Equal Opportunities. This implies absence of discrimination based on race, sex, religion, or other irrelevant considerations. This also implies that newborns need to have equal opportunity to develop their potential, i.e., "equality of life chances." [9]

Proposition 4

Pure redistribution that blunts the principle of merit is unjust unless the degree of redistribution is acceptable to all behind a veil of ignorance.

In order for institutional arrangements to be acceptable to free and rational persons with no predetermined interests, so that a society can be called just it must also have just laws, effective law enforcement, and just punishments. Just laws are proscriptive in a way that is agreeable to all members of society "behind the veil of ignorance" about where they would belong in society. They specify what behaviors are unacceptable and need to be punished. Just laws must also be made known to and easily understood by people. If they are known to some people but not to others offenders may be arbitrarily victimized because they happen not to be aware of the laws. They must minimize any arbitrariness both in design and in implementation. In other words they should not be enforced randomly or selectively.

Proposition 5

A just society must have laws that clearly and unambiguously define what behaviors are lawful and what behaviors are unlawful, and that are agreeable to all members of the society if they were behind a veil of ignorance about where they would belong.

Just laws need to be complemented with just punishments. Following the requirement of non-arbitrariness, just punishments must be commensurate with the nature and severity of the offence; they must not produce "spill-over" punishment on innocent people (explained below); and they must be well defined and precise so that the relative and absolute level of severity of each punishment is clear to the judge, which is necessary if the judge is to determine what is the appropriate punishment in each case.

Proposition 6

A just society needs to have just punishment to complement the just laws.[10]

All of the above has to do with arbitrariness externally imposed from the environment or internally given by virtue of inborn differences. There is still another aspect of arbitrariness that arises from the *interaction* of inborn characteristics and the environment. This has to do with differences in tastes and differences in attitudes towards risk. Assuming that we are all behind a veil of ignorance and do not know what kind of tastes we have, a just society would respect free choice about lifestyle and would minimize victimization due to peoples' different tastes and different attitudes towards risk. A just society should also strive to reduce opportunities for law offences (such as corruption) that attract risk-loving people to commit the offences and then punish them severely. In other words, a society that provides a 90 per cent success rate for an attractive (tempting) criminal offence and hands out very stiff punishment is considered less just than a society that offers a 1 per cent success rate for the same criminal offence and hands out a less stiff punishment.[11]

Proposition 7

A just society should not discriminate against people because they happen to have different tastes or different attitudes towards risk.

Proposition 8

Given the same deterrence effect, improving the chances of catching and convicting a law offender while reducing the severity of the penalty will make the society more just. This is desirable as long as the benefit of the improved justice is greater than the cost of improving the chances of convicting an offender. A corollary of this proposition is that a low chance of conviction coupled with very severe penalties is not as just.

5. APPLICATION I: THE CONCEPT OF EXPLOITATION AND EQUALITY OF OPPORTUNITY

Karl Marx in his *Capital* propounded a theory of surplus value and argued that a capitalist society is unjust because capitalists expropriate value created by labor. The reason why they could do this, according to him, lies in private ownership of capital. According to our analysis, and accepting his theory of surplus value of labor for the moment for the sake of argument, if private ownership of capital were arbitrary his argument would be valid. If, however, capital is not arbitrarily assigned to people, and everyone has the same opportunity to accumulate capital and run a business in a free and open market, then Marx's theory of exploitation would be invalid. Rather than ascribing exploitation to the ownership of capital, our theory of justice would imply that exploitation should be ascribed to unequal opportunities. Those who through no merit of their own enjoy more or better opportunities than others are the exploiters. Those who through no fault of their own suffer from a lack of or diminished opportunities are the exploited.

It may be argued that some people are born to belong to the capitalist class, while others are born to belong to the laboring class. Equal opportunity, it is held, does not exist in the capitalist society. This may well be the case, but if this is the case, injustice is still attributable to unequal opportunities rather than to the ownership of capital.

Completely equal opportunities for all is very difficult to achieve, given the vested interests now prevalent in all real societies. However, following Rawls' dictum and forgetting our identities and our ownership or lack of wealth, equal opportunities would require at least the following conditions:

- non-inheritance of wealth, status, and power implying a 100 per cent inheritance tax and an absence of caste or class distinction for all new-borns;[12]
- equal opportunities for nurture and for education for all children,[13]
- freedom to participate in all markets as suppliers or as consumers;
- equality of all before the law.

These conditions ensure that everyone have the same *initial conditions* to start their lives and that they face the same *rules of the game* throughout their lives. The concern for unequal inheritance is shared by many famous economists and intellectuals, including John Maynard Keynes:

> Since the end of the nineteenth century significant progress towards the removal of very great disparities of wealth and income has been achieved through the instrument of direct taxation—income tax and surtax and death duties...[Carrying this process much further has been deterred] mainly, I think, by the belief that the growth of capital depends upon the strength of the motive towards individual saving and that for a large proportion

> of this growth we are dependent on the savings of the rich out of their superfluity.....[U]p to the point where full employment prevails, the growth of capital depends not at all on a low propensity to consume but is, on the contrary, held back by it.....[I]n as much as an increase in the habitual propensity to consume [caused by a fiscal policy of heavy death duties] will in general...serve to increase at the same time the inducement to invest, the inference commonly drawn is the exact opposite of the truth..... This particularly affects our attitude towards death duties; for there are certain justifications for inequality of incomes which do not apply equally to inequality of inheritances (Keynes, 1936, pp.372-374).

The elimination of inheritance to many is a radical idea. Some may think that being allowed to accumulate and to leave bequests will not only satisfy an inherent human instinct but will also provide an important motivation for people to invest and to work. The desire to accumulate a bequest for children, however, should be reduced if, through government provision of equal nurture and education opportunities, parents are assured that their children will not be disadvantaged because no one is enjoying a headstart over others. The concern about blunting an important drive that is potentially important for human progress may also be misplaced, to the extent that historically many men and women of achievement made their contribution entirely out of their quest for expanding human knowledge, a desire for creativity, and an urge to overcome nature's constraints to human freedom. Musicians like Mozart and Beethoven, scientists like Newton and Einstein, mathematicians like Euclid and Von Neumann, artists like Van Gogh and Leonardo da Vinci, even entrepreneurs like Bill Gates and Alfred Nobel, make their achievements not because they have children to whom they want to leave a huge bequest.[14] Indeed, if there is the assurance that one's children have equal life chances compared to others people may be free to pursue their own interest. As a result there may even be more Mozarts, more Edisons, and more Einsteins.

Institutionally provided "equal opportunities for nurture and for education" does not imply the elimination of parental responsibilities for loving care. Parents can continue to give all the love they can, but they will not be inhibited by the need to leave a bequest for their children in pursuit of their own life goals.

6. APPLICATION II: CRIME AND PUNISHMENT

Applying the principle of non-arbitrariness to the study of crime and punishment, we can say that crimes are unjust, and that laws, an effective judiciary and a penal system that deter crimes contribute towards establishing a just society. Crimes are unjust because they arbitrarily redistribute welfare and increase residual risks for everyone. Laws, judiciary, and punishments that deter crimes make a society more just because they reduce residual risks.

Applying the principle of non-arbitrariness to the study of crime and punishment, there is a case for the judicious application of corporal punishment. Unlike imprisonment which tends to have arbitrary spillover effects on innocent people, corporal punishment is essentially personal. Prison terms take parents away from their children, husbands away from their wives, sons and daughters away from their parents. Prison terms take away the opportunity for the offender to earn an income, and impose the burden of feeding, accommodating, and caring for the offender on society.

To the extent that the offender's identity is revealed he/she and his/her family members are often disgraced and discriminated against by others. This disgrace or discrimination is over and above the punishment handed out by the judge. The degree to which a person hurts from the disgrace depends on his psychology, which varies from person to person thus rendering the "extra-punishment" arbitrary. Our theory of justice suggests that an offender's identity should not be disclosed, but the severity of the punishment should be adjusted to a level high enough for it to serve as a deterrent. Formal, judicially given punishment should shoulder all the responsibility to serve as a deterrent and should be as severe as necessary for effectiveness. Informal, non-judicially given punishment like disgrace or discrimination should not be used as a deterrent—not because the latter is ineffective, but because the latter is inherently arbitrary.[15]

In societies that place value on human dignity and morality, corporal punishment is often considered uncivilised and cruel. There is also the concern that if corporal punishment has to be commensurate with the severity of the crime, excessive use of violence against a human being will sometimes be inevitable. Actually, corporal punishment is not necessarily more cruel than imprisonment. The psychological damage of long prison terms has not been adequately understood. What is worse, financial considerations mean that the administrations of most prisons cannot prevent an inmate from being bullied, mugged, molested, or even murdered by other inmates. This is certainly potentially more inhumane than judiciously applied and medically supervised corporal punishment. Moreover, the severity of corporal punishment does not have to be positively related to the physical damage or impact done by a cane, a whip, or other penal gadgets. It can be positively related to the number of times the punishment is applied over an extended period of time. Thus, for example, a minor theft may warrant two whippings. A more serious one or a repeated offence may warrant two whippings per week for four weeks. A robbery may warrant four whippings per day for a month.

The case for corporal punishment based on justice grounds is that much stronger considering that the cost to different individuals for the same prison term may well be quite different. A single parent who has a two-year old at home and has a regular job may find his and his family's life shattered by a six-month prison term and the loss of his job. Someone else who is single and has never had a job over the last ten years may find the six-month prison term "a piece of cake." The abhorrence for physical pain, on the other hand, is universal.[16]

7. APPLICATION III: LABOR MARKET AND SOCIAL SECURITY

In some countries there exist laws that prohibit discrimination based on sex or race, discrimination against people with certain disabilities, and discrimination against older workers. Using the *ex ante*, Rawlsian approach discrimination based on sex or race is unjust because individuals behind a veil of ignorance are arbitrarily subjected to discrimination as they are selected by nature to fall into a race or a sex category. However, it should be noted that discrimination against older workers belongs to a different category because old age happens to everyone who lives long enough. If jobs are scarce and promotion prospects are scarce, then mandatory retirement, —which is considered a form of age discrimination, may equalize lifetime employment opportunities among all citizens. If everyone behind a veil of ignorance prefers such a scenario mandatory retirement *will be* consistent with justice. However, mandatory retirement for a much more capable person in favor of a younger, far less capable person may not be in the social interest. A mechanism for dispensing with mandatory retirement under pre-specified circumstances is not arbitrary and thus may also be just.

In order to achieve non-discrimination in the labor market, institutionally there has to be sufficient incentives for people not to discriminate. Women used to be and may still be discriminated against because the expected cost of hiring women or their productivity may be less favorable than that for men because they may become pregnant and may need maternity leave. Older people may be less favored if the cost of providing health insurance or the expected cost of providing for retirement benefits is higher for older workers than for younger workers. Physically or mentally handicapped people may be less likely to be considered for work if employers find them generally less profitable to hire compared to other workers. Legislating against discrimination generally comes to no avail because in a market economy successfully surviving competition requires firms to be lean and to minimize cost. Imposing heavy penalties on some employers who are caught in a discriminatory act when competition forces all employers to engage in discriminatory behavior when they have the opportunity is unfair and unjust (corollary of Proposition 8). This suggests that providing financial incentives that offset the inherent unattractiveness of women, the disabled, and older workers (other things being equal) is just.

In sheltering employers from the higher costs of hiring women, the handicapped, and other disadvantaged groups, state-provided social security will reduce discrimination in the labor market. At the same time it may foster fair competition among firms, to the extent that the social security cost burden is more evenly distributed among firms. In the People's Republic of China state and collective enterprises with a long history are now disadvantaged compared to newer private and foreign-funded enterprises because they are burdened with a heavy bill for retirees' benefits. As a result their ability to compete on the basis of merit is compromised. From another perspective state-provided social security is a direct application of the insurance principle, providing a safety net where private insurance fails to provide the necessary protection. However, social security should not be meant to be vertically redistributive as this would blunt the working of the principle of merit.[17]

8. CONCLUSIONS

In the foregoing we have argued that the Harsanyian-Rawlsian, *ex ante* concept of justice is the only concept of justice that is "institution-relevant," and have examined how principles of institutional design can be derived and applied from this concept of justice. In concluding this chapter, it is useful to emphasize that this concept of justice is itself derived from the assumptions of rationality and fairness. It is also useful to note that the theory is consistent with a large degree of autonomy at the individual level and with the libertarian ideal of a minimal state, in contrary to what some critics of the Rawlsian theory of justice believe.[18]

Our distinction between fundamental justice and incremental justice adds to the axiomatics about the concept of justice, an excellent survey of which is found in Kolm (1994), who has distinguished between direct justice and indirect justice, and discussed the Aristotelean distinction between distributive justice and compensatory justice, as well as various logical issues arising from or underlying the concept of justice. We believe our newly introduced distinction is useful, and has helped us avoid unnecessary controversies. In response to Aristotle's assertion that "justice is equality" Kolm (1994, p.971) had asked: "why is justice equality?" We provided an answer in suggesting that equality can be interpreted as equality in the position from which people make judgments about what is good and what is bad social choice--i.e., impartiality, or everybody being behind a "veil of ignorance." The rationale of this hypothetical exercise is *ex ante* welfare maximization through optimal choice of institutions.

An important advantage of the *ex ante* approach to social welfare maximization is that it avoids the "incessant quarrelling" and "uncertainty" about each act's consequences in the absence of prior agreement of rules and institutions that Mill (1972, pp.761-764) noted. Sen (1995) had stated that "To try to make social welfare judgments without using any interpersonal comparison of utilities, and without using any nonutility information, is not a fruitful enterprise." (p.8) This is certainly true with respect to the social ranking of alternative outcomes, that some practical circumstances will require. However, any resulting social choice will still likely be controversial. On the other hand with *ex ante* welfare maximization of "the" individual (all individuals are identically situated *ex ante*) under a veil of ignorance there should be no controversy.[19]

We maintain that the eight principles of just institutions are derived logically by deduction from the basic premises of fairness, rationality, and aversion to large risks. Without denying Arrow's point that real life persons have different backgrounds and are unlikely to have common views about what is just and what is not when incremental changes to real life situations are under consideration, we maintain that we are likely to share common views about *fundamental justice*. Indeed, the assumptions of rationality, fairness, and aversion to extreme risks *dictate* the principles of just institutions as described above.

Failing to make the distinction between fundamental justice and incremental justice is the reason behind much unnecessary controversy. As we explained, given the diverse background and interests of different individuals there can never be concensus over incremental justice. The United States will not do justice to its citizens by opening its door to free immigration, even though such a policy will be seen to be just by many others. Redistributing incomes from the rich to the poor, similarly, will please many people but it ignores the reasons behind the existing distribution of incomes. It may be regarded as arbitrary because freely choosing, rational human beings behind a veil of ignorance may not approve of such *ex post* redistribution, even though they would all rationally approve of instituting a safety net to reduce *ex ante* risks.

While the concept of fundamental justice is linked to the Harsanyian-Rawlsian hypothetical proposition of situating everyone behind a veil of ignorance, it is still relevant to the real world. The eight propositions are all relevant to the world and provide clues as to how our institutions may be improved even though they do not say anything about incremental justice or the merits of or demerits of an *ex post* welfare redistribution.

The principles of just institutions are consistent with a high degree of autonomy. Indeed, to the extent that individuals are assumed to value freedom and autonomy, institutions that limit freedom and autonomy unnecessarily will not have passed the *ex ante* test for justice. Of the eight principles described above, the principle of equal opportunity has been held to be inconsistent with autonomy (Fishkin, 1983). According to Fishkin, there is a "trilemma" and inherent incompatibility among three important principles: the principle of merit, the principle of equality of life chances, and the principle of autonomy of the family. He cited the case of a society that is dominated by a warrior class and noted that "fair competition" according to the principle of merit would inevitably favor the children of the warrior class at the expense of others. Equality of life chances would appear, then, to require state interference into the rearing of children, which would mean a loss of family autonomy (pp.30-43). Without disputing the logic of Fishkin's discussion, it must be pointed out that the merit of the Rawlsian justice concept lies in providing an approach towards evaluating and designing institutions. Rather than defining "the" just society and distinguishing it from unjust ones, the Harsanyian-Rawlsian approach offers a way to differentiate "Rawlsian improvement" from "Rawlsian deterioration" in the same way that the Pareto efficiency concept allows us to tell "Pareto improvement" from "Pareto deterioration." Application of the Rawlsian justice concept does not, therefore, require perfect equality of life chances. Reducing the inheritance of wealth, status, or political power, state provision of resources for nourishing and educating children, fair and open competition, a healthy safety net provided through a carefully designed social security system, better laws and a better penal system will have gone a long way towards establishing a just society.

NOTES

1 John Stuart Mill made a similar point when he wrote: "human happiness is the sole end of human action, and the promotion of it the test by which to judge of all human conduct; by whence it necessarily follows that it must be the criterion of morality, since a part is included in the whole." (Mill, 1969, p.234)

2 I owe Prof. Yew-kwang Ng for pointing this out to me.

3 This is a departure from the "maximin" "Rawlsian utility function" discussed in the literature. As pointed out by Arrow (1973, p.251) and noted by Posner (1981, p.100) the maximin principle that gives value only to the utility of the worst outcomes in the utility distribution implies strange results. Aversion to extreme risks is consistent with the double-hump utility function as discussed in Friedman and Savage (1948).

4 The *ex ante* approach to welfare maximization is obviously endorsed by Mill. In a letter to George Grote, Mill argued that "human happiness, even one's own, is in general more successfully pursued by acting on general rules, than by measuring the consequences of each act." (Mill, 1972, Vol. XV, pp.761-764) A modern example of this approach can be found in Garratt amd Marshall (1994), which described a "contract theory of public finance of college education" in terms of *ex ante* welfare maximization. The logic of this approach is underscored by an interesting question raised by Wasserman (1996): should we divide something evenly among everybody or should we give the total to the lucky one who wins a fair lottery--given that the sum of the values of the divided parts may be much less than the value of the total.

5 The distinction between *ex ante* and *ex post* judgments is related to but different from Sen's (1995) distinction between judgement over "decision mechanism" and "social welfare judgments." The *ex ante* approach to social welfare maximization, as discussed in this paper, and judgments over "decision mechanisms" as referred to by Sen, are common in that they are both not concerned with realized utilities or welfare. They are different in that the *ex ante* approach is concerned with expected utilities, while Sen's discussion about decision mechanisms is concerned with the satisfaction of formal axioms such as consistency.

6 If there is cardinal measureability of utility and utility can be compared, one could simply add up the utilities and seek the social state with the biggest number. But Arrow did not assume cardinal measureability and did not assume interpersonal comparability of utility.

7 This is defined as "Pareto risk efficiency" in Ho (1981) in contradistinction to Pareto efficiency which is defined in respect of *ex post* utilities of different individuals.

8 Sen (1992) notes the differences inherent in men in terms of the capability to convert primary goods to substantive freedom. Thus he argues that a theory of justice must take adequate note of such differences. (p.148)

9 Here we refer to equality of life chances in the *ex ante* sense. Affirmative actions are incremental and thus not part of the implications here.

10 Just laws and just punishment constitute only one component of "institutions." They are given special attention because, unlike a free market economy and a social safety net, they are not implied by the other propositions.

11 This does not mean that spending more on improving the detention rate while reducing the penalty (thus preserving the same deterrence effect) is always justified. In principle justice should be pushed only to the point where its marginal benefit is equal to its marginal cost.

12 100 per cent inheritance tax is not recommended in the absence of the other conditions. If the government can ensure equal nurture and education for all children and there is equality before the law, then parents will be more ready to accept zero bequest. Moreover the inheritance tax should not rule out gifts of an emotional nature.

13 Plato's *Republic* suggested not only that the birth and upbringing of children should be done in common but also that children should not know who are their true parents, just as parents should not know who are their offsprings. Such an arrangement was proposed apparently as a means to ensure equal opportunities for nurture and for education.

14 Bill Gates expressly says that he will not leave a large bequest to his heirs in a newspaper column. See *Hong Kong Economic Journal*, October 8, 1996.

15 There was a case in Hong Kong several years ago wherein a university student was convicted for shoplifting. The formal punishment was modest, but the act became front-page headline news in several local newspapers. The poor girl, unable to face the disgrace, committed suicide.

16 The abhorrence for physical pain is unlikely to be equal among different people. The degree of variation, however, is *assumed* to be acceptable.

17 Redistribution is not impermissible in a just society. Some degree of redistribution should be agreeable to rational individuals behind a veil of ignorance. See Proposition Four.

18 Nozick (1974) represents one of the foremost libertarian critiques of Rawls. Nozick's interpretation, as correctly pointed out by Kukathas and Pettit (1990), is not a correct representation of Rawls, even though Nozick provided "the outline of a libertarian alternative, but not to undermine Rawls's theory." (p.91)

19 Using a somewhat different approach, Kolm (1996) also proposes to adopt "the general philosophy of the the definition of an egalitarian ideal with priority of unanimity," the essence of which lies in arrangement such as the following: "prefer a more equal allocation except if everybody opposes it, and a less equal allocation if everybody prefers it." (p. 161)

Part 2

MICROECONOMIC RISK MANAGEMENT

Risk is a fact of life. Yet the social cost of risk is very much subject to social management. Human beings face all kinds of risks. On the micro level, there are, among others, the risks of being hit by traffic accidents, falling sick, being victimized by criminals or being treated unfairly, having money deposited in a bank that fails, and living older than retirement provisions have been prepared for. Chapter 5 looks at the case of protection against health care costs. Chapter 6 looks at the case of protection against litigation costs. Chapter 7 looks at deposit insurance. Chapter 8 examines the problem of aging and public pension design.

Chapter 5

HEALTH CARE DELIVERY AND FINANCING: IN SEARCH OF AN IDEAL MODEL

There are three models of health care delivery and financing: the market model, the professional model, and the bureaucracy-dominated model. The National Health Service of the UK and the Hong Kong government-funded health care system represent the professional model, although both are supplemented by the bureaucracy-dominated model (through the Department of Health) and private suppliers. The US system is predominantly market-based. The Canadian system, on the other hand, is bureaucracy-dominated. Regardless of the which model one follows, the incentives have to be right in order to achieve efficiency and effective protection for the public. This chapter will seek out the basic features of such a system.

1. INTRODUCTION

There are essentially three models of health care delivery and financing. The first is the market-driven and administratively decentralised "survival of the fittest" model (or "the market model"). The second is the professionally dominated "social welfare maximization" model (or "the professional model.") The third is the bureaucracy-dominated model (the "Niskanen model"). These three models seldom apply in pure form in the real world. In particular, it is not possible to demonstrate that the health care system of any particular country fits the "Niskanen model" very well, because no bureaucrat will declare that he pursues his own self interest while in public office. While the Canadian system was criticised for being dominated by bureaucrats to the detriment of both patients' and doctors' interests,[1] it was also hailed as a possible solution to the under-insured but costly system of the US.[2]

Under the first category are included both the more traditional fee-for-service model and the managed care model, with the former often complemented with third party insurance. Under the second category are various designs which vary in quality and effectiveness but which are all aimed at *maximizing social welfare* as perceived by welfare-minded professionals and bureaucrats. The institutional framework allows professionals much leeway to act independently but there is little room for them to profit for their professional decisions. Under the third category is the bureaucracy-dominated, self-interest maximization model (Niskanen, 1971) under which the welfare of medical service suppliers and that of patients are subordinated to the *self-interest* or convenience of regulator-bureaucrats. In the literature on health care reform and in practice, the first two models are always seen to be competing with each other in terms of social welfare maximization. The market driven model is not by design social welfare maximizing, but many economists still believe that the invisible hand of the market will be more effective in enhancing social welfare than one that sets out to maximize social welfare in the first place. The third model is not meant to compete with the other two models in terms of social welfare maximization, but does enjoy some advantages, as discussed below.

Section 2 and Section 3 will outline the central features of the market model and the professional model respectively. Section 4 will discuss briefly the bureaucracy-dominated model. Section 5 will explore how the best features of the market model and the professional model can be achieved through a unique form of government intervention that can be described as "excessive burden insurance." We shall see in the next Chapter that this principle of excessive burden insurance is equally applicable to the case of legal aid, and is an important direction that civilised societies of the world can take to improve social welfare.

2. THE MARKET MODEL

The U.S. health care system of today can be said to be the prototype of the market model. This is not to say that the U.S. governments, federal, state, or local, do not interfere with the medical care market. They do, in fact in a big way.[3] The distinguishing feature of a market model for health care is that the market is given the dominant role in determining how much and what to spend on in health care, because market forces are believed to lead to the most efficient outcomes. Patients are supposed to fare better when they are given the choice to select their doctors, their insurers, and their pharmacists. Doctors, therapists, and pharmacists are supposed to give the best services if they are rewarded according to the services that they provide at market-determined rates.

Following the market model, the United States has a sizeable population without any health insurance coverage.[4] This is quite unlike most other developed countries, where citizens are all under some kind of protection, with or without direct funding from the government. The underlying assumption is that while the Government should insure the poor (Medicaid) and the old (Medicare), those who are neither poor nor old should have the choice to buy health insurance or not. Unfortunately, not all poor are entitled to Medicaid, and not all old enjoy the same kind of care,[5] and not all among the uninsured voluntarily opted for no insurance.

By choice or otherwise, we know that "the uninsured have less access to care, use less care, cannot obtain specific health care services, are twice as likely to be hospitalized for conditions that can be averted by outpatient care (such as acute asthma attacks), and have a higher risk of death when they go to the hospital."[6]

Among those who are insured, most are now covered in "managed care" plans. The hallmark of such plans is prepayment or "capitation." The caregiver is paid when an enrollee enrolls in a plan, and not at the time when he actually uses the services. Such an arrangement has the obvious advantage of giving caregivers the incentive to save costs. But this incentive to save cost can be contradictory to the interest of patients. Obviously, caregivers are constrained in the extent to which they can sacrifice patients' interests. If they consistently sacrifice patient interest, they will fail to attract enrollees. Yet, according to Kuttner (1998) Health Maintenance Organizations (HMOs) may give the sickest people poor service because driving such people away is in their interest.

In the United States, nearly three out of four HMOs are for profit. Some 62 per cent of HMO members are enrolled in for-profit plans in 1998, as compared with 12 per cent in 1981. There are all kinds of HMOs. Some opted to be generous and tried to target at the young and healthy, like the Oxford Health Plans. Others, like the U.S. Healthcare, opted to be stingy and expose their doctors to financial risks if caring for their patients become too expensive. The financial performance of these HMOs varies greatly from one to another. The fact remains, however, that enrollees ultimately have to test their luck. Doctors, too, are highly subject to the vagaries of the market. Meanwhile, managed care under market auspices has produced a "double paradox": "The more patients chafe under the constraints of utilization controls, the more they demand a choice of doctors—not realizing that the various doctors affiliated with a plan have similar or identical financial incentives to constrain costs. And the more plans try to offer a choice, the further they stray from the system-wide integration, prevention, and case management that are the supposed advantages of HMOs." (Kuttner, 1998)

3. THE PROFESSIONAL MODEL

The Hospital Authority (HA) in Hong Kong is the prototype of the professional model. The HA in 1999 manages over forty hospitals, which range widely in size and scope of services. Each year the HA is given a budget by the Hong Kong Special Administrative Region Government. The budget is allocated to each hospital according to some formula that takes into consideration the volume and composition of caseloads of each hospital. Each hospital has a Hospital Chief Executive who is an experienced doctor-administrator. The HA itself is run by professionals who are hired on terms that are set independently from the Hong Kong SAR civil service. The British National Health Service (NHS), especially during the period prior to the recent market-oriented reforms, was another fine example of the professional model. Doctors are paid a salary and are not according to the volume of their work.

The underlying principle behind the professional model is that the medical profession is in the best position to serve the interest of patients, provided that the profession is given the latitude to act independently and paid a salary commensurate with the returns expected from investing in training. Medical professionals are assumed to have the integrity to engage in ethical practice. The biggest advantages of the professional model are two. One is that it is free from the problem of "supply-side moral hazard"—doctors will not, given their salaried status, knowingly supply a service that does not serve the patient's interest. The other key advantage is that it puts the medical professional in center stage. His decisions are not circumscribed by bureaucratic interference, and are not swayed by market forces. The main objection against the professional model is that it may limit the choices open to patients, and that, not being subjected to the forces of the market at all, caregivers may not be sensitive to the needs of patients. Without the goad of competition, services may not improve, and costs may be higher than necessary.

The professional model in practice turns out to be very attractive to consumers of health services. Surveys in Hong Kong and in the U.K. suggest overwhelming support and general satisfaction with the system. Jinks, Pharm, and Shayegan-Salek (1997) described the NHS as "a proud British achievement, the expression of over 40 years of a sustained commitment to the ideal of providing 'effective health care as a public service to all who need it.'"[7] Ho (1997a) found that Hong Kong citizens were in general quite happy with the HA system, and many indeed were prepared to pay more taxes in return for an even better service.

Both the HA in Hong Kong and the NHS in the UK are predominantly funded by the general tax revenue. User charges are nominal or nonexistent, and this is putting pressure on the system to reform. Still, as a professional model, the HA in Hong Kong is administratively independent of the government. While the NHS is under the direct jurisdiction of the Minister of Health, medical professionals are deeply involved and are heavily relied upon both in the administration and in the delivery of health services. Although the NHS has undergone a major reform through the nineties trying to introduce some element of competition the general consensus is that there was little overall measurable change. In particular, the professional culture remained intact. According to Le Grand (1999), "those working in the NHS—whether doctors, nurses, manages, or ancillary staff....felt that they were engaged in the provision of a public service, with provider relationships (both with each other and with their patients) based more on considerations of mutual trust than on adversarial competition."[8]

4. THE BUREAUCRACY-DOMINATED MODEL

There is a fine line and yet material difference between the bureaucracy-dominated model and the professional model. Obviously no bureaucracy-dominated healthcare system can work without significant input from medical professionals. The conceptual bureaucracy-dominated model, however, constrains the medical professional so much so that professional autonomy—a dearly treasured aspect of professional practice and the basis of professional self-respect—is severely circumscribed. The Canadian health care system, under the duress of fiscal pressures, had succumbed to bureaucratic interference to a degree that it could be described as an example of bureaucracy-dominated model.[9]

For many years the Canadian health care system had been the envy of Americans.[10] It had achieved universal access to high-quality health care, and the resources committed, in terms of the percentage of the GDP devoted to healthcare, are far less than that of the United States. The Canadian system is quite a unique one, in that public financing of health care goes hand in hand with the prevalence of private practice.

The Canadian system had been heavily supported by the federal government. As the federal government went more deeply into debt, however, federal funding for health care expenditures was sharply reduced. In Ontario, under the Savings and Restructuring Act, physicians were at the mercy of the minister of health, who can "unilaterally close hospitals, set physicians' fees and tell physicians where they can work and what services they can provide. He can remove at will their right to practice medicine in the province. He can view confidential medical records and disclose the information for any reason. Government inspectors can seize medical records without a reason, a warrant, or the patient's consent. Inspectors can…rescind payment after the fact for physician services deemed to have been 'unnecessary.'"[11] Patients complained of long waiting times for emergency care and for specialized surgical services. It is not true, however, that bureaucrats are necessarily insensitive to patients' needs.

The main advantage of the bureaucracy-dominated model of medical care is that it can be fiercely expedient for achieving certain policy goals identified by the bureaucracy. The fear is that it may be insensitive to the aspirations of the medical profession and the needs of patients. While this fear can be misplaced, because the bureaucracy may well be enlightened and sensitive,[12] too much is left to chance so that in general neither consumer (patient) groups nor the medical profession is satisfied with it.

5. TOWARDS AN IDEAL SYSTEM

We now know that an ideal health care system must have certain ingredients. First and foremost, health care services provided under the main health care plan must be heavily subsidized and yet priced in such a way as to provide the right incentives for both suppliers and consumers. That is, suppliers of health services must not have the incentive to over-supply or to under-supply services, while consumers should have the incentive to take good care of their own bodies and not to over-use the system. Second, consumers must be protected from excessive burden. That is, medical care expenditures needed for body "maintenance and repair" must not be so costly as to plunge the consumer into financial difficulties. Third, for-profit private sector medical practice and hospitals should operate against a background of an adequate and sound publicly-funded, professionally-run medical care system. This will ensure that all private practices will provide quality care or such particular and specialized services that they are normally not covered by the public plan—because otherwise patients will leave them.

By nature, medical care is costly. Modern medical care requires highly precise and specialized equipment, well-trained professionals, and knowledge-intensive drugs. Without subsidies many people may be denied the needed medical care. Voluntary private insurance does not work because private insurers tend to reject those who need medical services the most. Mandatory insurance may work but there are two catches. One is that the poor may still need to be subsidized. The second is that charging fees to the insurer could lead to over-supply of medical services ("supply-side moral hazard"). Without an appropriate fee charged to consumers, moreover, consumers are likely to over-use services and less likely to take good care of their health ("demand-side moral hazard").

The logical conclusion from this argument is that a fee reflecting the direct cost of providing the service, exclusive of any overhead cost, should be charged to consumers. Such a fee would be neutral to suppliers, because on the one hand suppliers will not under-supply services since any extra costs arising will be covered, and on the other hand they will not over-supply since no extra profit can be gained. Private health service suppliers will need a lump-sum transfer from the government to cover their overhead costs. This arrangement will allow the best of professionalism manifest itself.

Even though households are held responsible only for the direct costs of medical care the cost of medical care may still be too large for them. To protect them from excessive burden, we can set up a *spending limit* amounting to, say, six per cent of the mean household income for a household of average size. Larger size households will have a larger threshold and smaller households will have a smaller threshold. Once the threshold has been exceeded, all the excessive spending on permissible items will be taken up by the government.

In some countries private hospitals are under-utilized while public hospitals are over-utilized. The excess capacity in private hospitals does not relieve the government of building more capacity among public hospitals. This is a direct result of the vast gap between charges in public hospitals and those in private hospitals. To eliminate such waste, it is necessary to equalize the charges. In particular, the charges prevailing in Hong Kong's public hospitals should be raised, while the charges prevailing in Hong Kong's private hospitals should be reduced. Under my proposal, private hospitals will be given the option to join the Hospital Authority system. If they join, they will be committed to charging patients standard fees for the standard services on a list. They will receive a lump-sum payment per year based on a formula reflecting their capacity and the range of services provided. They will receive user-charges direct from patients up to their yearly spending threshold and from the government after they have breached the thresholds.

Private hospitals may charge full fees independently if they do not receive any lumpsum subsidy from the government. All private hospitals can also charge fees independently for services which are not on the "standard service list."

Sweden has a similar system as proposed in this chapter. From June 1999 Sweden has a spending ceiling of 900 krones (about US$100) per year for care and 1800 krones (about US$200) for drugs per person. The Swedes never need to worry about excessive health care expenditures. Yet Swedish health care expenditures as a percentage of the gross domestic product has remained stable or has fallen, while most countries experienced an increase.

One might question the wisdom of setting a uniform yearly spending limit for the entire population. In particular, why is it that a very rich person should be entitled to the same spending threshold and thus receive the same subsidies from the tax-payer as an average person? Should a poor person be subject to a smaller spending threshold or be exempted from any threshold altogether? Once it is realized that "the tax-payer" consists of none other than the richer members of the community the apparent inequity of allowing the rich to benefit from excessive burden insurance disappears. As for the poorer members of the community, it is possible to give them a smaller threshold at, say X per cent of the standard threshold. I would also propose to charge these poorer patients fees that are discounted X per cent, so that regardless of rich or poor, everybody with the same health care needs would progress towards exhausting the annual spending limit at the same pace.

The universal access principle or principle of universality discussed herein contrasts with the "Able Pays More" principle that are sometimes advocated by some politicians. On the surface, universal access to subsidized health care is unfair. However, when a "rich" patient gets subsidized care, the implicit transfer that he gets is sourced either from himself or from other "rich," tax-paying, individuals. There is no distributionally perverse transfer from the poor to the rich. There is only a transfer from the healthier taxpaying individuals to the less healthy taxpaying individuals. It is not apparent that this is undesirable in any way. Indeed, because universality is administratively simpler than limiting access to subsidized care to the poor, it is an eminently sensible principle in the conduct of public policy.

Another important consideration that we must bear in mind is that while few would disagree with the general idea that those with a greater ability to pay should pay more, the "able" is not indefinitely able. There will come a point when even the "able" finds it hard to come up with the resources to support a very costly treatment. Thus there is a need for protection against excessive burden even for the rich, and for those who have saved for "the rainy day."

The pitfalls of the "saving for the rainy day principle" do not spare the Medisave program of Singapore. Under the Medisave Plan Singaporeans contribute 6 to 8 per cent of their incomes towards the Medisave sub-account in the Central Provident Fund.[13] Realizing the pitfall Singapore later introduced the Medishield program to provide catastrophic insurance in 1990. Another pitfall is that if the accumulated savings are too big the enrollee would be tempted to use the accumulated savings on health services even when such services have a low value.[14]

6. CONCLUSIONS

It is important to point out that any health care system is subject to some drawback. There is, in a word, no perfect system. We should, however, find the best practical system. The best practical system must:

- be administrative feasible and not too costly;
- provide protection against unexpected excessive burden for all;
- provide protection for chronic patients;
- incorporate sufficient incentives on both the supply side and the demand side to ensure efficiency so that the overall burden to society will be minimized;
- provide the greatest degree of choice and freedom for patients possible;
- allow sufficient autonomy to medical professionals for them to do a good job;
- provide protection for patients against unprofessional practice;
- provide room for private health care professionals to operate.

This is not a list of impossible things. Actually, with today's computer technology we can easily build a system that records the "eligible health care expenditures of a household" and ensure that no household spend beyond the "excessive burden" threshold. Any eligible expenditures within the year beyond the threshold can then be taken up by the government. This takes care of the first three desirable features.

A key proposition developed in my work on health economics (Ho, 1997a) is that efficiency of health care delivery requires charging patients an appropriate fee and compensating caregivers at an appropriate rate. Charging patients appropriately not only will help avoid abusive utilization of the health care system, but will promote preventive activities and encourage people to adopt a healthy lifestyle. Charging patients for standard services according to standard charges means that we need to compile a list of the eligible health services to be covered and the charge rates. In practice the charge rates need not be fine-tuned to reflect the conceptual marginal costs precisely. The key is that they should not be so remunerative to the supplier that the supplier is tempted to oversupply the service.

"Seamless health care" can be achieved by covering both primary, secondary, and tertiary care, and even accident and emergency care, whether supplied by public sector providers or private sector providers, under the same "excessive burden insurance" plan.

The professional model works best when it is not subject to the sway of market forces or the influence of the financial motive. Public funding of health services provides the necessary environment for professionals to work with autonomy. Still, the "market model" should be given a role to play too, in those areas of the health care market which are not considered basic. Consumers should be given the freedom to buy the services that they want at prices which they agree to pay. Bureaucrats are in the best position to serve as the overseer to ensure that complaints from consumers receive independent and professional investigation. They also serve a coordinating role and act as a bridge among the public, the professionals, and the market.

Nobel Laureate Amartya Sen is right when he argued that an assessment of inequality in general should go beyond figures on income and wealth. As he explains, "Quality of life depends on various physical and social conditions, such as the epidemiological environment in which a person lives. The availability of health care and the nature of medical insurance...are among the important influences on life and death..." (1995, p.35) He argued that it was no coincidence that a dramatic rise in life expectancy occurred in the same decade as the National Health Service of Britain emerged, i.e., 1941-51. (*op.cit.*, p.12).

Consistent with the same logic, the Director General of World Health Organization in 1981 explained that "health for all" is a holistic concept (Roemer, 1993, p.335). Not only does it require universal access to primary care with adequate referral services to more specialized care, but it also implies a commitment on the part of the government to promote the advancement of all citizens on a broad front of development. This, however, cannot be done through a one-way delivery of services from the government to the citizens. This has to be predicated on the emergence of a greater awareness and a sense of responsibility on the part of the citizens to take care of their own well being. We argue that *making citizens pay* for the direct cost of health care is an important element in this strategy. We also argue that this need not compromise accessibility, provided that we have in place a system of protection against excessive burden, such as proposed in this chapter and currently in practice in Sweden. Justice, equity, and efficiency can go together, while the market, the professional, as well as the bureaucrat can all have a role to play to further these ends. Certainly bureaucrats need not be content with acting out the role as portrayed by Niskanen in his early book.

NOTES

1 See Arnett, Jerome C., Jr. (1996).

2 See "Whither a Health Care Solution? Oh, Canada," *Businessweek*, March 21 1994, 56-57. It was hailed again by Dr. Marcia Angell, Editor of *New England Journal of Medicine*, as superior to the American "insane" system at the annual meeting of the British Columbia Medical Association. See *National Post*, September 4, 2000.

3 In Fiscal 2000, President Clinton requested a total budget of $400.3 billion for the Department of Health and Human Services, representing a 6.6 per cent increase over Fiscal 1999. The biggest expenditures are for Medicare (53.6%) and Medicaid (28.6%) Inclusive of other smaller items, total "mandatory (entitlement) outlays" amount to some $359.8 billion. In addition, under "discretionary programs" the Health Resources and Services Administration has requested a budget of $4.1 billion and runs some 746 community and migrant health centers for low income and uninsured individuals and families. The budget for the Food and Drug Administration is not huge, but has a big impact on the health care market through its regulation of drugs and food products.

4 The proportion of American without health insurance increased from 14.2 per cent in 1995 to 16.1 per cent in 1997, when the uninsured population reached 43.4 million (See Kuttner, 1999).

5 Part B of Medicare requires voluntary participation through the payment of a monthly premium.

6 "The Medically Uninsured: Will they always be with us?" *New England Journal of Medicine* (the Sounding Board), Vol. 334, no.17, 1103-1133.

7 In *Health Care Systems Around the World*, edited by M.L.Lassey, W.R.Lassey, and M.J.Jinks (1997).

8 Le Grand, Julian (1999) "Competition, Cooperation, or Control? Tales from the British National Health Service," *Health Affairs*, May/June.

9 With the Federal Government's fiscal position swinging back into surplus in 1999 there is a good chance that bureaucratic interference with health care will be reduced noticeably.

10 A formal proposal for health care reform modeled after the Canadian system was put forward by Senator McDermott and 92 other House Democrats. See "Whither a Health-care Solution? Oh Canada," *Business Week*, March 21, 1994.

11 Jerome Arnett: "Ontario's Health Care: a Pox on Doctors and Patients," *Asian Wall Street Journal*, 10 March 1996.

12 As Naylor (1999) pointed out, Ontario does have a comprehensive waiting list management system. When coronary artery bypass graft (CABG) queues grew to intolerable levels, as happened in 1990 and 1997, the Ministry of Health responded with major capacity expansions that quickly reduced the length of the queues.

13 Those below 35 contribute 6 % up to a maximum of S$360 while those 45 and above contribute 8% up to S$480.

14 Singapore has set up a maximum for the accumulated Medisave account savings to contain the distortionary effects. Contributions in excess of the maximum are transferred to the CPF Ordinary Accounts.

Chapter 6

LEGAL AID AND JUSTICE

In many ways legal aid resembles health care. There is an imperative, on grounds of justice, to provide legal aid and to provide health care to those who cannot afford it. Both legal services and health services are performed by professionals whose knowledge about their trade is not shared by the users of their services. Both legal and health services can be so costly that they may stretch the limits of users. Schemes to protect users from both the heavy cost of legal services and that of health services are subject to moral hazard and information asymmetry problems.

1. INTRODUCTION

Legal aid is commonly seen to be an important cornerstone for a system of justice in a civilised society. Certainly justice would not be justice if access to the judiciary process were limited only to those with the means to seek redress through legal proceedings.

When legal aid was first introduced in the United Kingdom in 1950, it was designed exclusively for civil suits. However, it was soon recognized that defendants accused of criminal offences need to be properly represented in a court of law if society's claim for espousal of justice is to be upheld. Today, in the United Kingdom, as in Hong Kong, legal aid is more liberally given for criminal than for civil proceedings. Indeed, in Hong Kong all people charged with criminal offences who require the services have been granted legal aid. The *means test*, passing which is normally required for civil suits, is routinely lifted by the Director of Legal Aid to make sure that the defendant has a fair hearing. Similarly, in the U.K., following the recommendation of the Widgery Report on criminal proceedings (HMSO, 1966), the proportion of defendants appearing on an indictable offence in a magistrates' court with legal aid rose rapidly, from 20 per cent in 1969 to 80 per cent by 1986.

Legal services is in many respects similar to health services. Like health services, legal services is performed by professionals who need long years of training. Like medical care, the outcome of health services is often not clear. One cannot predict success or failure in litigation, just as one cannot tell for sure whether a surgical operation will be successful or not. Similarly, very often one cannot tell how much will the litigation costs be, or even how long the litigation process is going to take. Like medical care, legal aid is prone to supply-side moral hazard and demand-side moral hazard. That is to say, lawyers, like doctors, may supply more services than are needed in order to benefit financially, while users of legal aid, like patients, may demand more services than social costs/social benefit considerations justify.

Under most legal aid schemes, applications for legal aid are subject to a means test as well as a merit test. Today (i.e., year 2000) in Hong Kong the *means test* requires that the total annual income and capital assets after paying the rent for the dwelling unit and an allowance for daily maintenance should not exceed HK$169,700 (about US$21756). The *merit test*, applicable only for civil suits, requires that an applicant must have valid grounds of seeking justice through the judiciary process and must have a reasonable prospect of success. The latter can be regarded as a "gate-keeping" mechanism to avoid abuse.

Because of the similarities between health care and legal aid, the arguments for excessive burden insurance principle that apply to health care also apply to legal aid. The idea is that even people with incomes commonly regarded as high may not be able to afford the expenses required in seeking redress through legal proceedings. There is a difference though. Whereas in the case of health care a yearly spending limit is perfectly sensible in the case of legal services probably a much higher, 10-year spending limit would be more appropriate. Unlike health care, litigation is in general not a regular need. It would not make sense to limit litigation costs to X per cent of the annual income.[1] I would propose that one should be responsible for litigation costs up to half a year's earnings. We would still need the gate-keeping mechanism in order to prevent demand-side moral hazard.

2. SUPPLY-SIDE AND DEMAND-SIDE MORAL HAZARD

Under many typical legal aid schemes, the lawyers acting on behalf of the aided persons are in private practice. This is more a result of political lobbying by a professional body than one of social design. In the United Kingdom, the Law Society, which administered the scheme until 1988, had offered a 15 per cent discount on legal aid work to avoid a salaried service. The fee-for-service mode of operation, however, is widely known to engender supply-side moral hazard. Gray, Richman, and Fenn (1999) found circumstantial evidence that is consistent with the supplier-induced demand thesis. In particular, a rise in the opportunity cost of time, such as an increase in mortgage business, was found to have a negative impact on unit costs and the volume of legal aid work, while an increase in the number of solicitors was found to have a positive impact. Richman, Gray, and Fenn (1999) believed that the smaller increases in criminal volumes than civil volumes between 1980 and 1995 may also be related to the fact that it is the police and the crown prosecutor, not lawyers, that decide whether or not to proceed with a criminal case (p.272).

Supply-side moral hazard is not the only reason that may cause a misallocation of resources and a run-up in legal-aid-related expenditures. If users of legal aid services do not bear the cost of using the services, they may use the services even though the benefits may not justify the costs. Rickman et. al. (1999) found that the propensity to litigate is much higher among those who do not have to pay anything than among those who are required to contribute toward the cost (11 per 1000 as compared with 1.79 per 1000, p.273). Although there is a gate-keeping mechanism in the sense that an application for legal aid must pass a test of merit to be approved and gross abuse of the legal aid system is unlikely, the perception that the legal services are "free" will lead to excessive utilization of the services. The fact is: even if there is "merit" the social benefits of proceeding with a case still may not warrant the costs involved.

3. FEES OR SALARIES? FEES AND SALARIES?

As long as lawyers are paid on a fee-for-service basis and lawyers make money from legal aid work, there is likely to be a "principal-agent problem." Even after 1988, when the U.K. Legal Aid Board took over the administration of legal aid from the Law Society, we could see the Legal Aid Board as the "principal" engaging an "agent"—the lawyer—to provide legal services for a client. Since the interest of the Legal Aid Board and that of the lawyers are not the same there will be no reason to expect that lawyers will behave in a way that best serves the interest of the Legal Aid Board. As long as users of legal aid services pay only a fraction of the cost of such services or nothing at all there will also be a tendency for over-consumption of the services.

The best solution to the supply-side moral hazard is remunerating legal aid lawyers with a salary at a rate that fully reflects the professional nature of the job. Salaried lawyers will consider each job in a professional manner, much as a technocrat employed in the civil service would. Lawyers hired to work in legal aid are hired for their belief in the cause of legal aid and their professionalism. Earning a salary, their decisions and activity in a case will be money-neutral and market-neutral.

Because the cost of litigation is difficult to determine before hand, even relatively well-off people—people who normally would not qualify for legal aid, may refrain from litigation. This would mean that real cases of grievance or injustice may not be attended to, and more important, this means that more of such cases will occur each year because wrongdoers have reasons to believe that their victims will not litigate. This is clearly unjust and welfare-diminishing.

To contain the problem of demand-side moral hazard and at the same time to achieve greater social justice, eligibility to legal aid should be extended to all citizens, and all users should be charged a standard fee for each hour of legal services used up to some limit. Unlike excessive burden insurance in health care, however, I propose a ten-year spending limit rather than an annual spending limit. This will be a much bigger figure, perhaps 60 per cent of annual income. The main reason is that whereas health care expenditures are regular expenditures that will occur year after year, litigation expenditures are usually much bigger and very infrequent. Following the principle of redistribution and helping the poor, I recommend that the poor should be subject to a lower spending limit and lower fees. This is much like what I recommend for health care.

In the United Kingdom, at the initial stage of a potential legal action, free legal advice and assistance, for up to two to three hours, are generally provided under the means-tested Green Form Scheme. Following the logic of excessive burden insurance, offering this service free is really not important, because the expenses are relatively small. What is important is excessive burden protection. The free service opens up an opportunity for abuse. Collecting this amount as well as fees for other services will goad citizens into more "preventive care," as individuals will become that much more careful in interacting with other parties.

To conclude this section, a direction of legal aid reform will be to allow the legal aid department charge clients fees up to a limit. The legal aid department will use these fees as well as allocation from the government budget to pay for the salaries of employed legal aid lawyers.

4. PROSPECTIVE PAYMENTS, CONTINGENCY PAYMENTS, AND LEGAL AID

Just as health reform proposals are full of suggestions for prospective payments, for example under the Diagnosis-Related Group (DRG) formula that pay hospitals according to the diagnosis of admitted patients, so the legal aid literature has recently attracted some discussion about prospective payments.

As Rickman et. al. (1999) explained, the introduction of "standard fees" for criminal cases in Magistrates' Courts in 1993 followed the prospective payment philosophy. It is, however, fairly complicated, not only involving different standard fees for different categories of cases, but also allowing graduated charges based on "the solicitor's report, audited by the Legal Aid Board, of the work demanded by the case." (p.274) "The solicitor may additionally claim percentage enhancements to the itemised rates, by demonstrating that the work was done with exceptional competence and dispatch, or that the case had exceptional circumstances." (p.274)

The advantage of prospective payments lies in containing costs and limiting the risks of clients. Lawyers receiving fixed prospective payments will have no incentive to waste time and money. Clients (the Legal Aid Department in this case), too, will know with greater certainty how much they need to spend on the legal proceedings.

As mentioned earlier on the Law Society had been able to use its influence to avoid a salaried legal aid service. As long as legal aid works through a private practice system, however, it is unlikely that standard fees can dominate, because there is considerable diversity in the complexity of cases. For this reason, it is not realistic to expect prospective payments will help contain costs significantly.

Another direction of legal aid reform is related to the introduction of conditional fee agreements (CFAs). Under CFAs the litigant need not pay the lawyer a professional fee unless the case is won. If there is nothing to pay unless the case is successful, one major inhibition for taking legal action when one feels unfairly treated will be gone. The need for legal aid will then also be reduced.

One problem with CFAs is that clients with CFAs will still have to pay for the expenses of the lawyer, and in case of losing the suit, for the costs of the other party. Because there is always a chance of loss, CFAs can never eliminate the need for legal aid.

5. CONCLUSIONS

Legal aid has generally been offered on the basis of two tests: the means test and the merit test. This chapter argues that legal aid, like health care, should follow the principle of universality. Because legal costs are difficult to estimate ahead of time and can be quite significant, people who do not quality for legal aid routinely avoid legal action for financial reasons even though they have been unfairly treated. This behavior is perfectly understandable but may not be socially optimal, because it may lead to more wrongdoing.

It is true that conditional fee agreements are making legal services more accessible to the average person, but as pointed out earlier, the worry over losing the suit and having to pay the legal fees of the other party could be inhibiting.

Universal access to legal aid, combined with a legal aid service that hires salaried lawyers as employees and charges clients for services used at cost up to some limit, will greatly enhance social justice. It will contain supplier-induced demand as well as demand-side moral hazard, and will put the justice system truly within access of people at large.

If victims of wrongdoing are more likely to litigate, potential wrongdoers will think twice before they would offend. Less offence will be perpetuated. Although under the principle of excessive burden insurance legal aid is available without means-testing, the demand for legal aid services could actually decline, if the number of offences is reduced. While the universality principle is followed, the proposed scheme allows the poor to be given a smaller ten-year spending limit and to be charged at a lower price, just like what was proposed for health care in the last chapter.

Of course, having a state-run legal aid system that is available on demand to all citizens does not remove the right of a citizen to engage a private lawyer to litigate for him. Like medical care, the free market will offer those who can afford it greater choice. The state, however, should ensure that no one is denied basic health care and redress through the justice system.

NOTES

1 Ho (1997) proposed, as the yearly health care spending limit, 6 per cent of median household income divided by the average number of members in the household for one individual. The annual spending limit for a specific household would then be this figure multiplied by the number of the particular household concerned.

Chapter 7

BANK DEPOSIT INSURANCE

In the wake of the Bank of Commerce and Credit (BCC) debacle the Hong Kong Government, then under British rule, issued a Consultation Paper: Deposit Protection Scheme (Monetary Affairs Branch, Government Secretariat, February 1992). Despite expected objections from the major banks the Monetary Authority under the new SAR Government is revisiting the subject, and is expected to come up with a decision about introducing deposit insurance into Hong Kong before too long. This chapter is adapted from a contribution in Deposit Insurance: Issues and Evaluation, edited by Y.C. Jao and published by the Chartered Institute of Bankers-Hong Kong Centre, July 1992. The argument presented illustrates an important principle of public policy, namely, that the rational behavior of individuals must be fully considered in the design of policy.

1. INTRODUCTION

The traditional role of deposit insurance has been mainly to prevent bank runs and thus to foster stability in the banking system. To the extent that this role has often been filled by the establishment of an effective lender of last resort, to whom banks caught in temporary liquidity crisis can turn, some have argued that there is no need for a deposit insurance scheme.[1] Yet deposit insurance continues to serve important functions in a modern society. It is argued in this chapter that one form of deposit insurance, namely one that provides full coverage for all demand deposits, 80 per cent coverage for all savings deposits, and 60 per cent for all other deposits, is likely to bring the most benefit to a modern society. The precise percentage numbers could be somewhat modified, but the spirit of full protection for demand deposits and lesser protection for other kinds of deposits is eminently sensible.

In Hong Kong "the Government has made it clear that liquidity support for *solvent* banks would be forthcoming from the Exchange Fund" (Consultation Paper, para. 2b). If this is the official policy the Exchange Fund will then become the official lender of last resort. Granted that the

Exchange Fund has at its command considerable reserves and its official capacity, depositors should have little worry that banks would fail to honour their commitments on grounds of liquidity. Yet the reassurance by the Government about the overall health of Hong Kong's banking sector cannot guarantee that all banks are sound. The statement in the Consultation Paper, that "The main protection [to depositors] must continue to come from having a supervisory system up to international standards," (para. 7) is hollow for the unlucky depositors who were caught in the Bank of Commerce and Credit (BCC) incident. For them there was no "main protection": they had to endure a long wait before the first instalment of repayment at 25 per cent of their deposits. In a typical bank failure, depositors had to wait a long time to get any reimbursement made possible in the liquidation process which could last for years.

2. THE SOCIAL BENEFITS OF DEPOSIT INSURANCE

The Consultation Paper argued that a carefully designed deposit protection scheme could perform two valuable functions:

- compensate small depositors either fully or in part in. the event of a *non-systematic* failure of any but the largest banks in a banking system; and
- enhance the stability of a banking system by raising the "crisis of confidence threshold" of the general public.

Actually, this significantly understates the value of deposit insurance.

By providing immediate liquidity to depositors affected by troubled banks, bank deposit insurance (BDI) may save hundreds of well-run businesses which may otherwise be directly or indirectly pushed into bankruptcy or closing down for not receiving money receivable or not being able to pay money payable.

By providing the assurance that one's own liquidity and that of one's clients will not suddenly dry up because of bank closures, bank deposit insurance will improve the investment climate for businesses. Employment, income, and tax revenue may rise as a result. In the absence of a sound BDI the costs of self-protection and the risks of being adversely affected by bank closures will have to be considered in running a business or in long term investment.

By minimizing the discrimination against smaller banks by depositors on grounds of size, such banks are better able to survive. Competition from the smaller banks improves the services at the larger banks and forces them to achieve greater efficiency.

By offering reliable, basic protection, depositors are relieved of the need for costly self-protection which may not even be reliable. For instance, depositors might, despite "having done their homework" and read all the annual reports of their banks, still fail to find any signs or warnings for problems that will surface later. Unnecessary bank-runs are yet another form of costly (and certainly rational given high information costs) self-protection that depositors cannot be blamed for.

By providing the same protection to the depositors of all banks rather than providing discretionary protection to individual banks the Government can avoid allegations of discrimination or unfairness.

By making it less painful to wind up sick and technically bankrupt banks the Government can avoid being pressured into saving such banks at great cost to society.

Once we are clear about the functions that a BDI serves we will be in a better position to work out the best design for such a scheme.

3. OPTIMAL COVERAGE

First, there is little ground for limiting coverage to any specific amount as proposed in the Consultation Paper and in practice under the U.S. federal deposit insurance. If protecting businesses is important, such limited coverage is likely to be grossly inadequate. Proponents of limited coverage either think of such limits as a way of conserving the DPS fund in the event a payout is necessary, or believe that larger depositors are less deserving of protection than smaller depositors. Yet setting a ceiling to protected deposits is neither an efficient way of conserving the DPS fund nor efficient in terms of risk management.

Bank deposits, especially demand deposits, are more in the nature of money than in the nature of an investment. Businesses and households keep money in the current accounts to settle bills, repay loans, or make advances to clients. Any disruptions to these transactions will spell trouble for otherwise sound businesses and their clients. Most of these accounts in Hong Kong do not earn interest, and there is no question of them being in the "high risk, high return category" (and therefore unworthy of protection). From the risk management point of view, there is a prerogative for them to be fully protected by bank regulators, who should ensure that all the transactions in the current accounts are not disrupted. In the absence of such protection, businesses will have to bear the cost of selfprotection even though official protection by bank regulators is far more economical. Society as a whole will have to bear the consequences should self-protection fail, as chain effects are bound to occur in the wake of such failures. As demand deposits are a rather small fraction of all deposits, 100 per cent protection will not pose a significant drain on the resources of the DPS fund. It yields, however, very significant social benefits.

A similar, though somewhat weaker argument can be made for protecting savings deposits. Such deposits are repayable on presentation of the passbook and at the automatic teller machines. These deposits are classified as part of M2 in the money supply, but they are about as liquid as chequable deposits. Characterized by low and uniform returns, they have little resemblance to risky investments. I recommend 80 per cent protection for all such deposits. A 20 per cent "haircut" will not excessively compromise the need to protect a highly liquid form of assets. At the same time it will more effectively help conserve the BDI fund than providing full protection up to a cash limit as is currently practised in the United States. It is well known that depositors are prone to splitting their deposits among several banks and accounts in order to gain fuller protection under the latter system. Such a rational response from among the depositors will unnecessarily increase transactions costs. On the other hand, the "haircut" approach will avoid the deposit splitting scenario and will also help conserve the incentive for all depositors to monitor the performance of their banks.

Finally, time deposits and deposits in foreign currency accounts are, in comparison with demand and savings deposits, much more in the nature of investment than in the nature of money. 60 per cent protection is recommended for these deposits. As these deposits comprise the greater part of banks' deposit base in typical economies, imposing such a limit to protection serves two important functions. It will help retain "market discipline" on banks, giving them an incentive to attract deposits on the basis of sound management of its assets and liabilities. It will also help conserve the funds of the BDI should a payout be necessary. It is hoped that this provision will, in addition, remove the objection of the larger banks that deposit insurance involves cross subsidization at their expense and in favor of the smaller, weaker banks.

4. FINANCING THE BDI

Those who believe in the user pays principle tend to reject any proposal to have the government underwrite a BDI. They think that bank depositors, being the beneficiaries from a BDI, should pay for both the insurance premiums and the administrative cost of the scheme. There would be no need for an officially backed credit line for the BDI.

On the surface, this seems to make sense and seems to be in the best interest of taxpayers who are then protected from unknown contingent liabilities. The logic leading to this conclusion, however, is flawed for two reasons.

First, provided that the charges are sufficient to cover all costs of the BDI in the long run, any temporary deficit due to a bank failure occurring prior to the accumulation of sufficient funds can be recovered over the longer term. Extending a line of credit to the BDI fund will not cost taxpayers anything, provided that a market interest rate is charged.

Secondly, if the BDS contributes to a more stable, healthy, and fairer banking system everyone benefits from it. It is a public good and the benefits extend beyond the bank depositors. In order for the BDI to yield the intended benefits, prompt recovery of the protected amount by depositors in the event of bank failures or suspensions is of utmost importance. In order to provide for prompt recovery of the protected deposits a sound deposit protection scheme should have access to financing when needed.

Actually, the limited protection as recommended in this chapter is unlikely to cost the BDI anything even in the case of a bank failure, because there are many cushions that help prevent the payouts from eating into the equity of the BDI fund. First is the equity of the shareholders. Generally, bank supervisors are expected to take action either to rectify problems found or to suspend the problem bank long before shareholders' equity has fallen to zero. Second, the "haircut" of 20 per cent on savings deposits and that of 40 per cent on time and foreign currency deposits mean that even if bank shareholders' equity has fallen below zero there is a good chance that the payout will be recovered by the BDI fund as the assets of the bank are liquidated. Moreover, new legislation can be passed to give holders of demand deposits priority over other creditors in their claims on the assets of a failed bank.

There has been considerable debate over whether the insurance premiums should vary among banks. The principle that insurance premiums should rise with risks is of course generally accepted. However, many people argue that varying the premiums charged according to risk is infeasible in the case of bank deposit insurance, because a bank whose insurance premiums are raised will be regarded as unsafe. Market reaction may aggravate the problems of the bank (OECD, 1987). Some people also think that as a result of direct supervisory regulation the risks of banks may have become similar. There will then be no need to vary premiums among banks.

Actually, risk-related premiums are not only feasible, but also highly desirable (White, 1991). The way to go about implementing risk-related premiums, however, has to be adapted to the unique characteristics of the banking industry. The specific proposal is that while uniform premiums are charged on similar deposits held in different banks, additional charges will be imposed on those banks whose risk-adjusted net worth has fallen below some threshold level. Thus, depositors will not be alerted of any change in total premiums charged. Potential trouble banks are given the grace of conducting their businesses as usual while having to pay for their excessive risk-taking. To make things simple, a surcharge of 50 per cent on total premiums paid may be imposed on the potential problem banks. Aware of the potential need to make such payments, banks will become more careful. Risk-related BDI premiums have preventive and not remedial purposes.

In line with the recommendation to cover different kinds of deposits at different percentages, it is proposed that depositors be charged at 100 per cent, 80 per cent, and 60 per cent of the standard premium rate for demand, savings, and other deposits respectively. The base for calculating the premiums to be paid should be the highest daily balance maintained on each account.

A case can be made that part of the cost of a BDI be financed from the general revenue. As argued above, a BDI improves the investment climate of a country and enhances the stability of the economy. Bank deposit insurance can also be justified on efficiency and equity grounds (Ho, 1991), both of which is valued by society at large. The establishment of a BDI will generate benefits external to the banking industry and depositors during better times as a result of improved investment climate. The benefits will be even greater during crises as a BDI saves healthy but otherwise ruined enterprises. Some depositors may like to have complete protection on all of their deposits. It is highly desirable that the Government encourages and facilitates the development of a private market in deposit insurance that offers additional coverage at commercial rates. There is no need to subsidize this market, because subsidies for the additional coverage are likely to blunt market sensitivity and amplify the moral hazard problem.

5. THE RIGHT PERSPECTIVE ON THE MORAL HAZARD PROBLEM

The moral hazard problem is common to all insurance schemes and it is real. Yet we must not exaggerate the problem. Rather, we should understand its nature and take the necessary measures to contain it. As Jao (1982) maintained, the existence of moral hazard problems does not in itself negate the value of insurance. The moral hazard problem generally refers to insured people reducing their effort in self-protection because insurance reduces the benefits of self-protection. In the case of deposit insurance it means that depositors will have less need to find out if their banks are safe. Unsound banks are then able to retain their clients and even to attract deposits by offering higher interest rates. The Savings and Loans (S&L) crisis in the United States has been partly attributed to the emergence of "zombie" S&L institutions, namely "living dead" thrift institutions that sucked deposits away from their competitors and bid down loan rates on high-risk projects, thereby sapping the strength of these competitors (Kane, 1989, P. 36-37). This was possible partly as a result of the practice of "capital forbearance" or leniency on the part of regulators, and partly as a result of the 100 per cent deposit protection effectively available to most depositors.

Yet while it is one thing to say that the moral hazard problem is real, it is quite another thing to say that deposit insurance will cause serious moral hazard problems. Kane (1989) and Davis (1990) have argued that the US problem was very much a result of regulators' procrastination. According to Kane, the Federal Savings and Loans Insurance Corporation's "single greatest mistake" was "to adopt irregular and misleading regulatory accounting principles that served to create important new opportunities through which insolvent and unprofitable thrifts could legally conceal their ongoing weakness." In particular, "The FSLIC's decisions in 1982 to lower capital requirements and to loosen its definition of what constitutes capital for regulatory purposes put many economically insolvent clients beyond the pale of close supervision." (P. 34) Republican Representative Jim Leach, a House Banking Committee member, who had warned in vain about the S&L problem for years, concluded: "It's the single greatest regulatory lapse of this century. It's the single greatest indicator of the defer-at-all-costs approach to government in this century. " (*Newsweek*, May 21, 1990, P 23)

The S&L crisis in the United States was also very much a matter of the "looting" of depositors' and eventually of taxpayers' money by the major owner or owners of the institutions. Davis (1990) documented many cases of such looting. One practice, for instance, involved the trading of a piece of property at ever escalating prices, with the thrift owner or owners pocketing lucrative fees for "negotiating" fake deals each time the property allegedly changed bad-debt loans to one's close associates. Thus, "to deftly rob a thrift… required only a fountain pen, a circle of close personal friends in the real estate and financial businesses, and the perfect freedom provided by the absence of regulation." (P 56) If the report of a journalist is no proof, an FBI investigator's conclusion perhaps should be more convincing. Sessions (1990) wrote:[2] "insider abuse is a major factor in almost all investigations involving failed financial institutions." The reason why failures of deposit taking institutions rise during economic downturns is that "Even though fraud is often a contributing factor in bank failure, it was an economic downturn that surfaced the fraud." (p.58)

The United States' S&L crisis, then, is more the result of a lapse in regulatory effort, partly attributable to the budget squeeze,[3] and partly attributable to the lack of political will. It was certainly not the necessary result of deposit insurance. Indeed, for over fifty years since the establishment of federal deposit insurance, few banks failed; the 1/12 of one per cent premium which had prevailed since the 1930s was found to be more than adequate to service the deposit insurance in the United States for decades. Annual rebates to insured institutions had been made since 1962 through the early 1980's. Premiums were reduced and as recently as 1983 and 1984 stood at 1/14 of one per cent and 1/13 of one per cent respectively (Cooper and Fraser, 1986, P 156).

Bank deposit insurance is now common in many industrial and developing countries. The history of BDI is mainly a happy one. Only in the United States and only in the 1980s did we find such a mess in the banking and S&L industries. Notwithstanding the moral hazard problem, deposit insurance does not in itself imply financial disaster. Only when it is in the form of full coverage of deposits and combined with lax regulation will it lead to serious problems.

The kind of fractional deposit insurance for all depositors as proposed earlier, plus additional, punitive charges on risky banks, will go a long way towards minimizing the moral hazard problem. Although we have recommended full protection of demand deposits, this should not be a serious problem as virtually all depositors who open a current account will have other accounts and indeed will keep most of their deposits in these other accounts. Exposure to some risk will make them vigilant, or at least will give banks an incentive to foster an image of prudent management of their balance sheets.

6. THE OPTIMAL DEGREE OF OFFICIAL DEPOSIT PROTECTION

The argument for fractional deposit protection has been made on grounds of coinsurance for the minimization of the moral hazard problem. But it can also be made on the grounds of optimization. In Figure 1, MC represents the marginal social cost of self-protection.[4] It includes the cost of monitoring one's banks, the costs arising from the diversification of deposits and assets rendered necessary because of a lack of official protection, and the costs arising from higher risks of self-protection. MB represents the marginal social benefit of self protection. It includes the benefit of improved market discipline on the behaviour of banks, reduction in otherwise-needed regulation that may distort bankers' behaviour, etc. Optimal self-protection occurs where MC cuts MB. Optimal official protection is of course one minus the optimal self-protection percentage. A 100 per cent self-protection is justified only if the intersection point occurs to the right of the 100 per cent self-protection point. While the precise optimal self-protection percentage must be determined empirically there is good reason to believe that optimal self-protection is lowest for demand deposits and highest for time deposits, as the costs arising from higher risks of selfprotection are certainly highest for demand deposits and lowest for time deposits. The proposed protection at 100 per cent, 80 per cent, and 60 per cent for demand, savings, and other deposits seems quite reasonable.

Figure 1.

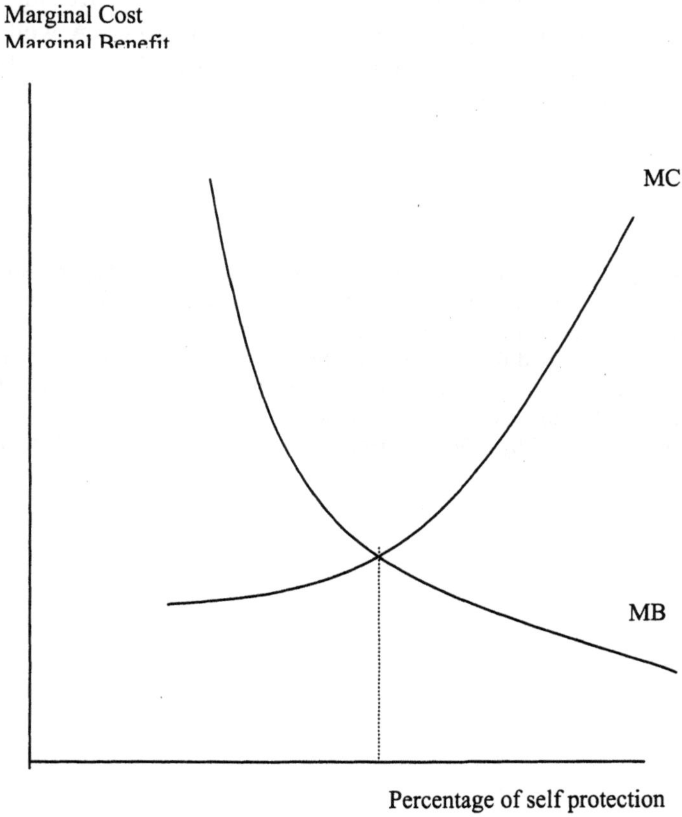

7. CONCLUSIONS

To conclude, a deposit protection scheme serves important functions in a modern society. Quite apart from protecting the interests of small depositors who cannot fend for themselves, it improves the business environment for firms, making them less susceptible to bankruptcy on account of other people's mistakes. It also makes the banking industry more competitive. Depositors of large banks today may congratulate themselves for enjoying good service and security of their deposits. But the good service of the large banks may be a result of competition from smaller banks which in the past could thrive because depositors had the impression that the Government would take over any failed bank. In the wake of the BCC incident we have observed a fairly significant shift of deposits from smaller banks to the larger banks. If the BCC shock ends up reducing competition in the banking industry the larger banks will become complacent or even arrogant with depositors. All depositors will then end up suffering a decline in the quality of service and even higher banking charges. A well-designed deposit protection scheme will protect an otherwise well developed economy from this unhappy eventuality.

NOTES

1 See "Symposium on Deposit Insurance," *Hong Kong Economic Papers*, No. 21, 1991.
2 Sessions was Director of the Federal Bureau of investigation Testimony Before the House Committee on Banking, Finance, and Urban Affairs.
3 Davis (1990) reported that in 1983 a starting thrift examiner was paid $14000 a year, turnover was immense, and there were fewer than 800 of them to cover the entire country (P 62). badly needed S&L examiners (P 22).
4 Deposits not covered by official protection are by definition under self protection.

Chapter 8

TOWARDS AN OPTIMAL PUBLIC PENSION SCHEME

Use the Insurance Principle to protect against longevity risks. Treat each cohort independently and adopt the Fully Funded Pension Principle for each cohort. Build in any redistributive elements explicitly and collectively as desired.

1. INTRODUCTION

Economists around the world are by now quite familiar with the pitfalls of a pay-as-you-go pension system. An aging society coupled with the prospect of increasing longevity is causing financial strains in public pension schemes from Europe to America.[1] (See Table 1) Calls for pension reform are heard everywhere. In the industrial world quite a few authors are talking about privatization of public pensions (Roberts, 1995; Dornbusch, 1995). A favorite model of pension reform is privatization Chile style.[2] This is an option (dubbed "personal security" in contrast to social security) considered in the recent report of President Clinton's Advisory Council on Social Security (*Businessweek*, Jan. 20, 1997, 26-27). Yet the superiority of this model is not unquestioned. Note, for example, MIT economist Peter Diamond's conclusion in 1993:

> We have come to think of privatization as a route to greater efficiency and lower costs. Thus, perhaps the most surprising aspect of the Chilean reform is the high cost of running a privatized social security system, higher than the "inefficient" system that it replaced. (NBER Working Paper, no. 4510, 1993)

It has been pointed out that the administration costs of public pension plans are likely to be under-reported (James and Palacios, 1995). However, under-reporting is unlikely to account for the huge gap between the administration costs of public and private plans (Mitchell and Zeldes, 1996, p.11). The U.S. Social Security Administration reported administration costs at less than 1 per cent of annual benefits while those of the life insurance industry are known to range from 12 to 14 per cent of annual benefits (Diamond, 1993, p.7). Economies of scale of management, economies of supervision, as well as economies arising from the dispensing of much of marketing costs, are likely to provide important cost savings attributable to the central administration of public pensions.[3]

Equally important, a "private social security system" is a contradiction in terms. Under such a system, each worker has his own account. Each worker and his employer are to contribute a percentage of the monthly salary into this account, and the funds accumulated are managed privately and the total amount inclusive of investment returns is repayable upon retirement. The only aspect that is "social" about a purely private system — the Chile model *not* being a true example because the government does guarantee a minimum pension and because it mandates a minimum requirement of annuitization — is that it is mandatory. A true Mandatory Private Provident Fund (MPPF) scheme — one that allows individual account holders to opt for lump-sum payment or to buy an annuity in the market place from voluntary underwriters, such as recently introduced in Hong Kong (Hewitt Associates LLC and GML Consulting Ltd., 1995, para. 33) — *either* fails to pool longevity risks (Eckstein, Eichenbaum, and Peled, 1985), *or* fails to deal with the high cost of voluntarily purchased annuity plans (Abel, 1986). It is also doubtful that workers stand to gain from employers' contributions. In a highly competitive world how much can be spent in compensation for labor is dictated by the market. Workers' pay and/or other benefit are likely to fall, thus offsetting employers' contributions. The set-up will not expand the real opportunity set open to workers.

On the contrary, employees see their opportunity set reduced because they are required to contribute the stipulated percentage of their salaries towards their retirement plans.[4] From this perspective, if the plan has any merit at all, the merit must be founded on the assumption that citizens do not know what is best for themselves (the assumption of *myopia*) or the assumption of *moral hazard*, namely that some citizens overconsume before their retirement, intending to take a free ride on public money to bail them out after they have retired. As we will see, even if the myopia and the moral hazard assumptions are valid, the MPPF is not necessarily the best option.

Abel (1986) has demonstrated the welfare enhancing property of "Fully Funded Social Security." With compulsory participation, fully funded social security overcomes the problem of "adverse selection." Adverse selection is the phenomenon of private, voluntary, insurance plans attracting "bad risks." Compulsory participation, through diluting the risks to the average level of those of the population, allows the rate of return to become higher than that on private voluntary annuities. With a higher, the *actuarially fair* rate of return based on population average mortality, and assuming exogenously given factor prices, both the steady state consumption of young consumers and the steady state level of bequests can be shown to be higher than would be the case under private, voluntary annuities.

Abel has, unfortunately, not addressed the problem of actual design for such a "Fully Funded Social Security." The fact is that practically all the public pension plans that we know today are either pay-as-you-go or partially funded. This chapter will explain how a "fully funded social security" system can be designed. It will be clear that the design is consistent with the spirit of the "generational accounting" framework as advocated by Auerbach, Gokhale, and Kotlikoff (1994).[4] Section 2 will present the salient features of the new model. Section 3 will provide an analytical investigation of the microeconomic and political economy properties of the model. Section 4 will conclude with a discussion of the longer term macroeconomic implications of a universal fully funded pension system. Finally, Section 5 will provide some brief concluding comments.

2. THE FULLY FUNDED PENSION FUND SYSTEM

Given the demographic trends of the world's population, economists generally agree that a pay-as-you-go type of pension system will ultimately require a rise in contribution rates, a cut in benefits, a postponement of the retirement age, or a combination of these. To avoid the predicaments of uncertain benefits or uncertain contributions a fully funded system, like that practised in Singapore or Malaysia (the "Central Provident Fund" model, Asher,1994), or a "Mandatory Private Provident Fund" model, seems necessary.

The spirit of a fully funded system is that workers should save for their own retirement needs. Post-retirement payouts should be "fully funded" by accumulated contributions rather than from the general tax revenue. According to Auerbach et.al. and citing from the Office of Management of the Budget, "even assuming a discount rate of just 3 per cent and a productivity growth rate of 1.25 per cent, future generations will still have to pay 65 per cent more (taxes) than current newborns." (*op.cit.* p.82) This presents a case of gross generational imbalance in U.S. fiscal policy, a problem underscored by generational accounting.[5] In general, only a fully funded system is compatible with the avoidance of arbitrary intergeneration transfers. However, a fully funded system does not require that *each individual* fully fund *his* own retirement needs. It is conceivable and desirable that each *generation* or *cohort*, rather than individuals, fund its own retirement needs.

The Universal Fully Funded Pension (UFFP) system proposed herein would have members of each age cohort contribute to and draw from the same pension fund. Rather than relying on the working population to support the retirees, each cohort finances its own retirement. The basic version of the scheme--with refinements to be introduced later--requires each member to contribute the same amount in each month during the contributing years and to draw the same amount each month during the payout years. The budget constraint is one simple equation which says that funds accumulated prior to the stipulated age for drawing benefits must equal the present value of post-retirement payout at the stipulated retirement age:

$$\sum_{t=0}^{N-1} C(1 + r)^t = \sum_{j=1}^{n} B/(1+r)^j$$

Here N is the number of contribution instalments in months. C is the monthly contribution. r is the effective average monthly real rate of return assumed, and is also used as the discount rate for the n instalments of payouts at B per month. Life expectancy is equal to the current age plus (N + n) /12.

Because there is little uncertainty over the life expectancy for a specified age cohort we can readily calculate the size of the required contribution to support a specified payout from the stipulated age through the end of the expected life for the entire cohort, given the long term real rate of return. If the expected life has increased at the stipulated payout age, say because of a breakthrough in medical knowledge, the budget constraint requires either that the payout age be postponed, or the payout be reduced. Each cohort being responsible for itself, it will have to make the choice. In principle, however, the payout should be large enough to cover a basic standard of living agreeable to the community. Individuals have, of course, the choice to top it up as they see fit from private savings.

The standard contribution, in general, may be borne by the employee or shared between the employer and the employee. Over the long run assuming that the market functions efficiently the split between employer and employee will not make any difference. A self-employed person, a housewife, and the unemployed has to be responsible for their own contributions unless he/she satisfies certain criteria for public subsidization, in which case the contribution is either in part or in entirety wholly paid by the government. The scheme also allows the government to subsidize an employee's contributions on grounds of lack of means. This set-up has the advantage of making otherwise implicit and unclear redistributive initiatives transparent. With a standard contribution and a standard payout, and providing a means-tested subsidy for contributions, the design will reduce the regressivity of existing pay-as-you-go plans arising from the longer lives of the high-income people and their steeper earnings profiles (James, 1995, p.6). It should be noted, however, that redistribution is not a central feature or an integral part of the scheme.

The UFFP needs to be phased in slowly. Clearly, for cohorts which have now reached, say, the age of 50, they have only 15 years to pay before reaching 65 (assumed to be the payout age). Accumulated funds by 65 would be small. The budget constraint would dictate that this cohort draw a smaller pension than cohorts that are younger when the scheme starts operation. In principle we can assume that the older people have accumulated more savings than the younger ones at the time the scheme takes effect. In addition, during the phase-in the government will have to provide assistance to the needy aged.

3. MICROECONOMIC/POLITICAL ECONOMY PROPERTIES OF THE UNIVERSAL FULLY FUNDED PENSION SCHEME (UFFP)

First, the UFFP is a universal, mandatory plan. It is therefore free from the problem of adverse selection that would characterize a true MPPF with voluntary annuity plans. The UFFP covers everybody, including employees, the self-employed, employers, housewives, and the unemployed. Everyone within the age group has to contribute unless a means test shows one eligible for financial assistance.

Second, the UFFP can easily accommodate any degree of redistribution desired, explicitly and without compromising the fully funded nature of the scheme. Any subsidy to contribution made to the poor is an explicit transfer that funds future payouts.

An interesting question is whether government contribution on behalf of the poor would invite a free-rider problem, as people attempt to declare an income below the threshold contribution level. Clearly, a system of policing to ensure that the subsidized do meet the requisite criteria, combined with necessary penalties to ward off fraud will have to be in place. It may be noted that the monitoring problem is not unique to UFFP and is part and parcel of any redistributive program.

Moral hazard is actually likely to be less serious under UFFP than under a MPPF that exempts the poor young from payment and makes transfers to the poor old. If transfers are made to the poor old through a means-testing mechanism the availability of the safety net for those without adequate savings will lure people to stay poor and avoid contributions. In contrast, under the UFFP young people with a temporariy decline in incomes are subject a means test that looks at their net worth. They will need to make contributions if they have sufficient savings.

Under the proposed UFFP *all* individuals are entitled to the pension for their cohort. Recent immigrants will collect benefits in proportion to the number of years of their contribution--regardless of whether their contributions have been subsidized. A recent immigrant starting to contribute, say, at the age of 50 will be entitled to (65-50)/(65-20) of the standard stipend when he reaches the age of retirement, which is assumed to be 65.

Third, the stipulated contribution is a flat amount, which makes it simple to administer. This contrasts with most public pension schemes in practice. Most public pension plans provide for benefits that rise with contributions and incomes. Such plans may have distributionally undesirable consequences because they accentuate the regressivity of many public pension plans earlier noted. In any case the direction of the implicit redistribution--progressive or regressive--cannot be easily discerned. In the case of the mandatory private provident fund contributions are income-related and are akin to a payroll tax. To the extent that low income people have to struggle to survive, MPPF that does not provide for public subsidization of contributions and does not exempt the poor from contributions may push the poor people to earlier death. If mandatory "private" provident fund schemes are modified to provide for public subsidization of contributions the schemes would lose their "private" character and resemble the UFFP.

Fourth, the benefit is also a flat amount, with the full amount payable on reaching the stipulated age but discounted if early withdrawal of benefits is deemed necessary because of health reasons. Its magnitude, clearly, depends on the size of the contributions and the rate of return to investment, just as illustrated in the equation described earlier. In principle, the amount should pass a test of adequacy but should be a basic amount. Individuals would be free to top it up as they please but would not be compelled into excessive provisions for retirement.

Unlike the *laissez faire* regime or the pure MPPF, the Universal Fully Funded Pension pools longevity risks and minimizes cost. Upon reaching the stipulated age members of the UFFP draw a monthly stipend as long as they live. The MPPF can, of course, be amended to require the non-discriminatory treatment of buyers of annuities. This will make it look like a UFFP.

As a fully-funded scheme, the UFFP, like the MPPF, is free from the risks associated with changes in the dependency ratio, and from the political risks of participants trying to extract a larger payout, which may affect the Old Age Pension Plan especially if the government is made an automatic contributor, along with the employer and the employee under the "Three-pronged Contribution Approach" as recommended by the Hong Kong Social Security Association. Any plan with the ultimate bearer of the financial burden hidden away is subject to the risk caused by the "free lunch" mentality. Under UFFP, the requirement that each age cohort obeys its own budget constraint eliminates the risk that members of a cohort may attempt to extract larger payouts at the expense of other cohorts.

Similarly, by setting up individual accounts and making the benefit-drawer responsible for his own contributions, the MPPF enjoys freedom from political pressures. Professor Diamond finds this a key attraction of the Chilean system:

> There is real appeal in individual accounts as insulation of the pension system from political actions to increase benefits without direct financing. (*ibid.*, p.19)

This advantage of the Chilean system, however, will diminish as the distribution of income in society gets more unequal. *The more unequal is the distribution of income, the greater pressure there will be for the government to exempt low income employees from the plan, and for the government to provide assistance for the poor old whose accumulated savings may be inadequate.* In Hong Kong under the mandatory provident fund introduced in 2000, employees with monthly income below HK$4000 are exempted. There will be political pressure on the government to raise this exemption level and on the government to support the poor old. The problem of moral hazard and politicization cannot be dismissed. Thus, the inability of the MPPF to provide universal, basic support for the elderly means that there will be demand for an extra tax-financed pillar for the needy. Such a pillar, unfortunately, may lure households into earning below the exemption level of income.

4. LONG TERM IMPLICATIONS FOR SOCIAL SECURITY AND FOR THE MACROECONOMY

Given the budget constraint listed above (p. 90), to the extent that the realized rate of return turns out deviating from the expected rate, actual payouts may deviate from expected payouts. However, while the realized rate of return may fall short of the expected rate for some cohorts it may exceed the expected rate for some other cohorts. While no one can insure such systematic deviations from the expected rate of return for an entire cohort momentarily, the government has a long time horizon and is in the position to offer, upon payment of the necessary premiums, a guarantee for some minimum real rate of return for funds invested by a cohort that desires to contain investment risks, by using surpluses for one cohort to tide over deficits for another cohort. This approach to deal with "correlated risks" will achieve *Pareto gains* for all generations which are exposed to such risks, which lack commercial insurers to protect them from such risks, and which are risk averse.[6]

Compared to a provident fund scheme which is in essence simply a form of forced savings, the Universal Fully Funded Pension is likely to result in smaller savings. This is by virtue of the fact that our capital markets are incomplete and imperfect. If our capital markets were complete and perfect the very idea of forced savings would be inconceivable, because those who prefer to save less can always borrow on the security of his future claims on his personal "forced" savings. In general, in view of longevity risks if the provident fund mode of old age security is adopted more savings will have to be made individually than are necessary to cover the expected life span. Although this means that investment is likely to be lower under the UFFP scheme than under the provident fund scheme we must not assume that more investment is necessarily desirable, as the benefit of higher current consumption should also be considered.

Because a provident fund scheme alone cannot guarantee a minimum standard of living for the elderly many of those who subscribe to a mandatory private provident fund scheme also believe that there should be a "mandatory publicly managed pillar" as well (James, 1995).[7] The coexistence of a heavily regulated MPPF with a public pension scheme is, however, administratively demanding. Moreover, the larger this tax-financed pillar is, the greater will be the distortionary effects associated with the related tax burden. Admittedly, the tax-financed subsidies for contribution by the poor under the UFFP are also distortionary. As always we have to find a balance between redistribution and allocative efficiency. Table 2 presents a comparison of the properties of the MPPF and the UFFP.

5. CONCLUSIONS

According to James and Vittas (1994) the most general recommendation and one that is relatively clear-cut and non-controversial is that old age security should be based on a multi-pillar system that comprises:

- broad based privately managed mandatory savings-annuity pillar to avert the results of myopia and incomplete insurance markets
- a carefully designed public pillar for redistribution to those in long term poverty, and possibly for insuring against correlated risks,
- tax-advantaged private pensions, and
- a purely voluntary savings pillar.

A multi-pillar system appears to be both logical and indeed the direction of reform being considered in Europe, America, and elsewhere (Ploug and Kvist, 1996; *Businessweek*, January 20, 1997). Two major questions remain, however. One is whether the private component of old age security should be mandatory or voluntary. The other is if there is still a role for public pension, how should it be reformed to be financially viable. Our analysis suggests that the mandatory private option to replace the public pension system is fraught with many problems, which would require a heavy dose of regulation to avoid. The pay-as-you-go public pension system, however, is subject to uncertainty and financial risks. On the other hand, a mandatory public pension system will deal with longevity risk far better than individual savings accounts or provident funds.

The fully funded pension system as proposed provides a mandatory pension that deals with myopia and incomplete insurance markets and offers government subsidization of contributions for the poor. It therefore accomplishes by and large the objectives to be achieved by the first two pillars as envisaged by James. The fully funded pension system is by design small scale allowing for "top-up" by individuals as they see fit. This recognizes the imperfection and incompleteness of capital markets, which make it difficult for individuals to transform excessively large future pensions into current consumption.

A recent article in a recent edition of *World Bank Development Brief* (August 1995) aptly remarks that "The future course of mortality is a major social risk that must be borne by some group no matter how retirement incomes are organized." The UFFP system discussed is predicated on the assumption that each cohort should be responsible for itself, so that no generation is burdened with the uncertainty of supporting another when mortality and demographics change. This is consistent with a concept of justice linked to Rawls (1972) as discussed in Chapter 3. If we all faced a "veil of ignorance" and were randomly assigned to different cohorts, we would probably have preferred a system like what was suggested, namely that each cohort saved for its own retirement.

Many countries have different pensions plans for different occupations, and some countries have different pension plans for employees and the self-employed (International Social Security Association, 1987; Noguchi, 1983). The proposed UFFP is based on the assumption that a mandatory plan should be universal, simple, and basic, and free from the vagaries of uncertain demographics, without inhibiting each occupation and each company from developing its own private schemes.

Table 1. Public Pension Expenditure as a Percentage of GDP in OECD Countries

Country	1960	1975	1980	1985
Austria	9.6	12.5	13.5	14.5
Canada	2.8	3.7	4.4	5.4
France	6.0	10.1	11.5	12.7
Germany	9.7	12.6	12.1	11.8
Italy	5.5	10.4	12.0	15.6
Japan	1.3	2.6	4.4	5.3
Sweden	4.4	7.7	10.9	11.2
U.K.	4.0	6.0	6.3	6.7
U.S.A	4.1	6.7	6.9	7.2

Source: Table 1 in Mitchell (1993).

Table 2. Comparison of Mandatory Provident Funds System and the Fully Funded Pension System

Criteria	Mandatory Private Provident Fund System*	Universal Fully Funded Pension
Financial Stability	Independent of changes in the dependency ratio	Independent of changes in the dependency ratio
Administration	Privately administered but publicly supervised; supervision potentially difficult if schemes are too numerous.	Centrally administered under a Board of Trustees for each cohort; funds can be "farmed out" to private fund managers.
Insurance Benefits	*Either* no insurance benefits and no risk pooling *or* high insurance cost because of adverse selection problems.	Insurance benefits because there is risk pooling for people with unknown lifespan.
Freedom from Political Risk	Contributors will have no incentive to boost scale of scheme on account of others shouldering the cost. But there will be pressure to provide for a tax-funded pillar for redistributive purposes.	Same. There will be pressure to provide for redistributive subsidies.
Distortion of Individual Choice and Sacrifice of Individual Freedom	Greater choice for investment outlets. Distortion to the savings/consumption decision can be serious if scale is large.	No individualized choice for investment for contributed funds. UFFP is small in scale to avoid distorting the savings-consumption decision.
Public Confidence	An individual fund could be subject to large investment risks. Public confidence generally higher compared to Pay-as-you-go schemes under adverse demographic trends.	Risk spreading for funds contributed by the entire cohort, and appointment of a Board of Trustees by members contribute to higher confidence
Redistribution	Requires a separate "pillar"	Redistributive provisions are explicit in the subsidies to contributions. The degree of redistribution a matter of public choice.
Coverage	Limited to employed people	Universal
Adequacy	Adequacy depends on total contributions of an individual. As a defined contribution plan it does not guarantee post-retirement incomes.	Any level of payout can be set so as to meet socially determined adequacy standards; larger payout would however entail larger distortions to choice.
Portability	Portable with transaction costs for plans that are employer-specific; question of portability does not arise for plans that have been chosen by employees	Question does not arise as there is just one central plan for each cohort.

* MPPF referred herein is a pure form of private provident fund that does not allow public contribution or provide for public guarantee of any sort. Allowing for public contribution on behalf of participants or providing public guarantee of a minimum pension blurs the distinction between MPPF and UFFP. A referee points out that some countries, such as Latvia, operate a version of MPPF that provides for government contribution on behalf of the unemployed, mothers, and students at the minimum wage.

NOTES

1 Prof. Robert Fogel in his 1993 Nobel lecture presented evidence that the mortality and disability rates for the elderly had fallen for longer than expected, with the result that the U.S. elderly population in 2050 was likely to be underestimated by the Census Bureaau to the tune of 36 million. Recent breakthrough in genome research is causing both excitement and anxiety because of unpredictable implications on longevity.

2 Actually the Chilean system is more properly represented as based on "an intermediate form of funding." The Chilean government guarantees a minimum benefit payable irrespective of the performance of the funds invested. (Mitchell, 1993, pp.27-28) Another well-known system, the Central Provident Fund (CPF), which is in operation in Malaysia and Singapore, is privately and fully funded but are publicly administered. See Asher (1994).

3 Central administration does not necessarily mean government management of the pension funds. It does mean, however, that there may be a monopsony (sole buyer) for fund management services. A board of trustees charged with administration of a public pension may "farm out" funds for management by private pension funds. Under such a setting the private pension funds would be in a weaker position to pass along marketing costs to consumers

4 If the capital market were perfect individuals could trade future payouts for current income. But if this were the case the very concept of *mandatory* provident fund would fall apart as no individual could be forced to save more than he would like.

5 Robert Haveman (1994) has raised some questions about the generational accounting framework, but conceded that it should serve "as a useful supplement to the annual budget." (p.110) The Office of the Management of the Budget (OMB) presented for the first time in history a tabulation of the lifetime tax rates of current and future generations in the FY 1994 budget.

6 Prof. Yew-kwang Ng pointed out that if we all face a Rawlsian "veil of ignorance," we may prefer some cross-subsidies between different cohorts to reduce uncertainty and increase expected utility. In the same spirit Ho (1981) introduced the concept of Pareto risk improvement and suggested that an arrangement that led to an *ex post* redistribution may be Pareto improving if all parties concerned are *ex ante* risk-averse and if the arrangement reduces everyone's risk exposure.

7 In Hong Kong a motion to establish a pay-as-you-go pension along with the mandatory private provident fund scheme was passed in March 1995 and again in December, 1995. See *Mingpao*, 14 December, 1995. It should be noted that motions passed in the Legislative Council in Hong Kong represent only recommendations that need not be implemented by the government.

Part 3

MACROECONOMIC RISK MANAGEMENT

Mismanagement of the macroeconomic environment has been the cause of major economic disasters including the Great Depression of the 1930s and the recent Asian Financial Crisis. Policy makers have traditionally been too preoccupied with bringing one or two indicators into line with their prior expectations to come up with the needed policies to bring about a stable macroeconomic environment which is needed for businesses to operate efficiently and to grow. Chapter 9 argues that in countries that adhere to basic rules of fiscal discipline and that allow real interest rates to stay around the long term rate of return to capital inflation risks have been successfully contained and often overstated Chapter 10 looks at the risks of interest rate and exchange rate fluctuations. It demonstrates that the misbehavior of our central banks have directly caused or aggravated major crises, including the Great Depression of the 1930s, the global stock market crash of 1987, the rise and fall of the Japanese economy, and the Asian Financial Crisis in 1997-98. Chapter 11 looks at the formation of asset price bubbles, and argues that the world needs better savings instruments that can provide true financial security. The concept of a real value unit of account is advanced. It is argued that the lack of a savings instrument of reasonable security drove asset prices in Japan sky-high in the 1980s. Sharp appreciation of the yen, by discouraging purchases of Japanese assets and encouraging sales eventually led to the crumbling of asset prices at home. It also led to a sharp fall in the yen value of foreign-held assets, creating a gigantic financial crisis. Finally, Chapter 12 will look at transparency, an important subject in macroeconomic risk management.

Chapter 9

THE RISKS OF MONETARY CRISES: INFLATION

Avoid malignant inflation. Abhor not benign inflation. Index debt instruments to prevent borrowers from getting a free ride from inflation. Never index to protect people from shortages.

1. INTRODUCTION

At one time, opinion polls indicated that inflation was looked upon as Public Enemy Number One in the United States. However, for countries which observe basic rules of fiscal and monetary discipline the dangers of inflation have been grossly overstated. It is not apparent that relatively high inflation, even going into the teens, would necessarily damage the economy. Hong Kong during the late seventies and early 80s routinely saw inflation going into double-digit levels (Table 1). Yet the economy went through rather turbulent periods (not of its own making)—with a major oil crisis and serious global recessions—largely unscathed. I have no intention here of preaching the virtues of inflation. It is important, however, to note that there are different kinds of inflation. Inflation can be innocuous and even beneficial, and inflation can be dangerous and even lethal.

Generally speaking, inflation that is caused by cost-push factors is relatively innocuous and may be beneficial. Inflation that is caused by an expanding money supply, on the other hand, can be very dangerous. While unbridled expansion of the money supply can ruin the market economy, modern societies that observe the basic rules of fiscal and monetary discipline should have nothing to worry about "excessive inflation." I shall elaborate on what I mean by basic rules of fiscal and monetary discipline below.

Table 1.

Hong Kong

Year	1975	1976	1977	1978	1979	1980	1981	1982	1983	1984
Inflation- CPI-A	1.2	3.4	5.8	5.9	11.6	15.5	15.4	10.5	9.9	8.2
Economic Growth	0.3	16.2	11.7	8.5	11.5	10.1	9.2	2.7	5.7	10.0

United States

Year	1975	1976	1977	1978	1979	1980	1981	1982	1983	1984
Inflation CPI-U	9.1	5.8	6.5	7.6	11.3	13.5	10.3	6.2	3.2	4.3
Economic Growth	-0.4	5.4	4.7	5.4	2.8	-0.3	2.3	-2.1	4.0	7.0

Sources: Gross Domestic Product 1961-1999, Hong Kong: Census and Statistics Department; Bureau of Economic Analysis and Bureau of Labor Statistics, US Government.

2. A HISTORICAL PERSPECTIVE

Before we go into the subject of fighting inflation, a historical perspective is warranted. We must realize that *in all of the history of mankind, every episode of hyperinflation was a result of one or more parties trying to unload the burden of shortage onto others in society.* Typically, it was started when the government "borrowed" money from the central bank to cover its expenditures. Typically, there was political and economic stability and acute shortages, and prices were rising.

For example, Yugoslavia in the early nineties was in the grasp of a deep civil war and the government simply could not raise the needed revenue through normal taxes to meet its escalating expenses. Like many earlier governments facing similar situations it resorted to the printing press to finance the war. As a result, it found itself in the grasp of very serious hyperinflation.

The Nationalist government under Chiang Kai-shek during the civil war with the Communists in China did the same, leading to the hyperinflation episode of 1946-49.

Although civil war was not the cause the German hyperinflation in the early 1920s this episode of hyperinflation was also the direct result of resorting to the printing press when government revenue fell dramatically on account of social and political turmoil.

Perhaps one of the most intriguing episodes of hyperinflation is that of Hungary from December 1945 to July 1946. At the outset, the country was beset with serious shortages and prices had been rising rapidly. The inflation was a natural reflection of the shortages, and would have diffused the burden of the serious shortages across the entire population as well as the government. The government, however, tried to avoid the erosion of the real value of taxes collected through indexing tax liabilities. The idea was to force taxpayers to compensate the government for any loss in real purchasing power between the time the tax bill was sent out and the time of actual payment. In January 1946, various banks also set up the so-called valorization accounts, which effectively indexed the values of deposits against inflation. Unfortunately, because the shortages were real the indexing could not eliminate the shortages. Even as depositors got back twice as much money as what had been deposited in the first place on the back of a doubling in the price level, there was no guarantee that when doubled-up money could buy the same real goods in the following periods. The price index went up from 100 to 39,623,000,000,000,000,000,000,000,000 within a year.

3. SOLUTIONS OR PROBLEMS?

When there are serious shortages, and output lags behind demand, prices have to rise. The inflation that arises because of the real shortages is Market's way of spreading and diffusing the burden. Everybody finds inflation burdensome, but the culprit is really not inflation but shortages. Given the shortages, which could be quite unavoidable, for example when there is an oil shortage imposed upon us externally, or when production has been disrupted by a war, the realistic way to deal with the problem is to bite the bullet. Some demands have to go unsatisfied. In such times of exigencies, rationing or inflation would be unavoidable. While rationing could be superior when it comes to distributing certain essential goods inflation could be the more efficient and the fairer way of dealing with the problem in most cases. In this sense, inflation is a "solution" to the shortage problem.

If we refuse to come to terms with the problem of shortages, and start turning to the printing press in an attempt to run away or get shelter from the problem of shortages, inflation becomes a problem. Inflation will take on a life of its own. Rather than prices rising in response to known shortages, various parties, armed with their loads of money, try to compete away the scarce resources from others. This competition becomes a negative sum game because when inflation takes on a life of its own the market ceases to function efficiently or at all. Production and division of labor and investment become ever more difficult.

4. BENIGN INFLATION

In contrast, imported inflation and cost-push inflation which are truly exogenous and do not originate from an increase in the money supply is mostly benign. As Table 1 shows, Hong Kong had double-digit or nearly double-digit inflation from 1979-1984, but the economy was spared the fate of two recessions as had hit the US. Along with the fairly high inflation, the Hong Kong dollar had depreciated right through October 1983, when it was linked to the US dollar through a currency board mechanism. But both the short-term and the long-term performance of the economy had not been jeopardized. While the inflation seems to adversely affect the livelihood of the people the true culprit is shortage—which can be artificial such as caused by the oil embargo under OPEC in the seventies, or natural disasters that result in large scale destruction of crops. The resulting higher prices effectively ration the scarce goods among people. Such inflation is in reality benign in character.

Because of certain constraints that include human nature as it is and institutions as they are, there is some resistance against wage declines and such resistance varies from sector to sector because of institutional reasons. For this reason, to expect price declines to exactly offset price increases as relative scarcity changes, thus keeping inflation at zero, is unrealistic. The efficient relative price changes are more likely to take place if prices either rise or stay put. The prices of those goods and services which have become more scarce relatively will then rise faster. Creeping inflation of this kind is benign.

Since the early 1970s many economists have accepted the concept of "natural rate of unemployment," believing that an attempt to reduce unemployment below this natural rate will engender accelerating inflation. The logic of this theory is that it is in the nature of the labor market to have some people "in between jobs." In a steady state, when peoples' expectations about inflation and actual inflation match, the natural rate of unemployment will result. An expansionary policy to reduce unemployment will result in the actual inflation running ahead of inflation expectation. Superficially attractive job offers will fool job seekers into accepting jobs sooner than otherwise, leading to a temporary decline in the rate of unemployment. Since people will not be fooled forever, the result is accelerating inflation.

Actually there may also be a "natural rate of inflation" which is "natural" or inherent in human nature and socio-economic institutions. If we tried to reduce inflation below the natural rate— that which is consistent with the public's natural resistance against wage declines—we could end up with rising unemployment. An excessively tight monetary policy aimed at forcing wage and price declines to offset concurrent wage and price increases may create unemployment. Indeed, it is the threat of unemployment that ultimately intimates workers into accepting reduced wages.

In a similar spirit that comes to terms with human nature and particularly workers' imperfect perception of reality, Akerlof, Dickens, and Perry (2000) suggest that employees' job satisfaction may be higher in periods of moderate inflation and rising nominal wages. They estimated that the employment- maximizing rate of inflation ranges from 1.6 per cent to 3.2 per cent. They categorically rejected zero inflation as a policy target.

5. MONEY GROWTH THE CAUSE OR THE RESULT OF INFLATION?

Nobel Laureate Milton Friedman taught that inflation is everywhere and always a monetary phenomenon. Professor Friedman argues that if the money supply does not accommodate, then all inflation, demand-pull, cost-push, or otherwise, would grind to a halt.

Prof. Friedman is right. All kinds of inflation can be choked off by keeping a tight grip on the money supply. However, just as with all other kinds of public policy, we have to consider the costs versus the benefits.

If there is shortage, prices will rise. Because we cannot expect prices of goods and services not in shortage to fall by exactly the amount as to neutralize these prices increases, generally shortages, even those that are not widespread, will result in a rise in the price level. The increases in the price level will result in a greater demand for money. In response to such demand, generally there will be a greater supply of money through the credit expansion process. The increase in the money supply is under these circumstances a result of the inflation, not the cause.

Of course, things can run the other way round. There can be excessive expansion of credit because the cost of borrowing is too low. The increase in consumption and investment may exceed the capacity of the economy to produce, and inflation may result. Because inflation renders money repaid worth less than money borrowed it further increases the attractiveness of borrowing. Inflation may then accelerate. Here the increase in the money supply is the cause of inflation. The overheated economy cannot be sustained, paving the way for a substantial economic downturn. Central banks would be wise to prevent economies from overheating.

6. INFLATION RISK AND MACROECONOMIC ENVIRONMENT MANAGEMENT

To prevent the economy from overheating does not require cyclical adjustments of interest rates, as has been practised in the United States and many other industrial nations. All that is required is to keep the real cost of borrowing within a relatively narrow range of 2.5 to 3.5 per cent, which corresponds to the real rate of return to capital that has prevailed for decades. As long as the real cost of borrowing is transparent to the borrower and kept at such a level, investors will not borrow to finance investments that can yield only a lower rate of return, so investment would not be excessive. Similarly, only consumers willing to pay such interest costs would borrow to finance their consumption expenditures. Consumption expenditures will also not be excessive.

In general, central bankers believe that there are the following approaches to monetary policy:

- Money supply growth targeting
- Interest rate targeting
- Inflation targeting
- Output targeting
- Currency board
- Discretionary fine-tuning

Money supply growth targeting, once a favorite approach advocated by monetarists, has largely fallen out of favor these days, primarily because the relationship between velocity of money and economic activity has changed tremendously with changes in technology and financial market innovations. Interest rate targeting, once advocated by Keynesians, has never really been considered seriously by central bankers. With possible changes in inflation expectations, keeping interest rates stable may not keep real interest rates stable, and under some circumstances could engender excessive demand and hence inflation because real interest rates could become negative.

Inflation targeting is practised by the Bank of England. Money is tightened up or loosened up depending on whether the observed inflation rate exceeds or falls short of the target rate. This approach is not satisfactory because inflation changes may be caused by non-monetary factors. As alleged earlier on, a purely cost-push inflation, from external uncontrollable sources, is essentially benign and so there may be little need to tighten up the money supply.

Some central bankers are uncomfortable with economic growth rising beyond certain levels and go about tightening up the money supply whenever the GDP grows "excessively." At one time, the Federal Reserve Board was thought not to tolerate a GDP growth in excess of 2.5 per cent. Such a target has proven far too conservative, so the Federal Reserve is now known to tolerate a higher rate of growth. The Fed, however, has never announced any threshold rate of GDP growth, leading to much market speculation. Because rapid output change can be a result of productivity improvement, an expansion in production capacity, a catch-up from a situation with much slack, etc., specifying any GDP growth rate as a dividing line between an overheating economy and one without overheating is subjective and unreliable.

Some economies, including Hong Kong since October 17, 1983, practise what is known as a currency board system. The currency is linked to a major international currency, typically the US dollar. Bank notes are issued on submission of US dollars at the official exchange rate. This system has the advantage of transparency and being rule-based rather than discretionary. Central bankers are spared the need to make judgments and will avoid judgmental errors.

Finally, discretionary fine-tuning refers to the freedom to tighten up or to loosen up the money supply whenever the economy shows signs of overheating or excessive cooling. It allows the enlightened central banker to exercise his wise judgment freely, but then it also allows the unenlightened central banker to tighten or loosen up monetary policy at the wrong time and thus aggravate fluctuations.

There is, of course, no perfect answer to the problem of monetary policy. But investors and consumers all prefer greater stability, other things being equal. The fact is, so far US monetary policy is seen to be cyclical, with a series of interest rate drops followed by a series of interest rate increases, and the swing from trough to peak can be a few hundred basis points. The rest of the world often follow these interest rate movements faithfully. This leads to excessively large gyrations in financial markets.

Given the shortcomings of these approaches to monetary policy I would like to advance the proposal of real interest rate targeting as a practical way of stabilizing the macroeconomic environment. I should like to point out the following facts:

- While it is true that real interest rates cannot be set and held at any arbitrary level, real interest rates can be held near the long term real rate of return to capital. In principle, the real interest rate target should correspond with the long term real rate of return to capital investment.

- The existence of indexed bonds that are now traded openly, both in the US and in the UK, means that real interest rates can be moved in the short term through open market selling and buying of these bonds.

The financial markets will feel assured if there is the announcement that monetary policy keeps the real cost of borrowing near the long-term real rate of return to investment. The financial markets know that such a policy will stabilize real borrowing costs, prevent the economy from overheating, and is credible.

7. CONCLUSIONS

When inflation gets out of control the damages to the economy can be catastrophic. Clearly, the risks of inflation should not be taken lightly. However, today we have ample safeguards against malignant inflation. Keeping real rates of interest positive and close to the long-term equilibrium rate of return to capital will avoid excessive borrowing and hence excessive private sector spending. Governments following basic rules of fiscal discipline by striving to maintain budget balance at full employment will help avoid excessive public sector spending. If these basic rules are followed, then there should be no worry about inflation. Indeed any residual inflation should be benign in nature. Being nervous against such benign inflation is counter-productive.

Just as inflation itself can be malignant or benign, so indexing against inflation can be harmful or beneficial. Hungary's experience shows that indexing inappropriately can be very dangerous. Hungary wanted to use indexing to protect everybody against the consequences of a real shortage. Of course that would not work. The ongoing inflation was benign and beneficial because it forced everybody to bear part of the cost of the shortage. Indexing savings and tax revenues against inflation when there is a real shortage is trying to achieve the impossible.

Indexing to force borrowers to face up to the real cost of borrowing is an altogether different animal. Because the cost of borrowing is indexed against inflation, borrowers are forced to face up to the cost of scarcity and so are prevented from borrowing too much. The inflation-indexed bond is a big financial market innovation that can help tame inflation and avoid arbitrary redistribution between creditors and debtors.

Chapter 10

THE RISKS OF MONETARY CRISES: CURRENCY CRISES AND INTEREST RATE GYRATIONS

Maintain real exchange rates and real interest rates at levels compatible with full employment. Defend full-employment compatible exchange rates wholeheartedly. Maintain real interest rates at close to the long term rate of return to investment.

1. INTRODUCTION

Currency crises are serious matters. They can be extremely destructive, pushing otherwise well-run enterprises out of business, eliminating hundreds of thousands of jobs, ruining families and lives. The Asian Financial Crisis of 1997-98 was particularly devastating. Wealth valued at hundreds of billions of dollars virtually disappeared overnight. The damage was certainly more serious than any natural disaster could have caused.

Many commentators trace currency crises to currency attacks, but for currency attacks to be successful, one or both of two conditions must exist. The first is that the values of the currencies in question are out of line with the economic fundamentals. This is a sufficient condition for currency attacks to be "successful." Here "success" may mean that the currency in question is actually devalued, or that domestic prices and domestic asset prices decline so much that real exchange rate adjustment is achieved without the nominal exchange rate itself adjusting. The second is that the central bank makes policy mistakes, has inadequate foreign exchange reserves, or has inadequate access to credit lines.

If the value of a currency is compatible with full employment and long term balance of payments equilibrium, we can say that the prevailing exchange rate is defendable even though there may be a balance of payments deficit in the short term. The central bank should, then and only then, use reserves and any available credit lines to defend the currency. Because the economic fundamentals are sound the economy will, in time, generate sufficient income for the central bank to repay its debt. On the other hand, if the values of the currencies are out of line with the economic fundamentals, then the prevailing real exchange rates are not defendable. Either the nominal exchange rate has to decline or domestic prices have to fall. There will be little point in trying to defend the currency. That is why, to this day I still think that George Soros did the UK a great service forcing the pound sterling to delink from the European Monetary System in 1992. Devaluing is not the end of the world. The devaluation of the British pound and the interest rate declines following the devaluation actually jump-started the economy.[1] In contrast, in 1997 virtually all the Asian economies hit by currency attacks tried to prevent further currency devaluation by increasing sharply domestic interest rates. The very high interest rates destroyed the economic fundamentals otherwise improved by the initial devaluations.

I have no doubt that the key to maintaining stability in the foreign exchange markets is to know the values of currencies which are economically sensible and therefore defendable, and to defend these values whole-heartedly and with international help if necessary. We must note that neither the regime of floating exchange rates nor that of fixed exchange rates can be counted upon to bring about economically sensible and defendable exchange rates. That is why both a floating exchange rate and a pegged exchange rate may lead to problems. The appreciation of the yen in the late 1980s and early 1990s when the yen was floating had caused Japan serious economic difficulties and is ultimately responsible for the weakness of the Japanese economy throughout the nineties. The *de facto* overvaluation of many South East Asian currencies prior to the currency crisis of July 1997 when they were more or less linked with the U.S. dollar also had invited major currency attacks. The linking of the pound sterling to the European monetary system prior to 1992 had caused the UK serious economic difficulties, pushing up its unemployment rate and hurting exports.

Currency attacks can potentially do good things and bad. As I had maintained earlier on, George Soros did the UK a great service by pushing it off the European Monetary System. After the pound sterling had de-linked from the European Monetary System, the Bank of England did not panic. Instead, it allowed interest rates to decline. This jumpstarted and brought about a dramatic turnaround of the British economy. Even today, the UK remains the strongest economy in all of Europe, enjoying a very low unemployment rate and a very strong fiscal position. On the other hand, Indonesia and Thailand suffered tremendously in the aftermath of the currency attacks. Backbreaking interest rates compounded the problems of already weak economic fundamentals. The economies slipped into major recessions.

2. THE ECONOMIC COST OF HIGH REAL INTEREST RATES

Just as overvaluation of the currency can derail an economy by rendering it uncompetitive internationally and choking off external demand, so high real interest rates can plunge an economy into recession by curbing domestic demand.

John Maynard Keynes drew the insight from the Great Depression in the nineteen thirties that maintaining "effective demand" at a level consistent with full employment or "demand management" is a prime responsibility of the government. In his *General Theory of Employment, Interest, and Money*, he clearly stressed the importance of maintaining interest rates at a sufficiently low level—if that was possible (pp.205-209). He was aware that interest rates should not be too low, otherwise "a state of true inflation will be produced." (p.202) But keeping interest rates low enough to achieve full employment could be difficult. "For example, in a country linked to an international gold standard, a rate of interest lower than prevails elsewhere will be viewed with a justifiable lack of confidence; yet a domestic rate of interest dragged up to a parity with the highest rate (highest after allowing for risk) prevailing in any country belonging to the international system may be much higher than is consistent with domestic full employment." (p.203)

Although the world has given up the gold standard for a long time this observation of Keynes is still relevant. When there is a lack of confidence in a currency, interest rates may have to be much higher than what is compatible with full employment in order to arrest a flight of capital. Yet backbreaking, high interest rates are unsustainable either.

Conceptually, there are different combinations of interest rates and exchange rates that are compatible with full employment. But depending on whether interest rates are higher (and exchange rates are lower) or the exchange values of the domestic currency are higher (and interest rates are lower), the mix of domestic demand and external demand in the total demand will be different. When interest rates go higher and exchange rates go lower, external demand will fill in where domestic demand falls short of full employment. On the other hand, when interest rates go lower and exchange rates go higher, domestic demand will rise to fill what is vacated by external demand.

If the (real) interest rates are higher than what is necessary to maintain full employment, investment will shrink and unemployment will rise, *unless the currency is devalued.* If the latter should take place and in the right magnitude, external demand would rise and restore aggregate demand to the level needed for full employment. Starting from a point where the level of aggregate demand is at the right level for full employment, if a capital flight should cause pressures to devalue and the central bank raises interest rates to defend the currency, aggregate demand would shrink, and the economy will slip into recession.[2] Since a recession will weaken confidence further, a vicious circle would develop. There would be new pressures for devaluation, and new pressures to raise interest rates. Eventually the economy would collapse. Apparently this was what happened with Indonesia and Thailand during the Asian Financial Crisis.

We have now accumulated a fair bit of knowledge about how high real interest rates and currency over-valuations do to the economy. Experiences in the United States, Canada, Australia, the United Kingdom, and Japan all tell the same story. Excessively strong currencies combined with high real interest rates always lead to recessions. Deep recessions mean joblessness for many and big fiscal deficits for governments. Investment and economic growth will slow down, implying long-term losses in productivity and welfare.

The surge in the fiscal deficit in the United States from 1981 to 1983, with the federal deficit surging from 2.6 per cent to 6.3 per cent of the GNP, was a direct result of the tight money policy of 1979-81. Following a similar tight money period from 1980-82, Australia saw its fiscal deficit surging from 0.34 per cent of the GDP to 3.7 per cent by 1984. In Canada, the fiscal deficit also rose sharply during 1981-84, thanks to a monetary policy that mirrored the tight money of Paul Volcker in the U.S. More recently, the recession of 1990-91 was a direct result of a policy of high interest rates and strong Canadian dollar through 1990/91. Tight money pushed Canada's unemployment rate above 11 per cent in 1992 and 1993 and the federal deficit above 6 per cent of the GDP. Only after monetary policy eased in the nineties did the Canadian economy bounce back to life and the budget deficit fall sharply. In the United Kingdom, prior to the de-linking with the European Monetary System in 1992 British interest rates were very high and the currency was overvalued relative to what was compatible with full employment. As a result both the fiscal deficit and the unemployment rate were very high. In 1992, George Soros successfully pushed the British pound off the European Monetary System. While the unemployment rate and the fiscal deficit, well known to be a "lagging indicator" continued to rise briefly and peaked in 1993, at 10.4 per cent and 7.3 per cent of the GDP respectively, both fell rapidly soon after. By 1998, the fiscal balance turned in a surplus, and the unemployment rate dipped below 5 per cent—an amazing and unique achievement among European countries. Japan is another case in point. Although its interest rates had been very low throughout the nineteen nineties, excessive strength of the yen was directly responsible for the bursting of the bubble, the stagnation of the economy and surging fiscal deficits. Chapter 11 will revisit the Japanese economy and its problems.

3. RULES VERSUS DISCRETION, CURRENCY BOARDS, AND COMMON CURRENCY AREAS

In recent years, interest rates are often hiked to avoid overheating so the economic expansion can continue. By definition avoiding overheating makes good sense, but what makes overheating is not totally clear. Judgement as to whether an economy is overheating is necessary, and a discretionary move in the interest rate is made on the basis of that judgment. The market is left to speculate about how the central bank acts, and capital flows and the security markets reflect these speculations.

Some economists believe that allowing so much room for the markets to speculate is not conducive to stability. They prefer rules rather than discretion. Rules are there for everybody to see, so everybody can act with anticipation that the rules are to be followed. The currency board, with the local currency effectively tied to a major currency, is one form of rule-based monetary policy. Hong Kong and Argentina are examples of economies adhering to a currency board system. According to many proponents of the currency board system, in order to foster credibility in the system, economies have to be prepared to take any economic pain required in defence of the system. If confidence is lacking, a capital flight will take place, and the outflow of capital will engender a tight money situation at home, potentially taking the domestic interest rate to very painful levels. According to the rules of the currency board, the monetary authority will have to be steadfast and relentlessly allow the course of adjustment to take place. This must involve unemployment and deflation at home. After all the painful adjustment, the real exchange rate will have been lowered and interest rates will have fallen back to more normal levels. Without the willingness to take the pain of adjustment, the currency board will have no credibility, and will not survive over the long run.

Because a currency board involves a currency linking to another currency it is akin to the idea of a "currency area" with one common currency.[3] In principle, if the Hong Kong dollar is linked to the US dollar at HK$7.8 to US$1 tightly and there is no question about the arrangement ever going to change, there will be no reason why Hong Kong interest rates should deviate from US interest rates at all. Any interest rate difference should quickly lead to arbitrage that will eliminate that difference. If there is no possibility that the Hong Kong dollar would devalue and if US interest rates are lower, no one will borrow in Hong Kong dollars, and Hong Kong dollar interest rates will decline.

In fact, however, the public perceives exchange risk to be real. So it is possible that the interest rates of a currency board currency deviate from the interest rates of the "host currency." During times of crisis, the "risk premium" can be very high. To avoid such high risk premiums the option of "dollarization" has been seriously considered in some currency board economies which have linked their currencies to the US dollar. The suggestion of dollarization should not be dismissed lightly, as between a currency board that links with the US dollar and a fully "dollarized" economy the advantages of the latter are overwhelming. The only real disadvantage is the political cost of giving up the local currency as a symbol of the identity of the country. There is the savings in transaction cost in the form of not having to convert one currency into another. Exchange risk and exchange risk premiums will be eliminated. Interest rates will be lower, contributing to a more favorable investment climate.

Starting in 1999 many European countries have accepted the euro as their common currency. For the time being it is circulating in electronic form, but in time the euro bank notes will circulate and will replace the DM, the French franc, the Italian lira, the Austrian schilling, etc. in the market place. The European Central Bank will take charge and a uniform monetary policy will be adopted. The euro zone certainly will be more tightly integrated as one organic economic system. But each of the constituent countries will no longer be able to depreciate or revalue its currency independently. The euro is an unprecedented experiment. With each constituent country being an independent fiscal system but all countries using a common currency and subject to one common monetary policy, there are risks that the prevailing monetary policy may be too tight for some regions and too stimulative for others. If the former want to stimulate their economies using fiscal policy deficits will occur. It waits to be seen whether this bold experiment undertaken at the turn of the century will prove to be successful in improving efficiency and promoting full employment (Sala-I-Martin and Sachs, 1991; Ho, 1993).

4. CONCLUSIONS

Maintaining exchange rates and interest rates at levels compatible with full employment is sometimes more easily said than done. The Thai central bank knew that the Thai baht was overvalued but tried to defend it. That led to a huge loss of foreign exchange reserves. In the end, on July 2 1997 it had to let the baht devalue. But the devalued baht was still under pressure, and foreign exchange reserves had been drawn down to very low levels. Further devaluation could lead to high inflation and panic and even more capital outflow. Raising interest rates was, under the circumstances, the natural way to stem the capital outflow in the short term, but it would undermine the health of the economy in another way.

In the end the Thai central bank raised interest rates sharply, and similarly did Indonesia and even Hong Kong. As expected the medicine worked in the short term, but plunged the economies into a deep recession.

These economies all should have resisted raising their real interest rates, if they had the choice. Instead, real interest rates were raised to back-breaking levels. If the United States had those real interest rates, the US would have plunged into a deep recession all the same. With deep recessions firmly in place, larger and larger fiscal deficits emerged.

How could these economies have kept their real interest rates at sensible levels and contained capital outflow at the same time? The answer lies in a credible international effort to achieve just this. The fact is: if the currency has been devalued to a level consistent with the economic fundamentals, the currency should be defendable at that level. An international lender of last resort should come in and assure the financial market that there is no more need to further devalue, and real interest rates should be kept in line with international levels. This international lender of last resort should not impose various conditions for lending that may actually kill the patient.

In failing to deliver just this medicine that the ailing economies needed, the International Monetary Fund attracted heavy criticism. Joseph Stiglitz was particularly disappointed with the IMF, which was insistent in prescribing a medicine of fiscal austerity. He wrote: "a student who turned in the IMF's answer to the test question 'What should the fiscal stance of Thailand, facing an economic downturn?' would have gotten an F." (Stiglitz, 2000) It is important that the whole world, not just the IMF, learn the lesson about what constitutes a macroeconomic environment favorable to growth and stability and work together to bring it about.

NOTES

1 A similar episode happened during the Great Depression in the 1930s. See Section 4, Chapter 17.

2 The point that a restrictive monetary policy can trigger a recession was supported by Ng (1999).

3 The path-breaking reference on optimal currency areas is Mundell (1963).

Chapter 11

SAVINGS INSTRUMENTS, BUBBLES, AND FINANCIAL CRISES

We badly need to improve the financial market's intermediary function between savers and investors. Savers need protection against inflation and foreign exchange risks and seek a positive return. The absence of such an instrument directly led to the formation of bubbles.

1. INTRODUCTION

Savers throughout the world are confronted with big dilemmas. No matter what they do with their savings, there are big risks. There are currency exchange risks, default risks, the risk that the real values of their savings are eroded by inflation, bank failure risks. There is, of course, also the risk that they may invest in dangerous bubbles. The problem is: even as they want to get shelter from risks they may actually be contributing to the formation of bubbles and are endangered by them.

This chapter tries to make a very simple thesis. The lack of a reliable instrument whereby savers can invest their money and secure a reasonable rate of return is at the heart of many financial crises. Inventing and bringing about such an instrument, then, will avert many a financial crisis.

I cannot, of course, claim that most financial crises are due to the lack of such an instrument. There are lots of theories explaining financial crises. Crony capitalism, inadequate regulatory controls, greed, the lack of a mechanism to avert moral hazard for banks, savers, and investors, over-confidence, herd behaviour, mishandling of initially containable problems...all have been said to have engendered financial and economic crises.

It is difficult to prove or disprove these theories. There is certainly an element of truth in all these theories, many of which can be attributed to highly authoritative observers and analysts.

Harvard's Jeffrey Sachs blamed the IMF, saying that Asia was brought to its knees in 1997-98 by a loss of confidence sparked by the IMF and its prescription of tight credit and bank closures ("The IMF and the Asian Flu," *The American Prospect*, March –April 1998, 16-21).

The IMF blamed the Asian Financial Crisis to "weaknesses in financial systems, and to a lesser extent, governance." "A combination of inadequate financial sector supervision, poor assessment and management of financial risk, and the maintenance of relatively fixed exchange rates led banks and corporations to borrow large amounts of international capital, much of it short-term, denominated in foreign currency, and unhedged...." (*The IMF's Response to the Asian Crisis*, May 1998)

Lawrence Summers (then U.S. Deputy Treasury Secretary) believed that "a combination of leverage and illiquidity" was the source of Asia's and "most financial problems." (October 14, 1998 address to the Philadelphia Bar Association) (*USIS Weekly Summary*, October 12-18, 1998)

Realistically, we should see financial crises as a system with a long standing, potential problem being triggered into a crisis situation by one or a series of short-term events. Without the potential problem being there in the first place, nothing would have happened. Without those triggers, too, the crises need not happen at those moments when they happened. As long as the potential problem remains, the seeds for crises will still be there, however. When the time is ripe they will eventually lead to crises of one sort or another. Although I agree with Sachs that poor management on the part of the IMF and, in addition, poor central bank policy were largely responsible for the gravity of the crisis, they cannot be the long-standing problem. Rather, the lack of a reliable instrument for savings and investment is the long standing problem and is at the heart of the Asian Financial Crisis.

If the world's savers had access to an instrument that could provide security and a reasonable rate of return, the formation of bubbles would be less likely, and as a result the bursting of bubbles would also be less likely to happen. We would have a financially safer, more secure, and less turbulent world.

2. THE NATURE OF BUBBLES

Let us take Japan's serious economic troubles as a case study. Japan's high savings rate is legendary and is sometimes held to be a positive factor for the economy. Yet it is actually very much the source of its economic woes. If the Japanese had consumed more, it would not have so much money to pump into real estate. The current account surplus would not have been so big. The yen would not have been so strong. And the asset price bubble would not have formed, let alone burst.

Imagine yourself being a Japanese in 1987. On the eve of the global stock market crash of that year, the Nikkei index had already breached the historical high of 26,000. At the time you knew that stock prices were high, and you knew that Japanese real estate prices were extremely high. But being thrifty and productive, you had to put your savings somewhere. It would be logical for you to put some money in the stock market, some money in real estate, and some money on overseas assets. Even if you were so conservative as to put all your money into bank accounts, it is likely that the banks will in turn lend the money to builders and home-buyers, finance the purchase of assets overseas, or directly acquire overseas assets.

There being many others in the same boat looking for a place to invest the money, it is no wonder that the Nikkei Index and property values continued to rise. Helped by a temporary but sizeable depreciation of the yen (see Table 1), by the end of 1989 the Nikkei was close to 39,000, while property prices also went higher, indeed by as much as 59 per cent since 1987. When the yen hit a new high in 1991, however, it became apparent that it made less and less sense to put more money into the domestic stock market and the domestic property market. Interest in acquiring Japanese assets reversed. Yet, thanks to an efficient manufacturing sector and a highly successful export effort, notwithstanding large capital outflows, the yen kept rising. The United States wanted the yen to appreciate in order to curtail the trade deficit with Japan. Between 1990 and 1995, the yen-dollar exchange rate moved from a low of 160 yen to the dollar to a high of around 80 yen to the dollar. As the yen appreciated, home assets, which were denominated in yen became even more expensive to international investors. The incentive to sell increased while the incentive to buy disappeared. No wonder property prices and stock prices came down. A couple of months after the yen's US dollar exchange rate peaked at around 80 yen to the dollar in April 1995, the Nikkei had fallen below 15000. The land price index had also been shaved by half. Commercial land was particularly hard hit. About 60 per cent of the peak value was lost.

While domestic asset prices plummeted, the value of overseas assets also declined in yen terms as the yen continued to appreciate against the foreign currencies. Because Japan is a net creditor nation, by definition Japan has more foreign-currency denominated assets than foreign currency-denominated liabilities. Appreciation of the yen will hurt the balance sheets of Japan's business sector by reducing the yen value of net foreign assets. It will then hurt indirectly those of Japan's banks even if the latter were prudent enough to ensure that their own foreign liabilities match with their foreign assets.

Table 1. Asset prices and exchange rates

Year	Stock Price Index	Property Price Index	Exchange Rate Yen/$	Economic Growth
1997	15258.7	44.9	129.9	1.4
1996	19361.3	48.6	116.0	5.1
1995@	19868.1	54.7	102.9	1.5
1994	19723.1	63.2	99.8	0.6
1993	17417.2	71.4	111.9	0.3
1992	16924.9	87.0	124.6	1.0
1991###	22983.8	103.0	125.2	3.8
1990##	23848.7	100.0	135.4	5.1
1989#	38915.9	76.9	143.4	4.8
1988	30159.0	61.8	125.9	6.2
1987	21564.0	48.3	138.5	4.2
1986	18701.3	38.4	160.1	2.9
1985	13113.3	33.6	200.6	4.4
1984	11542.6	31.3	251.6	3.9

Source: Bank of Japan

Data for the Land Price Index is for comprehensive use in 6 major cities and is cited from *Statistics of Japan* 1998 published by the Statistical Bureau of Japan.

Note: Stock price indices are for end of the month at end of the year; the land price indices are average values for the year.

\# 1989 saw the stock market hit the peak and the yen hit a trough

\## 1990 saw the property market jumping following the sharp surge in the stock market the previous year.

\### 1991 saw the yen rising to a nearly all time high having reversed a brief depreciation against the dollar in 1989. Property prices peaked.

@ April 1995 saw the yen touching 80 yen to the dollar, then weakened rapdly. The weakening of the yen triggered a dramatic rise in stock prices that lasted about a year.

Why did the stock market bubble burst in 1990 and the property price bubble burst in 1991 is not an easy question to answer. Ito and Iwaisako (1995) could not find a valid explanation for the stock price increase in the second half of 1989 and the land price increase in 1990 using any asset pricing model based on fundamentals or rational bubbles. The evidence does show, however, that exchange movements certainly played some role. We know that stock prices are much more sensitive to emerging economic trends and they tend to lead property prices and turns in the macro-economy. The yen's depreciation in 1989 increased the attractiveness of Japanese assets and triggered a boom in asset prices. It also slowed the outflow of Japanese capital. The excessive stock price increase, coupled with the realization that the yen's depreciation in 1989 was only a temporary blip triggered a sell-off in 1990. The sharp declines in the stock market in turn aggravated the property sell-off in 1991.

One would ask why in the long years of secular appreciation of the yen, from 360 to the dollar early 1971, through around 125 yen to the dollar in 1988, nothing serious happened. The evidence however is quite clear that during these years Japan had invested aggressively in enhancing its productivity and overseas. Through such investments, it managed to preserve its competitiveness so that the manufacturing sector was still going strong in 1988, notwithstanding an already strong yen. *Over the years, however, the accumulation of savings and the absence of alternative instruments of investment inevitably had driven domestic asset prices to higher and more dangerous levels.* The yen depreciation in 1989 apparently gave investors a pleasant surprise. The prospect of yen appreciation having run its course drove investors to euphoria, and stock prices climbed to new highs. When investors learnt that the yen was to resume its appreciation, however, a major sell-off occurred.

In Hong Kong, there was a similar story. Like Japan, Hong Kong also has a high savings rate. While Japan's high savings were fuelled by a very successful manufacturing sector which enjoyed long periods of growth, Hong Kong's high savings were not only fuelled by strong growth. For many of Hong Kong's households, low cost public rental housing means that they could save huge sums of money as their incomes increase. Indeed, Hong Kong's public housing tenants were known to be the most cash-rich and the biggest savers compared to private housing tenants, private housing owners, or the subsidized homeownership scheme housing owners (Watanabe, 1998).

In 1987 the government announced a new policy requiring the richer public housing tenants to pay higher rents, even market rents for those proven to have the ability to do so.[1] This sent a strong message to public housing tenants, who then started to snap up private housing units in droves. This sent the prices of entry-level homes higher. But the owners of entry-level homes, finding that their homes could fetch good prices, also were in the position to trade up, i.e., to buy better, larger, and newer units. During a time of high inflation, trading up and otherwise investing in the home were eminently sensible. The home was held to be the best inflation hedge. The absence of alternative and reliable inflation hedges led to a long spell of property price increase in Hong Kong that lasted through the hand-over of sovereignty in 1997.

3. INDEXED GLOBAL BONDS AND THE WORLD CURRENCY UNIT

These considerations lead readily to the idea of introducing better instruments of investment for the world's savers. An ideal instrument should protect savers against inflation and exchange risk. These instruments would be issued by borrowers of different stripes, including sovereign governments. They will be rated for risk just as traditional bonds are. Savers will buy those with the preferred risk-yield combinations according to their own needs and preferences. These bonds, called indexed global bonds, are to be denominated in what is called "a standard real value unit of account." Because each of these units, by design, buy the same amount of a composite world output, these bonds offer protection against inflation risk as well as diversification for exchange risk. (See Ho, 2000.)

The proposed unit of account will be called the "World Currency Unit (WCU)." It is based on the GDP of five major economies in a chosen base year. The five economies all have totally convertible, freely traded currencies, and include the United States, the Euro zone, Japan, Canada, and Australia.[2] The sum of the GDPs in the base year, translated into US dollars from their original currencies, is scaled down to equal US$100 and forms the basic unit. Let Q_{i0} be the GDP of country i in base year 0, where country i is one of the five countries/economic entities in terms of gross domestic product. In the base year:

$$1 \text{ WCU} = \lambda \sum Q_{i0}.e_{i0} = \text{US\$ } 100 \qquad [1]$$

where λ is the scaling factor
i is any of the five major economies
e_{i0} is the exchange rate converting one unit of the currency of i into US$ in base year 0.

As a constant value unit ("*valun*," to use Coats' terminology, see Coats, p.7) the nominal value of WCU may change. No matter how the nominal value changes, however, its real purchasing power is the same, because by design it would buy the same basket of output. The nominal value, in US dollars, at time t is equal to:

$$\lambda \sum Q_{i0} .(P_{it}/P_{i0}).\, e_{it} \qquad [2]$$

which merely says that the initial basket of goods should be revalued at today's prices and translated into US dollars.

To the extent that bonds denominated in the WCU are available, savers who need an inflation hedge can buy these bonds rather than properties and stocks. Because such bonds are effectively based in a basket of currencies and protected against inflation if a Japanese saver in the late eighties could buy these bonds, he/she would have obtained a reasonable rate of return that reflected the real rate of returns to investment, and would have been subjected to minimal exchange risk. Similarly savers in Hong Kong could have bought these bonds as a hedge against inflation rather than properties. The excessive "bubble building" of the early nineties could have been avoided.

4. THE NATURE OF SOVEREIGN RISKS AND THE WCU

International investors are familiar with the existence of "sovereign risks." Sovereign risks are risks not directly stemming from the credit-worthiness of the borrower per se, but are associated with the economic, social, and political stability of the country in which the borrower is domiciled. Exchange rate gyrations are one important aspect of sovereign risk. If the currency of the country depreciates significantly, the lender will inevitably get into deep trouble, *no matter what currency the loans or the bonds are denominated.* If the loans are denominated in the local currency, the repayment may be worth nothing when translated into the currency of the lending country. If the loans are denominated in the lender's own currency, the lender appears to be protected, but the borrower will have great difficulty honouring the repayment. Either way the lender will suffer huge losses.

The fall of Peregrine Investment Holdings in Hong Kong in January 1998 was a case in point. Peregrine Investment Holdings was Hong Kong's largest investment bank and had been highly profitable and regarded by the investment community. Yet, because of the dramatic depreciation of the Indonesian rupiah, it suffered huge losses and had to declare bankruptcy. Because it had lent heavily to the well-connected Indonesian transport enterprise Steady Safe, when the rupiah was caught into a free fall, Steady Safe simply could not repay its debt. As recently as July 1 1997 the rupiah was still trading at 2431 rupiah to the dollar. By January 1998 it was trading at over 15000 rupiah to the dollar. Yet the Indonesian economy had been considered an "outstanding performer" in the *1997-98 Pacific Economic Outlook* (PEO), which was published in 1997 by the Pacific Economic Cooperation Council. The following were the exact words from the PEO: "Given the challenges faced by Indonesia in 1996, economic performance was outstanding. Real growth edged ahead, inflation dropped significantly, and domestic investment grew at an unprecedented rate." (p.14)

While Indonesia had a large outstanding foreign debt, its current account deficit in 1996 was only about 4 per cent of the gross domestic product and was deemed sustainable (p.36). Although hardly innocent of corrupt practices and nepotism, Indonesia's dramatic economic decline would not be warranted by macroeconomic fundamentals. It was a victim to the contagion, and Peregrine was in turn a victim to the economic melt-down instigated by the plunge of the value of the currency.

Many commentators believe that the Asian Financial Crisis had much to do with the problem of moral hazard.[3] The problem of moral hazard was predicated on the explicit or implicit link of the various Asian currencies to the US dollar, which had given investors a false sense of security. Excessive lending to the Asian countries was attracted by high interest rates, buttressed by the belief that there was little exchange risk. One could blame the lenders for lack of the prudence to avoid excessive risk. One could blame the borrowers for lack of the prudence to invest in more sensible projects. But in this game even lenders and borrowers who are highly reasonable and sensible get hurt. Once a currency gets into free fall, no one will be spared. Such is the nature of sovereign risk. If the obligations were denominated in World Currency Units, it is highly unlikely that a currency would go into free fall against the WCU. Both lenders and borrowers would be better protected.

5. EXCESS CAPACITY AND BUBBLES

If the unavailability of a reliable instrument of savings is a contributor to bubbles, so the lack of demand for final output is certainly no less important a contributor to the bursting of bubbles. Particularly during times of inflation, the urge to look for an inflation hedge may mean the pouring of large sums of money into real estate or the stock market. Even if money is invested in productive capital, however, the build up of excess capacity may also lead to serious problems. In a sense, these two aspects are closely related. If people spent more and saved less, there would be less excess capacity and the amount of savings looking for investment outlets would also be less. Some commentators have argued that excess capacity was the "root cause of the [Asian Financial] crisis."[4] Indeed, in both Korea and Thailand very serious excess capacity problems in the manufacturing industries emerged prior to the crisis. In a sense, the overbuilding of office buildings and even residential blocks are also a manifestation of excess capacity. If the Japanese had spent more and saved less, certainly its economy would have been stronger. Even today we should worry as much about excess capacity and excess savings as about overheating. Should Alan Greenspan raise interest rates and curtail spending, or should he stimulate more demand to absorb the excess capacity that is plaguing the world?

Adam Smith's insight sheds light on this question. Smith (1776/1961) was vehemently against high interest rates. Rather than helping to allocate the world's scarce capital efficiently, excessively high interest rates are destructive. At eight or ten per cent, according to Smith: "the greater part of the money which was to be lent, would be lent to prodigals and projectors, who alone would be willing to give this high interest... A great part of the capital of the country would thus be kept out of the hands which were most likely to make a profitable and advantageous use of it, and thrown into those which were most likely to waste and destroy it." (p.379)

6. CONCLUSIONS

Notwithstanding years of innovation and inventions, our financial intermediaries have not performed very well. We have seen massive problems in Japan's banks. We have seen system failures in Mexico and then in Asia. We have seen gyrations of the exchange rate under a freely floating exchange rates system that crippled an otherwise strong economy such as Japan. We have seen regimes of pegged exchange rates that led to moral hazard and eventually had to give way to the free float. In the former case a "floating exchange rate" floated out of line with economic fundamentals and engendered an economic decline. In the latter case a pegged exchange rate parted with economic fundamentals, got so overvalued that a crisis occurred. According to Ito, Ogawa, and Sasaki,[5] one common feature of the countries caught in the Asian Financial Crisis was a *de facto* peg to the US dollar. The Thai baht was theoretically tied to a basket of currencies, but "the US dollar had an overwhelming weight in the basket since 1985." The Indonesian rupiah was on a slide system with a narrow band, where the slide was adjusted for the inflation rate difference between Indonesia and the United States. The Korean won had also informally tied to the US dollar. Prior to the currency crisis of July 1997 all currencies had appreciated in real terms vis-à-vis the US dollar. An important lesson from all this is that the world's exchange rates should be *realistic*—should reflect the fundamentals of the respective countries, so that full employment and sustainable growth can be achieved. *Neither floating exchange rate nor pegged exchange rate can, by itself, prevent the exchange rate from assuming unrealistic, economically damaging levels.* Hot money flows driven by changing expectations and political pressures can lead to overvalued currencies in floating exchange rate regimes. Nominally fixed exchange rates will also not work either, because of divergence in monetary policy and real economic performance among countries.

My analysis suggests that the introduction of a standard real value unit can help stabilize the financial markets and improve significantly the financial intermediation function of banks. Investors can issue bonds denominated in such units. As such bonds by virtue of their denomination units are based in multiple currencies sovereign risk associated with major exchange rate movements will be reduced. With sovereign risks minimized, bond issuers can be assessed fairly and independently of sovereign risk considerations for their own credit worthiness. Similarly, banks can offer deposit accounts denominated in such units, so that savers holding money in these accounts can be spared of the need to look for alternative, risky inflation hedges. Sovereign nations can, if they choose, link their currencies to this unit of account. Because this unit of account has a diversified basis, the likelihood of the home currency being subjected to extreme devaluation or revaluation pressures will be smaller than if the home currency were linked to a single currency.

If bubbles form when savings have nowhere to go but various asset markets, it is globally rational to consume more. An increase in consumption will absorb the excess capacity of our manufacturing firms and reduce global unemployment, and will restore the rationality of investing in productive capacity. Only investing in productive capacity and in research and development can enhance our welfare over the long term. If demand for existing products is low, investments in productive capacity will not be profitable. In contrast, investing in bubbles may be profitable—as long as one could get away before others ahead of the bursting of the bubbles. This was exactly what happened before the great stock market crash of 1929, as we will see in Chapter 17.

Globally, therefore, we need more consumption at the turn of the century. To stimulate more consumption and more investment, we need lower real interest rates. This appears to run counter to the Federal Reserve's policy. Given that the United States already has a very low savings rate and is enjoying historically low unemployment rates, moderate tightening is sensible. Globally, however, the world in 2000 still has a high unemployment rate, widespread excess capacity, and a lack of interest in real investment. Lower global interest rates will stimulate more demand and foster a healthier investment climate. Contrary to what may be feared lower interest rates will not cause bubbles. Bubbles are caused by a lack of opportunities for productive investment and a lack of reliable instruments to preserve the value of savings.

NOTES

1 According to Housing Authority (December 1990) "With the implementation of the Housing Subsidy Policy on 1 April 1987, tenants who have resided in public housing for 10 years or more with their houshehold income exceeding the Subsidy Income Limit (SIL) are required to pay double net rent plus rates. The SIL is twice the Waiting List Income Limit which is reviewed on an annual basis."

2 These economic zones are representative in that they comprise the world's major industrial zones as well as major producers of primary goods.

3 Sarno, Lucio and Mark P.Taylor (1999) "Moral Hazard, Asset Price Bubbles, Capital Flows, and the East Asian Crisis: the first tests" *Journal of International Money and Finance*, 18, 637-657.

4 Christopher Wood, "Embrace Creative Destruction, " *The Wall Street Journal*, October 13, 1988, p.A22.

5 "How did the Dollar Peg Fail in Asia?" NBER Working Paper 6729, September 1998.

Chapter 12

TRANSPARENCY

"If there is one thing I've learnt in government, it's that openness is most essential in those realms where expertise seems to matter most."

Joseph Stiglitz, The New Republic, *April 17, 2000*

"...the East Asian financial crisis of 1997-1999 has highlighted twin reform areas. These are financial sector strengthening and corporate governance reforms..."

Issues, PECC, June 2000

1. INTRODUCTION

The subject of transparency deserves much attention, not only because it is frequently mentioned in discussions of financial crises, but also because of its direct relevance to the subject of macroeconomic risk management.

In the past, it was not uncommon that central banks kept the foreign exchange reserves secret. Even in Hong Kong, the composition of foreign exchange assets was not disclosed until quite recently. Giving the markets information about how much foreign exchange is held as reserves was thought to be too dangerous, because speculators could observe its fluctuations and would know the opportune time to attack the currency.

Even within the banking sector, the Hong Kong and Shanghai Banking Corporation used to hold an "inner reserve" into which profits can be transferred and out of which money can be paid out to stabilize the current year's profit. There was then a total lack of transparency about exactly how well the bank performs. This practice did not end until the early 1990s.

Is transparency good or bad for stability? In the science of military maneuvering revealing one's strengths and weaknesses to the enemy would be an unforgivable mistake. Why then is this criticism about lack of transparency?

2. TRANSPARENCY OF FINANCIAL REPORTING

While many other factors were also mentioned, both the Mexican peso crisis in 1995 and the Asian Financial Crisis in 1997 had been attributed to the lack of transparency in financial markets (Montgomery, 1996; Grenville, 1999; Rodrigo, 1998). Rodrigo thus said of the Asian Financial Crisis:

> It resulted from the explosive conjunction of serious internal flaws masked by lack of transparency, interacting with the natural volatility of global financial markets.

The problem with a lack of transparency is that because market participants do not see the problem when there is a problem, the problem grows and remedial actions are delayed. The benefit arising from increased transparency is therefore largely preventive. When one's actions are laid open for everyone to see one would avoid doing things that are obviously against the public interest. Without transparency one is apt to be less responsible. Officers of banks may lend to people close to them at terms that may not reflect the underlying risks and may lend when they should not lend at all. Company directors may engage in insider trading or other practices at the expense of shareholders and the public. Still another problem is that without transparency market participants will be much more prone to speculation and herd behavior as a self-protection mechanism. Such behavior is consistent with human nature as discussed in Chatper 2.

It is true that if a bank gets into trouble, the trouble could magnify when there is transparency. Depositors, realizing the problem, may all move their funds away in self-protection even though the problem may not be so serious. This disadvantage of greater transparency will be ameliorated once deposit insurance has been introduced into the system. Because depositors are protected against the risks of their bank failing, large scale bank runs can be avoided. Moreover, under a proper, transparent form of corporate governance and the watchful eye of the market and bank regulators, banks will behave, company directors will be accountable, and the benefits from greater transparency can be achieved.

3. TRANSPARENCY OF POLICY OBJECTIVES AND TARGETS

If we want to have a more stable world with more stable financial markets, we want to minimize surprises. One way to do this is to spell out clearly our policy targets and objectives. In an attempt to reduce market uncertainty, the Bank of Canada, for example, recently adopted explicit inflation targets and modified its operational framework, hoping to achieve greater transparency and minimize speculation (Gonzales-Hermosillo and Ito, 1997). One key advantage of currency boards, a subject now very much in vogue, is its transparency and policy-by-rule rather than policy-by-discretion nature. Under a true currency board system banknotes are issued against full (100 per cent) backing of the linked currency at the official link rate. According to Kurt Schuler, there are not many "orthodox," "true" currency boards around these days. An orthodox currency board is supposed to be entirely passive, and would not engage in any form of open market operations and would certainly refrain from intervening in the stock market, like what Hong Kong did in August 1998. A true currency board will have 100 per cent backing of the currency, but even Argentina, whose peso is now tied to the US dollar at a one-to-one ratio, is not committed to 100 per cent backing. Like most things in life, the benefits of a rule-based system have to be balanced against the costs. It is well known that under a currency board system the monetary authority has given up its discretionary power on monetary policy. Not only does the exchange rate rise and fall with the anchor currency, interest rates also have to follow that of the anchor currency. Not only do interest rates have to rise with those of the anchor currency—often against the macroeconomic needs of the local economy, but they also may have to rise more when the market is not fully convinced that the currency board will last at the prevailing exchange rate.

But being rule-based and transparent does not necessarily mean that the monetary system has to be a currency board in the "orthodox" sense. I have proposed that Hong Kong adopt a system of linking the currency with a basket of currencies under a currency board-like arrangement (Ho, 1990). Such a system is fully transparent as the proposed basket is simply the well-known effective exchange rate index, which in the case of Hong Kong is an index of the exchange value of the Hong Kong dollar against 15 currencies including the US dollar. I proposed that the official Hong Kong- US dollar link rate be continuously adjusted in order to bring the effective exchange rate index to the target level. Exactly because the rule is transparent, market speculators and arbitrageurs will help achieve this. If, say, the US dollar rises in the foreign exchange market, the Hong Kong effective exchange rate index will be pulled up, and the Hong Kong –US dollar exchange rate has to be reduced if the original effective exchange rate is to be maintained. Before the official announcement, therefore, market speculators and arbitrageurs will sell the Hong Kong dollar. As a result the value of the Hong Kong dollar in terms of the basket will be restored to the old level.

Alternatively, the monetary system can be one that is based on linking with the World Currency Unit as suggested in the last chapter. The mechanics are no different from that of a currency board and are fully transparent. Compared to linking with one anchor currency, linking with a basket of currencies or linking with the WCU will achieve greater flexibility and stability.

4. CONCLUSIONS

Whether we like it or not, the world values transparency and is moving towards greater transparency. The main benefit from having transparency in corporate governance is increased accountability, so that people who wield power will not be able to abuse their power. Potentially harmful or unfair practices can thus be avoided. The benefit from transparency is therefore largely preventive.

Rule-based policies are more transparent than discretionary policies. The main benefit from having rule-based policies is reduced uncertainty. Because rule-based monetary policies tend to be inflexible there is a price to pay for this reduced uncertainty. However, some rule-based systems are more inflexible than others. We have now the knowledge and the technology to adopt more adaptive rule-based monetary systems. Currency-board-like systems that link a local currency to a basket of currencies and to the WCU are superior to systems that link to a single currency. They are less likely, through pulling the currency's exchange value up, to plunge the local economy into recession or, though pulling it down, to drag the local economy into inflation.

I cannot agree more with Prof. Stiglitz about the importance of intelligent, open debate on important public policy issues (see the opening quote in this chapter). Although the subject of privatization of public housing had been discussed for quite some time in Hong Kong before the announcement of the Tenant Purchase Scheme on December 8, 1997, there was no public consultation at all regarding the terms and conditions of the final scheme. I was shocked when it was announced. Despite multiple articles appearing in the South China Morning Post by this author criticizing the policy (Ho, 1997d, 1998c), the scheme had been announced and offered to tenants. As we can see in Chapter 18, the policy led to Hong Kong's worst recession in history and plunged many homeowners into net debtors.

Part 4

RESOURCE ALLOCATION AND REDISTRIBUTION

The market has traditionally been hailed as providing an ideal mechanism for efficient allocation of resources. There are, however, serious limitations to the market. There are very good reasons why the market cannot replace the Government when it comes to providing certain key services. Chapter 13 looks at the issue of "optimal government size." The conclusion is that there is indeed an optimal government size, but it comes about automatically after the right decisions have been made in particular public policy areas. There is no point in trying to work out the optimal government size in the first place. Chapter 14 and Chapter 15 take a look at two important policy areas, namely education and housing, where the role of the market and that of the Government are both indispensable. Chapter 16 looks at redistribution issues, and suggests that what society needs is a true safety net. I shall argue that Government has a key role in providing "basic jobs." These Government-provided basic jobs form an important safety net for the able-bodied. In addition the society needs an income-based safety net for the more seriously handicapped.

Chapter 13

OPTIMAL SIZE OF THE GOVERNMENT

The concept of optimal size of government, like the concept of optimal city size, is not very meaningful. A government or city with the "optimal size" means nothing if it does not function well because it is ill-structured. On the other hand, if all the government functions are taken up by the government to the optimal degree and the people in charge are well organized, the problem has been solved and there is no need to talk about the optimal size of the government.

1. INTRODUCTION

All societies need a government. A number of important functions have to be taken up by governments because the private sector is not in the position to do the job fairly or properly. These include the maintenance of law and order, fostering a favorable macroeconomic environment for the private sector to operate ("macroeconomic risk management"), setting up and running a social security system that provides a safety net for those hit by misfortunes, ensuring the provision of infrastructure and those services which may be under-provided if left entirely to the market. In the Introduction to this book, I have maintained that any government that satisfies the needs of society by delivering these needed goods and services can be said to be a substantive democracy. In this chapter, I argue that if a government takes up those tasks that it can do better than the private sector can, and if it performs these tasks at a scale that is optimal, then the size of the government will be optimal. The size of the government should not be considered a public choice parameter because having achieved the "optimal size" means nothing if the government is not doing its jobs properly.

2. BENEFIT-COST ANALYSIS AND BUDGET BALANCE

These days the financial markets expect governments to balance their budgets. Whether we like it or not, a government that runs an ongoing deficit is seen to be fiscally imprudent. Even though theoretically an ongoing fiscal deficit can be part of a long run equilibrium and a growing economy could service an ongoing fiscal deficit indefinitely if the debt-servicing cost is a fixed percentage of the GDP, the financial markets will grow nervous. Largely reflecting the widespread belief that prudent governments should balance their budgets, while Europe prepared for the monetary union, the Maastricht Treaty required that the fiscal deficit of any member country should be no bigger than 3 per cent of the GDP. In a similar spirit, the Basic Law of the Hong Kong Special Administrative Region stipulated that the SAR government would adopt a policy of balanced budget, and that the government "should spend no more than its revenue." However, the revenue of the government is not fixed. We can raise more revenue or less revenue. The edict of spending no more than the revenue does not really specify how much to spend and how much to raise. Ultimately, however, efficiency dictates that the government should spend the money if the benefit of the spending is larger than the cost. So long as the benefit justifies the cost, it makes sense to raise that extra revenue and to facilitate that extra spending.

To put it simply, under the balanced budget requirement a government can be bigger or smaller. Given the size of the GDP, if the government gets bigger, the private sector gets smaller. With resources available to the private sector being smaller, the real interest rate tends to go higher. But this does not mean that a smaller government is always better than a bigger government. Any government has to justify its size by looking at each policy variable. When each policy variable is set right, the government is optimal. There is no need to worry about the optimal size of the government.

3. LAWS

Just like everything else, the introduction of laws and regulations involve costs and benefits, and it is the consideration of these costs and benefits that should determine whether a specific law is to be introduced. The costs include the costs of legislation, the costs of compliance, and the costs of enforcement. These costs include both economic and social costs. To further the public interest, any law that brings more benefits than costs should be enacted; any law that brings more harm than good should not be. In general, the more laws we introduce, the bigger will be the government, and the more constrained private sector businesses and households will be.

There is really no point in saying that something by nature should or should not be legal. In Hong Kong, it is an offence in law for passengers to talk to the bus driver when he is driving. This would be unthinkable in some other countries, but is obviously intended to ensure that the bus driver will not get distracted. Nowadays, in many countries not wearing a seatbelt while driving is illegal. Using a handheld mobile phone while driving is also illegal in some places but not in others. To this day people are still debating whether euthanasia should be legal or illegal. In some jurisdictions, drivers are not allowed to make right turns when the red signal is on. In other jurisdictions, they are allowed. Speed limits are set higher for similar roads and road conditions in some countries than in others.

In general, laws define what behavior is acceptable and what is not. Making a behavior illegal and hence punishable by law may bring benefits, in the form of protection of citizens and their properties against the harm caused by such behavior, greater peace of mind achieved for not condoning behavior believed to be immoral, improvement of public safety and hygiene, etc. But it also brings all kinds of costs. *The test of whether a behavior should be made illegal is really costs versus benefits and this is an empirical question that needs to be studied carefully, case by case.* Because values change over time, the benefits and costs of laws will also change over time. What is legal today may justifiably become illegal tomorrow and what is illegal today may justifiably become legal tomorrow.

There is an ongoing and lively debate about whether addictive drugs should be legalized, and this serves as an interesting case study for the concept of optimal government size. Clearly, making drugs illegal will increase government size. One would need a big anti-drug squad, a bigger police force to fight street crimes, bigger and larger number of prisons, and devotion of more court-time to drug and drug-related crimes. This is the cost we have to pay. Are the benefits big enough to justify the huge outlay? There is little question about the power of addictive drugs. They simply overwhelm the physical system of the body and readily overpower the mind. But is keeping drugs illegal an effective way of reducing drug addiction?

Many economists believe that drug law enforcers are spending too much money on the war against drugs and that the costs of the drug laws outweigh the benefits of the drug laws (Miron and Zwiebel, 1995; Niskanen, 1992). They argue that the huge public expenditure on fighting drugs and crimes could be better spent on education and on health. Opponents to drug legalization fear that legalizing drugs will lead to much more widespread use of these drugs. More human beings will be enslaved by drugs. Productivity and health will suffer.

Given the potency of powerful drugs, full legalization of drugs and drug trafficking is risky. While the benefits of legalization could outweigh the costs, the costs to health and productivity arising from more widespread use and greater consumption could also vastly outweigh the benefits. It is a gamble that responsible public policy makers cannot afford to make.

Still, we need to recognize that addictive drugs can never be completely eradicated. What this means is that the fight against drugs has led to higher prices and drug addicts are pushed into criminal activities and drug trafficking rather than giving up the habit. In this light, destroying seized drugs is really a silly thing to do. Rather than destroying these drugs, seized drugs should be confiscated and administered to the known addicts under security and clinical supervision. This would be the worst nightmare for drug traffickers, because it will reduce the demand for street drugs, lower street drug prices and undermine their profit.

What does this approach of criminalizing drug trafficking and decriminalizing drug use mean for the size of the government? I suspect that the size of the government will tend to go down, but we may need to set up an official drug-buying agency that will buy quality drugs at the lowest prices possible from countries where the drugs are available. This agency would supply the drug clinics whose mission is to help drug addicts kick the habit if they want to and feed the habit if they so desire. These clinics would be manned by doctors, counselors, and other professionals. This way, drug addicts would be treated like patients and we would reduce the number of deaths from overdose or from taking drugs loaded with various impurities. We would supply drugs to addicts at low cost while giving them all the help they deserve to kick their habits. Drug smuggling and drug pushing would still be a criminal offence punishable by law. Because drug trafficking would become much less profitable but is still illegal we can expect them to decline. Drug use can also be expected to decline.

This example about drug use decriminalization and drug trafficking criminalization shows that the size of the government in the aggregate should not be a policy variable. There is no scientific basis for limiting the percentage of the GDP devoted to public spending at any pre-specified level.

4. GOVERNMENT SUBSIDIZATION OF ACTIVITIES AND THE USER PAYS PRINCIPLE

There are two good reasons why the government should subsidize a productive activity. The first is that the activity may bring benefits that are external to the producer, so that the output may be under-provided if not subsidized. The second is that the activity may involve heavy fixed costs, so that charging users the marginal (direct) cost of the service will not pay for the full costs of setting up and running the facility.

The external benefit argument is discussed in most textbooks and will not be elaborated here. The heavy fixed cost argument is discussed in some books,[1] but is not as well known. In particular, it is common these days for governments to assert the user pays principle in providing services, as if every service should be self-financing if it is to be efficient. Nothing is further from the truth. Unfortunately, people do not recognize that the user pays principle really says that users should pay the full marginal cost of a service ("marginal cost pricing"), but not the full average cost. Requiring users to pay the full average cost is often inefficient. On the other hand, having to subsidize users for the use of a service on an ongoing service can be most efficient. All over the world, most underground mass transit systems require governments to subsidize their operations. Because underground mass transit systems are very costly to build and to operate, requiring users to pay the full average cost so these systems could operate without a loss is generally unrealistic, except in places like Hong Kong where the density of the population and the volume of passenger traffic are exceptionally high. Yet most people would agree that these systems are mostly a good investment for the economy. Charging passengers below the full average cost is the only way to keep these systems optimally utilized. Even if it is possible to charge higher fares and to make the systems profitable it will be socially undesirable to do so.[2]

5. PRIVATIZATION OR GOVERNMENT-RUN OPERATIONS?

These days it is also widely believed that privatization is good. If there is no overriding reason for the government to step in, such as to defend the public interest when there is a major divergence between social and private costs or benefits, the private sector should take over the operation. The government should only retain those activities which the private sector simply cannot engage in because of a potential conflict of interest or because it cannot possibly maintain itself.

Although belief in a small government and in privatization certainly antedated Margaret Thatcher, there is little doubt that Thatcher is the single most influential missionary for the gospel of privatization. However, having looked at the evidence from the experience of privatization of many countries, Tittenbrun (1996) concluded that "the available evidence on productive efficiency performance of public vs private enterprises is insufficient to prove that the former are inherently less efficient than the latter." (p.115) Ownership is not the most important determinant of efficiency. Rather, the existence of competition or the lack of it has much to do with efficiency. Tittenbrun further noted that, since some industries are characterized by large fixed costs and significant economies of scale, the allocatively efficient level of output and price would lead to a loss for the producer and is not feasible as a pure market outcome. It follows that profitability cannot be used as a reliable indicator of allocative efficiency. A profit-maximizing firm in a decreasing cost industry will set output and prices at levels different from the optimal levels.

Tittenbrun (1996) notes correctly that publicly owned enterprises tend to be subject to greater political pressure than private enterprises. He found "a lot of evidence" suggesting that politicization is the main cause of the "inefficiency" of public enterprises that do not perform so well. As a result, public enterprises may have greater difficulty in laying off redundant staff, may pay higher salaries than will their private counterparts, or may provide more generous fringe benefits. From this light, the problem of "inefficiency" for public enterprises may be more a redistribution issue than an efficiency issue. In China, the reform of state owned enterprises is beset with one big problem, which is the public policy consideration of avoiding excessive unemployment and social instability. If these enterprises are doing all these things, which may be desirable in their own right, then not being so profitable may not necessarily mean that they are intrinsically inefficient.

From the public policy point of view, it is important to ensure that enterprises, private or public, are accountable and that they operate under an environment of fair competition. If public enterprises are implicitly given policy responsibilities, we should ask ourselves whether these policy goals are really important and whether giving public enterprises such responsibilities is the best way of achieving the policy objectives. Public enterprises need not be financially self-sufficient, if they are characterized by large fixed costs and significant economies of scale. But subsidies should be in the form of lumpsum payments rather than in the form of underwriting against losses *per se*.

6. EFFICIENT TAXES AND REVENUE SOURCES

If governments should be as large as it is economically efficient to be, we will need to raise sufficient taxes or alternative revenues to run them. Revenues can take one of two forms: land-based revenues and non-land based revenues. In a growing economy land-based revenues can be very important and can dominate other forms of revenue.

Hong Kong is a case in point. For years it had been the envy of the world. Economic growth had been sustained for three decades at high rates; tax rates had been the most favorable known to the world; and land prices, though high and rising, had not undermined the former British colony's ability to compete in the world. Capital continued to be attracted to Hong Kong, while Hong Kong products continued to sell all over the world.

Hong Kong's success testifies to the validity and viability of the Henry George tax model, which says that we can keep tax very low if the government taps its revenue from land, and that is economically efficient.

Notwithstanding the "bursting of the property bubble" after the handover of sovereignty, I maintain that, for Hong Kong as for other economies, keeping taxes low and tapping land for revenue is the way to go. Traditionally, the Hong Kong government sells land leaseholds in public auctions, collects land premiums from land developers that convert land use from one use to another, collects stamp duties from land transactions, shares the profit of land developers and banks that finance mortgage loans through the profits tax.

If taxes are kept low the private sector will be encouraged to invest and to produce, since the product of hard work will not be taxed away. Provided that law and order is maintained, social and political stability is maintained, the bureaucracy is free from corruption, and the government allows the market to operate freely, the private sector will deliver the best of entrepreneurship and will invest aggressively. Land prices will rise, and the government will collect handsome revenues both directly from land and indirectly from land through profits and income taxes. This is the success story of Hong Kong over the thirty years before the handover of sovereignty. As to why Hong Kong's property bubble burst, Chapter 18 will give a full explanation. Suffice to say at this point that property prices may rise or fall in the short-term, but secular economic growth means that over the long run property prices will rise, and land remains an excellent and dependable source of government revenue.

7. CONCLUSIONS

Optimal resource allocation means that every type of resource should be put into one use as long as that use brings more benefit than if it were put into another use. This is true within the public sector, within the private sector, and between the public sector and the private sector. The test of optimality is always marginal benefit--marginal cost comparison. Any attempt to bring in any form of "rules of thumb" constraint to public spending is unscientific and anti-welfare. There is no need to worry about the "optimal size of the government." Instead, we should keep asking ourselves: do we have the right policy and the optimal policy parameters?

NOTES

1 For example, Richard Lipsey and Paul Courant (1996) *Economics*, 11th edition, Harper Collins, p. 267-268.

2 See Frankena, Mark W. (1979) *Urban Transportation Economics: Theory and Canadian Policy*, Toronto: Butterworths, Chapter 5.

Chapter 14

EDUCATION POLICY

"The adults in schools must have the power and the authority to make decisions on the spot, decisions that may differ from school to school, depending on the circumstances and the individual children involved."

Diane Ravitch, Introduction,
Brookings Papers on Education Policy 2000

1. INTRODUCTION

There are plenty of studies that show that education provides attractive rates of return. Both social and private rates of return have been estimated at double digit levels (Psacharopoulos, 1994) for most countries, although a more recent study came up with a much lower, approximately 6 per cent social rate of return to education for the UK (National Committee of Inquiry into Higher Education, 1997), The reason why estimates of the social rates of return are always lower than those for the private rates is that the calculation of the social rates of return takes into account the social investment into the education process. Private rates of return, on the other hand, are estimated on the basis of the private opportunity costs of acquiring the education. It should be noted that, typically, estimations of the social rates of return ignore external benefits on society such as lower crime rate and increased literacy that allow more effective functioning of the government. The importance of education is widely recognized and is reflected by the large budget devoted to education by governments all over the world.

Foremost in the agenda for an education policy is *curriculum design*. Education builds various kinds of skills and influences the way people perceive themselves and the world. Skills obviously directly affect an individual's ability to engage in economic production and in "household production." Because what counts in one's utility function include both tangible and intangible qualities or "attributes," as had been discussed in the chapter on human nature (which include "mental goods" and "mental bads"), the design of the school curriculum is of utmost importance. The school curriculum certainly should cover general job-related skills, communication skills, and cognitive skills, but it should also cover "life skills." Life skills include social skills, stress management and coping skills, problem-solving skills, and self-management skills. Education should contribute to the production of happiness-enhancing attributes such as self-respect and the respect for others, and help people minimize the production of happiness-ameliorating attributes, such as self-pity and jealousy.

Another important policy concern is to create an environment that encourages the emergence of quality schools and quality students. Crucial to this is a system that respects autonomy, choice, and fair competition. This provides *the environment that will promote the efficient production of education output.*

Assuming that we have an environment that allows the education output to be produced efficiently, the next important policy question is what constitutes the *optimal combination of quality and quantity of education output.* Assuming efficiency, quality would be equivalent to providing more input per student-year. Quantity has two dimensions: the number of years of education per student, and the number of students enrolled in each level and each type of education.

Still another important policy concern is the funding of education. Should education be publicly funded? How about private schools? Should students bear a part of the cost of education and if so, how much?

Finally, there is the question about the diversity of education. Should we provide more vocational or professional education or more general education? How shall we decide between this mix?

This chapter will explore these questions using the framework introduced in the beginning of this book.

2. CURRICULUM DESIGN

This is not the place to discuss the details of curriculum design. One basic principle of economics, and one that we must bear in mind, however, is that all components of the curriculum compete for the student's scarce time. There should therefore always be a "systems perspective." Rather than each subject trying to defend its turf we should consider the total time available and the balanced needs of the student. Only those components which will serve the student's long term interest best should be included. As much as the authorities may want to dictate the full curriculum on schools, they should not preempt schools and teachers, who should be given the autonomy to bring into their school curriculum elements that they regard important for the children under their care, for they have direct contact and interactions with their students and know their needs and abilities better than anyone else. Over the years each school may have its own success stories and schools can then learn from one another.

There is no question that basic language literacy and numeracy skills are essential to effective communication and learning so the school curriculum must definitely provide adequate coverage of these subjects. Students should clearly also learn to know more about their own community and the world. But more important, they should learn how to live peacefully with others and with themselves. The way to do this is not to tell them what is right and what is wrong, but to go into history and literature and human case studies to alert students to the consequences of alternative ways of life and let students decide for themselves what is right and wrong.

As the chapter on human nature argues what affects human happiness is not just market goods and services but also mental goods and mental bads, which are in turn affected by perceptions and attitudes. A school curriculum that helps create mental goods and eliminates mental bads is economically as productive as firms that supply market goods and services are. This is over and above the human capital investment aspect of education. It is useful to use the example of the concept of success for illustration. A feeling of success or achievement is certainly conducive to happiness. If the education system builds a concept of success based on *relative performance* a large number of school children will suffer from a totally unnecessary mental bad. When success is interpreted in relative terms, students tend to see others as enemies rather than friends. On the other hand, if the education system builds a concept of success based on reaching new heights for each person, then all school children (and future adults) will be able to enjoy the mental good called "success" as long as they all try hard and realize their own potential.

Designers of school curriculum should realize that many children come from unhappy families. They need to learn how to relate to their parents and brothers and sisters and friends, particularly how to respond when they are unreasonable or even mean. School children should also learn about parenting. Only when they know how to be parents and learn about the problems faced by parents can they relate to their future children, and can they communicate more effectively with their parents.

The authorities should standardize only part of the school curriculum and probably a greater part for lower grades but should exercise less control for higher levels of education. Students in higher grades should have greater choice over programs and curricula, which may be more vocational and career-oriented or more academically and intellectually oriented, depending on their aspirations.

3. EFFICIENT PRODUCTION OF EDUCATION

Maintaining Fair Competition and Standards of Excellence

Efficient production of education requires motivated teachers and motivated students. Among other things, a necessary condition for teachers to be motivated is that they can see the results of their own effort. If, for historical or other reasons, a secondary school keeps getting the best students year after year while another keeps getting the worst students year after year, teachers in the "good" schools may find that they can put in a minimum effort with little apparent adverse effect on performance. On the other hand, those schools that keep getting the worst prepared students may find that they are being unfairly treated, because teachers in these schools never get a break. Students groomed to become competitive would leave for schools with better names, while new enrollees continue to be poorly prepared.

Generally, a system that allows students to compete for school places will end up with preferred schools with preferred students. Such a system is good up to a point. There is no harm and indeed a lot of good in putting the sharpest minds together. But if the whole lot of students are ranked and slotted to schools that correspond with their ranks it is likely that some schools will be labeled "undesirable" and will be left with "undesirable" students. Such a system will inevitably create a lot of pressure on students and parents. To the extent that schools that are least preferred are assigned the worst-performing students there will be a labeling effect on these students and the teachers in these schools will have a hard time helping the students overcome their sense of failure. Under such a system the fear for being assigned a lowly rated school will put great pressures on students and parents. Such a system, which allows some schools to take the best students and forces some others to take the worst students is, however, most definitely a socially destructive and an inefficient way to educate our students. It is socially destructive because at an early age students are trained to see success in relative terms. Given such a system, it is no wonder that primary school students in Hong Kong felt so much pressure from the public examination that would categorize them into the five bands.[1] It is also highly inefficient because teachers in the preferred schools will not need to perform in order to attract good students, while teachers and students in the to-be-avoided schools are demoralized. Students tend to see themselves as failures and teachers have a rough time maintaining order in class, let alone teach effectively.

Actually, in order for schools to run efficiently, a dose of healthy competition, allowing students and schools to compete on an equal footing is highly desirable and even necessary. One proposal is to allow the top 10 or 20 per cent of students from a public examination to choose their own schools. This is just like the current banding system in Hong Kong. The remaining 80 to 90 per cent of students will, however, be randomly allocated to various schools according to the nearest location. This way, the most preferred schools may continue to have the best students for a while. If they do not perform well, however, any one of the other schools may attract away the outstanding students in the next rounds of public examinations from them. The other schools will enroll students covering a whole range of abilities.

Under this arrangement, if students do very well they will have their choice of the secondary school, but if they do not do so well, it is not the end of the world. There will still be elitist schools. A typical secondary school, however, will have a student body with a full range of abilities. For maximum teaching efficiency students of similar abilities may be grouped together. Because this is done within the school any labeling effect will be kept to a minimum. Moreover, provided a student improves he can easily move up to a class for higher abilities. Such a "migration" is certainly easier within a school than from one school to another.

The Role of Public Examinations

Both public examinations and the presence of elitist schools that will take the top students from the public examinations are necessary to instill a sense of purpose and to generate greater awareness of one's performance. Both will help enhance efficiency. Because all the other, non-elitist, schools have a similar student base they can compete on the same footing. Provided that they build up sufficient reputation they can attract the top 10–20 per cent of students and become one of the elitist schools.

Empowerment of Parents and Autonomy of Teachers

Also important to the cause of efficiency is respect for teachers' autonomy. Teachers working in the classroom know best how students respond to different teaching methods. Bureaucrats can provide schools and teachers with information and different perspectives, but should really leave it to the teachers as to how they go about teaching their students.

This principle finds testimony in Bill Clinton's praise of the charter schools in the US. Charter schools are public schools that operate with little government intervention and union interference. According to Clinton, "We now have enough evidence that the charter school movement works… Very often we see charter schools provide an even greater atmosphere of competition that induces kids to work harder and harder to learn."[2]

While it pays to give teachers greater autonomy to exercise their professional judgment and creativity in the classroom it should be recognized that teachers are human beings and are subject to their own likes and dislikes and human weaknesses. Like all workers and professionals they should also be held accountable. A recent issue of the *World Bank Economic Review* contained studies suggesting that it pays to give parent greater involvement in the management of schools. Positive results in terms of lower dropout rates, lower teacher and student absenteeism, and more effective learning (Volume 13, September 1999) from parent participation in school management have been documented.

In recent years, there is more and more discussion about the use of education vouchers as a way of enhancing efficiency and choice. The idea of education vouchers is to allow parents and students to have choice outside the public school system for education. The subsidies implicit in a public school place can, under the voucher system, be transferred, if the student so chooses, to a private school of his own choice. The biggest fears about an education voucher system are two. First, while in principle students can choose schools under the voucher system it could end up with schools choosing students based on socio-economic background, as a result of which there could be social segregation and less equal opportunity rather than more. Second, allowing students to opt out of the public school system could undermine the finances of the public school system and hurt those students that remain in public schools. As long as these problems can be contained, perhaps through limiting the face value of vouchers to only a fraction of the funding support implicit in a public school place, the voucher system, by enhancing choice and competition, should have positive effects on education quality.

There is an imperative to defend and improve the public school system. A good public school system is our chance to ensure equal opportunity to education. A completely privately funded school system would leave out children from the poorer families. Having a public school system and at the same time allowing students to take part of the funding to a private school[3] not only will give students from poorer families the choice to enroll in private schools, but will give public schools a healthy dose of competition. However, allowing students to take the full funding to a private school will drain too much resource out of public schools and will put them at a disadvantage.

4. FUNDING

Considerations about social justice and equity dictate that the government should ensure that basic education is available to all. This would mean that the public purse should *fund* basic education. Funding basic education is not restricted to paying for the running cost of schools but also implies paying for a significant percentage of the training cost of teachers. This is to ensure that a career in teaching is sufficiently attractive to high quality candidates. Given that a good primary education is an important aid and even a prerequisite to a good secondary and even university education, the returns to primary education have often been underestimated, as pointed out by Appleton, Hoddinott, and Knight (1996). Making sure that teachers are well qualified and motivated, and equipping schools adequately is well worth the while.

As argued earlier, those parents who choose to send their children to private schools should have the prerogative to do so, provided that they take only a fraction, perhaps fifty per cent, of the average funding cost to the public school system.

A big question is whether the government should provide sufficient funding for post-secondary education to be accessible to all who want it.

The argument in this book is that each student should get the education he deserves. Everybody deserves basic education, but not everybody deserves higher education. Higher education investment should be made only as long as the benefit is larger than the cost. The benefit of higher education investment is larger than the cost for some individuals but not for others. The investment in quantity should be made only as long as the marginal net benefit from extending the education to the next competent student is positive. The investment in quality should also be made only as long as the marginal net benefit from spending more on an individual is positive.

Since higher education brings returns to the individual, is there a reason to use public money on higher education at all?

Public subsidization of higher education will raise the private rate of return from education. This will make the study program more attractive. If the opportunities for enrolling in these programs are limited, the subsidy will make the program more competitive. The increased competition will increase the quality of students enrolled in those programs. So the question we should ask is whether the benefit of having better-qualified students to enroll in these programs outweigh the costs. For example, making medical students pay a greater percentage of the cost of their education will reduce the private rate of return for enrolling in the medical school and will reduce the attraction to students. Competition for the medical school will become less keen. As a result the quality of students enrolled in the medical school will decline. Public spending on medical education therefore can be seen as a spending to enhance the quality of our future doctors.

5. CONCLUSIONS

Education prepares a person for living in the society. Living in the society means work, socializing, being with one's own family and being with oneself. Certainly education means a lot in terms of happiness, both for the one receiving the education and for others. The curriculum is of utmost importance because a badly designed curriculum will certainly result in our younger generation badly prepared for society when they leave school.

Giving parents the choice between public school and private school is fine as long as the public schools are fine. It would be tantamount to giving up the poor and depriving children from poorer families the opportunity to decent education if the public school system is poor. Giving poor parents education vouchers to buy education in private schools is not the answer. As Lazear (1999) testifies, quality private schools charge high prices. Giving parents education vouchers and giving up the public school system is abrogating the responsibility of providing a decent education to all. Public schools should be given a fair chance to compete. They should be given adequate resources and should be allowed to tap students covering a full range of abilities. Within the public school system the choice to opt for personally preferred schools should be given only to the top 10 to 20 per cent of the students. If schools tap different qualities of students they will not be able to compete fairly.

In principle, investment in education should be carried to the point where the marginal benefit of extending the education to more people is reduced to equate with the marginal cost. This means that a blanket statement in favor of universal education at all levels for all is not warranted, unless it can be proven that extending the education to more people continues to yield net social benefit. In general, the latter is probably true with basic and perhaps even secondary education, but quite unlikely with university education. For an individual, optimal education investment requires that he receive as many years of education as it takes to reduce the marginal benefit of an extra year of education to the cost of doing so. It is highly unlikely that the optimal "intensity" of education would be the same for all individuals, with their different aspirations, interests, and abilities. Before extending the number of university places, therefore, we should assess the marginal benefit and marginal cost of doing so. A good place to start is to assess the extent to which existing university students benefit from their degree programs and whether there are other social benefits or costs.

Since enrollment in a university is voluntary, we may assume that the fact student continue to enroll in university suggests that the private rate of return from university education is sufficiently attractive. The latter seems to be borne out by various studies. For example R. Blundell, L. Dearden, A. Goodman & H. Reed (1997) found a substantial wage premium, between 12 and 18 per cent for men and between 34 and 38 per cent for women, enjoyed by university graduates over non-university graduates. Such wage premiums calculated for the average university graduate, however, do not imply that we should expand university enrollment, because "marginal students" may not benefit from the education and may earn much lower returns. The fact that students enroll in universities in expectation of gain is not good enough a reason for expanding enrollment. Students may think enrolling in university is a good gamble. But from the social point of view it may not be. People are known to take actuarially unfair bets. That does not mean that socially the bets are worthwhile. Extending university education to an additional student may entail a marginal cost that is larger than the expected marginal benefit.

The extent of unemployment among university graduates in many countries such as the Philippines and India suggest globally and particularly among less developed countries, higher education enrollment ("quantity") may have expanded too fast when in fact the investment should have been in quality. Widespread illiteracy or half literacy suggests that for basic and secondary education investment in both quality and quantity has been inadequate. Grim career opportunities awaiting many university graduates in a number of countries suggest that investing in quality, rather than quantity, is the way to go. It is high time we use benefit-cost analysis, rather than political rhetoric, to determine the further development of education.

NOTES

1 This is the system in place in Hong Kong for many years. The Special Administrative Region is proposing to collapsing the five bands into three. This is far from adequate, as students enrolled in the third band will continue to be labeled as failures.

2 Quoted in Abby Goodnough, "Clinton seeks some control of charter schools," The New York Times, May 5, 2000.

3 Alberta in Canada offers students the opportunity to take half of per capita public school cost to private schools. See West (1997).

Chapter 15

HOUSING (WITH A DIGRESSION ON TRANSPORTATION PRICING)

Those in charge of housing policy should be mindful to maintain the "flow" in the housing market. Public involvement in the housing market should be limited to providing the low-income households with decent but basic shelter; otherwise it would preempt the private market.

1. INTRODUCTION

Governments throughout the world, regardless of their ideology and political orientation, have participated in the housing market to a greater or a smaller extent. Food and shelter are regarded as basic human needs and both certainly receive considerable attention from governments.

Food and housing are "private goods" which are bought and sold in the market place. Yet if people cannot afford food and housing malnutrition and poor housing conditions result. This is regarded as unacceptable in an affluent society. In principle, an income transfer could allow the poor to meet these basic needs and exercise some choice, and it could be superior to a transfer in kind. But the poor, on receiving an income transfer, may not spend it on food and housing to the extent most people feel comfortable. This is why governments often choose to issue food coupons and to subsidize housing. For this reason housing can be called a "merit good."

Public policy to boost housing consumption among the poor can take the form of demand-side subsidy, supply-side subsidy, or outright production for the poor. The problem with demand-side subsidy is that the subsidies may end up boosting the rental income of landlords without improving the housing conditions of the poor. Because the poor have little means to buy new housing, housing for the poor is never commercially profitable to build. As a result the poor rely on a process of "filtering down" to obtain their accommodation. Filtered-down housing refers to old, run-down housing vacated by those who have become better off and able to move for better housing. If the supply of such filtered-down housing is limited and inelastic with respect to rent, giving the poor rental subsidies may benefit landlords more than tenants.

This is why typically governments use supply-side measures to help the poor live in better housing. Contracting out the construction, subsidizing production, or taking charge of the construction directly, many governments make sure that new housing are built for the poor according to certain specifications and avail such housing to those satisfying specified eligibility criteria at subsidized cost.

2. SUPPLY OF RENTAL OR OWNED HOUSING?

For many years—indeed over two decades up till 1978—Hong Kong provided low-cost rental housing for the poor. Singapore's Housing and Development Board (HDB) went the other way. Singapore's Home Ownership Scheme was introduced as early as 1964. Because Singapore adopted the subsidized home ownership approach from an early day, today over 90 per cent of families living in HDB flats owned their homes. In contrast, on the eve of the transfer of sovereignty more than 70 per cent of Hong Kong's public housing population lived in rental flats. In terms of coverage, Singapore's public housing program had provided homes to 86 per cent of the entire population, a ratio far higher than Hong Kong's 50 per cent.

The public housing program in Hong Kong was from the first day intended only as a kind of interim housing. It was very low-cost and very low quality, although today quality has improved significantly. The public housing program in Singapore, in contrast, was intended to provide permanent, quality homes even in the early sixties. According to the HDB, "Even towns built in the early years, such as Toe Payoh town come complete with a town centre, children's playground, swimming pool, shops, markets, cinema, library, and light industries to provide employment for residents. All the transportation and commercial facilities are also linked up to serve residents."[1]

The public housing program in Hong Kong was intended to help the poor; that in Singapore was to help the poor and the middle-class people as well. Obviously Hong Kong's model left much more room for the private sector than the Singapore model.

More important, because the low income people in Hong Kong paid very low rents (less than 10 per cent of the median household income among the tenants) and because the economy had gone through years of strong growth, many households in the low cost rental housing were able to accumulate a huge amount of savings. When the Home Ownership Scheme

(HOS) housing was first introduced in 1978, the 8400 units attracted 36,000 applications, many of which were from public housing estate tenants. As a matter of fact, the government intended that the public housing estate tenants, by purchasing HOS units, would vacate their rental units and make room for those waiting in line for public housing. This is why public housing tenants were exempted from the income eligibility requirements that would apply to other applicants for HOS housing. HOS housing was priced at a 30 to 50 per cent discount from estimated market prices. Successful applicants for HOS housing were selected through a lottery, and from the first day until 1997 obtaining a ticket to buy HOS housing had been considered equivalent to winning a lottery.

In Singapore buying and owning a HDB housing flat was encouraged through the following means:

- From 1968, Singaporeans were allowed to use their Central Provident Fund savings for the 20 per cent downpayment and monthly repayment of the mortgage loan;
- The income ceiling is frequently reviewed "such that every 9 out of 10 Singaporeans are eligible to enjoy the benefits of public housing."
- Buyers are charged very low, HDB-sibsidized interest rates and had the option to repay the mortgage loans over a period up to 25 years.
- Rental tenants are offered a discount of 30 per cent off the selling price, or S$10,000, whichever is lower and can obtain a mortgage loan of up to 100 per cent of the discounted price.

Compared to Hong Kong's property prices, HDB homes are quite affordable with prices in 1998/99 ranging from about S$130,000 to S$400,000. Because HDB homes account for 86 per cent of Singapore's population and clearly dominates the market. In other words, the HDB "calls the shots." Although since 1991 private developers have been invited to tender for the design and construction of public housing flat, they continue to have only a tiny room to play in Singapore's housing market. However, there is no discontinuity in the housing policy.

In contrast, Hong Kong's housing policy underwent a few rather significant changes. These included the introduction of HOS housing in 1978, a policy to make the richer tenants pay higher rent that was first endorsed in 1986, and the announcement of the Tenant Purchase Scheme in December 1997, which allowed sitting tenants to buy their units at a deep discount.

To provide an option for richer tenants to buy better, less subsidized, housing was a great idea. The policy to make the richer tenants pay higher rent was also a great idea. Both policies increase the "flow" in the housing market. Tenants whose economic circumstances had allowed them to move out of subsidized rental housing moved out. Those waiting in line moved ahead. The richer tenants also moved onto better housing.

The policy in Hong Kong for many years had allowed HOS owners to resell their units in the open market after 10 years. Many of them did, and they realized a good profit (they had however to pay back to the Housing Authority the implicit land cost subsidy). With the profit they could afford to pay a high price for a better home. This has set off a stream of homeownership upgrading that has proved highly profitable for developers, decorators, brokers, bankers, retailers, lawyers, homeowners themselves, and the government.

3. THE OPTIMAL POLICY

Public Housing vs the Market

A public housing program that sets out to satisfy the housing needs of 86 per cent of the population normally does not make much sense. But Singapore obviously did a good job in its town planning and in meeting citizens' housing needs. Notwithstanding the apparent success, however, there is a price to be paid. Moreover, Singapore owes its success to historical and particular reasons including the Central Provident Fund, a forced savings program that became a backbone to the housing program. The price is that there is little room for private developers to play in the Singapore housing market, Singaporeans' choice of housing has become rather limited, and taxes have to be much higher than otherwise.

Low Cost, Basic, but Decent Housing

In principle, a public housing program should aim at assisting the low-income people. It should provide *low-cost, basic, but decent housing only to those who qualify* and should disallow the richer people from enjoying the implicit subsidy. This restriction is both for justice reasons and for efficiency reasons. The richer people normally would have opted for better housing. Only very low rent would keep them in relatively low quality housing because they place only a small value on living in such conditions.

Given the policy objectives of a public housing program, limiting implicit housing subsidies to the target group is no doubt a correct policy. Unless announced on the first day, however, such a policy will prove difficult to implement, as Hong Kong's experience has shown. Hong Kong faced considerable opposition from tenants and politicians when it tried to introduce a "Housing Subsidy Policy" that would make the richer tenants pay more. For too long Hong Kong had allowed full secure tenure to tenants once they had been admitted into public housing. Against all these difficulties and in the face of expected protests from tenants, however, the Housing Authority finally managed to announce, in November 1986, that families who had lived in public rental housing for ten years and whose income exceeded the prescribed would start paying double rent as from April 1988.

"Conditional Bidding"[2]

When the supply of public housing is larger than the number of target group households, there will be a need to increase the supply of public housing. But if the supply momentarily cannot meet the requirements of the target group, it becomes necessary to ration the available supply among the eligible people. One way of doing so is to use the first-come-first-served principle. The other and a far better way is to allow the eligible households to bid among themselves: whoever pays the highest price will get the unit—through either an outright purchase or a rental arrangement. This can be called "conditional bidding"—conditional in the sense that one's bid is conditional on one's being eligible. The "conditional market" becomes segmented from the free market, as any resale will also be restricted to the target group. The advantage of this arrangement is that everyone within the target group can bid for any unit, which will then find its "conditional market price." Each unit will go to the highest bidder within the target group and all the target group players will not have to wait. This means that each unit will realize its greatest valuation among the entire eligible population. Any tenant or owner can vacate or sell his unit and rent into or buy another unit from the conditional market.

The logic of excluding those outside the target group to bid is that given that all those within the target group have similar abilities to pay, any household who will not pay as much as others does so only because the unit is not as valuable to him as it is to others. It is not because others have higher ability to pay and on that account outbid him. Because the public housing program is designed in the first place to assist the low-income people, there will never be any leakage of housing units to outside the target group. The government will then not need to commit so much resources to the public housing program.

In practice, once a household has moved into a public housing unit it is not easy and certainly politically painful to ask him to leave. If a household is to leave, he has to leave voluntarily. Given that this is the case, a policy of making richer tenants pay higher rent, and enforcing the rule of resale only to eligible households should do the trick. If richer tenants have to pay higher rent, there will be little to gain in terms of rental savings for them to stay on. If owners have to resell only to eligible households, there will be little hope of reselling at a profit. Speculative holding of public housing units will be less likely.

Maintaining the "Market Flow"

If public housing is basic and is restricted to households who are within the target group, then those who have become better off will want to leave the public housing units when they can afford it. The income elasticity of demand for housing being positive and close to unity for high income households, (O'Sullivan, 1996, p.389) better-off households will have a great incentive to leave if the quality of housing is "basic."

Given that the units though decent are basic, the desire to realize a better life will automatically lead many households who are ready for better housing to leave. More of the eligible households will then benefit from the public housing stock. At the same time there will be a stream of households entering the private market.

In order to facilitate this transition, Hong Kong's introduction, in 1978, of "Home Ownership Scheme" housing that offered better quality housing than rental public housing, is quite a good idea. The Home Ownership Scheme housing in Hong Kong, however, is also subsidized. Accordingly currently some eligibility criteria apply. As was pointed out, however, the Hong Kong Housing Authority exempted existing public housing tenants from the income eligibility criteria if they want to buy HOS housing, in the hope that this will encourage them to vacate their subsidized rental units.

In principle, as long as the HOS housing is of better quality than the public rental housing, and not quite as good as new private housing it will find buyers only among the lower middle income people. *There will be no need to maintain eligibility criteria and HOS housing can be sold at full market prices.* These full market prices may still imply a subsidy, but this does not matter. Such HOS housing will serve a purpose. It will enable more of the low cost rental housing tenants and some of private housing tenants to buy a first time home. With this kind of arrangement people should be free to sell and buy HOS housing without restriction.[3] Because those who opt for better quality have to buy in the private market, the market flow can be maintained. This flow is very good for the economy, as it will generate a lot of jobs and side-benefits throughout the economy. On the other hand, upgrading the quality of rental public housing to approach that of HOS housing is a poor policy because it will reduce the "flow" in the housing market. Tenants in rental public housing will not move out. Turnover in the housing market will become lower.

4. CONCLUSIONS

The proposal of "conditional bidding" and segmenting the public housing market from the private housing market may not find much favor among free market economists. In particular, it may be felt that disallowing public housing owners from selling their units in the open market is tantamount to not realizing the full market value of these units. However, such segmentation is equitable and efficient. It is equitable because the housing subsidy is intended only for the target group. It is efficient because it minimizes the public resources required to help to target group. As Chapter 18 points out, failing to segment the market in an attempt to privatize public housing quickly can lead to economically disastrous results.

Segmenting the low-cost housing market by spelling out that buyers of subsidized public housing must not resell to people outside the target group will reduce the opportunity for these owners to realize a capital gain. If this condition is not in place, for every unit that is resold to people outside the target group, the government will have to build a new unit in order to maintain the same stock of low cost housing units for the low-income people. Clearly segmenting the low-cost housing market this way will minimize the amount of resources that the government has to devote to housing the poor. There will be less pressure to raise taxes, and more of the poor people can be housed better faster.

The Singaporean Housing and Development Board states its mission as: "We provide affordable homes of high quality. We promote the building of communities." There is no right or wrong for the government body to take on such responsibilities, but it does mean that with the government taking on such policy missions, the private sector will have less room to play under such a government philosophy, and taxes will have to be higher. If this is what the community knowingly chooses, that would be fine.

In a system that prefers to allow the private sector to solve the community's housing problems and to restrict the government's role to assisting the poor, "homes of high quality" should never be built by the government. The government should build decent but basic homes, so that when the poor have become better off they will turn to private housing.

NOTES

1 See http://www.hdb.gov.sg/isoa034p.nsf/factsonhdbview?OpenView
2 The argument is given in greater detail in Ho (1988) and Ho (1995a).
3 The Hong Kong Housing Authority used to impose a 10-year period of residence before an HOS owner can sell his unit in the open market. This rule has now been relaxed.

A DIGRESSION: TRANSPORTATION PRICING

Before closing this chapter, it is useful to refer to one key principle in resource allocation, which is that prices should reflect (marginal) costs and the pricing structure should also reflect the cost structure. Called the Efficient Pricing Principle, it is fundamental to achieving efficient resource allocation. In contrast, full cost pricing may be inconsistent with efficient resource allocation.

Marginal Cost Pricing and Optimal Departures from MC Pricing

The Efficient Pricing Principle is best illustrated with transportation pricing. In general, in a mass transit system, the marginal cost of providing a passenger with a trip service is very low, and it does not vary much with respect to the length of the trip. Given that the transit system is up and running, taking an additional passenger, when there is not much congestion,[1] will have little effect on total operation costs, implying that the marginal cost of a passenger trip may be quite close to zero. This cost may also not vary significantly with the length of the journey. The efficient pricing principle would suggest that the fare would be rather low and would not vary much with respect to the length of the journey. If this principle is not followed, and instead fares are fixed at such levels as to attempt a full cost recovery in the name of the user pays principle, chances are that, with the exception of very densely populated cities and very heavily used routes, the system will be underutilized.

Following the efficient pricing principle to the letter, however, implies that the government may have to subsidize the operation costs of the system heavily. This in turn implies having to raise tax rates. Raising taxes, however, is known to hurt economic efficiency. If the inefficiency caused by having to raise taxes is even worse than the inefficiency of raising fares above marginal costs, then it will not be wise to raise that much tax and it will be wise to allow fares rise above marginal costs. This departure from marginal cost pricing makes sense strictly on cost benefit principles. That is, if a departure from marginal cost pricing produces more benefit (in terms of allowing tax rates to stay low and thus avoiding "excess burden") than costs (in terms of underutilization), then it should be allowed.

Because long distance passengers are more ready to accept higher fares than short distance passengers, they are less likely to be driven away when fares are raised above marginal cost. So raising fares for them may not cause so much underutilization. For this reason it will make sense to charge long distance travel at a higher rate than short distance travel.

Thus, in a second best world when taxes have to be raised to finance the operations deficit in a mass transit system, the Efficient Pricing Principle has to be modified.

Efficient Pricing Structure Principle

The Efficient Pricing Principle requires that the pricing structure follow the cost structure. This is best illustrated with the pricing of taxi services. There are actually several cost components in a taxi-passenger trip. First, there is the cost of "booking" the driver and the taxi for the time of the trip. This cost element strictly varies with the duration of the trip. Second, there is the fuel and additional maintenance cost associated with the trip. This cost element is closely related to the distance traveled. Finally, there is a "passenger-pick-up cost", which is the cost of the taxi waiting in line, that of cruising in the streets or the cost of going to the passenger pick-up point in response to a telephone call. This last element can be treated as roughly fixed although there obviously is some random element to it.

In general, the fare structure does not reflect this cost structure and this gives rise to problems. There are complaints against drivers discriminating against short-trip passengers. Such discrimination occurs because normally the fares do not reflect the fixed pick up cost. As a result taxis have to bear the additional pick up cost for picking up another passenger.

Drivers are also wary about going into heavy traffic. When they are caught in heavy traffic, even though there is often a "waiting time" charge this charge may not even cover the cost of the time of the driver and the rental cost of the taxi. As a result there are often arguments between the driver and the passenger. Drivers may want to take a more roundabout route to avoid the congestion, while passengers may object.

For all these reasons it makes sense to structure the charges to include three elements: a fixed charge to reflect the pick-up cost, a time-based charge to reflect the rental or booking cost of the driver and the vehicle, and a distance-based charge to reflect additional marginal costs that are related to the distance traveled.

NOTES

1 If there is congestion, so that taking on an extra passenger increases the waiting time and discomfort for other passengers, the marginal cost will be very high reflecting the time and discomfort cost. Fares should be correspondingly much higher.

Chapter 16

SOCIAL SAFETY NET AND REDISTRIBUTION

1. INTRODUCTION

Income distribution has traditionally been an important concern of policy makers and policy analysts. Historically, extreme inequality in income distribution has been cited as a major contributor of political and social instability, and is considered by some to be one of the reasons for the economic depression of the 1930s. However, from the humanitarian point of view, *it is far more important to have a social safety net than to have an effective program of income redistribution.* A social safety net will of course have distributive consequences, but is not intended to be distributive.

Traditionally, people think of a social safety net as income support for the needy. In particular, if someone is hit by some misfortune and is unable to fend for himself because he is sick or disabled, the safety net will come to his aid, and will reduce his suffering tremendously. A social safety net transfers income, not so much because the recipient is poor but because he has been hit by misfortune beyond his control. Income redistribution, on the other hand, simply transfers income from the "have" to the "have not."

This chapter wants to advance one doubtlessly controversial idea, which is that *access to a basic job is a human right and an important social safety net.* These days an able-bodied person may have great difficulty getting a basic job, which is defined as a job that offers an income that can maintain the daily subsistence and satisfy the basic needs for social life. Since what constitutes a basic pay is certainly subject to the subjective judgment about what is subsistence and basic needs for social life, there is little point in trying to be very precise about the dollar amount for the salary of a basic job. However, both the idea of access to a basic job for the able-bodied and that of providing adequate income support for the disabled and the physically disadvantaged are important elements of a respectable social safety net.

2. ACCESS TO A BASIC JOB AND MINIMUM WAGES

The minimum wage was recently advanced as a redistributive tool (Freeman, 1996). According to Freeman, "an appropriately set minimum [wage] can be a modestly effective redistributive tool." (p. 640). The effectiveness of the minimum wage would be particularly enhanced if the social welfare system complements the minimum wage by enhancing in-work benefits (pp.644-645).

Freeman does recognize, however, that the minimum wage will potentially reduce the availability of jobs (p.648). From a theoretical point of view, if the minimum wage is set at a sufficiently high level, there is no question that jobs will disappear. The current debate about the employment effects of the minimum wage is whether a minimum wage set at a low level will also adversely affect job availability.

David Card and Alan Krueger (1994) presented a case of minimum wage increasing jobs. In that particular case, the minimum wage was raised in one region (New Jersey) relative to that of a neighboring region (Eastern Pennsylvania). Employment in the region with raised minimum wages was found to increase. The reason behind this phenomenon, however, may be that workers from other regions, particularly better workers from other regions, are attracted to the region. Because of the increase in productivity the demand for labor curve or the marginal product curve of labor shifts to the right at the same time as labor supply increases. The increase in employment in New Jersey may well be at the expense of employment elsewhere. From this perspective, a nation-wide increase in the minimum wage may reduce employment.

Economists usually find minimum wage legislation ineffective as a means to improve the well-being of workers (Baumol and Blinder, 1991, pp.773-774). First, it does not increase the incomes of those whose wages are higher than the minimum wage. For those workers whose wages would have been lower than the statutory minimum wages, only a few will be employed at the minimum wages. The rest will be denied the opportunity of employment altogether. In the industrial world, where minimum wage legislation generally applies, the unemployment of unskilled, younger workers who are supposed to be the major beneficiaries of the legislation, is often serious. These groups are clearly hurt by the policy.

To ensure that the workers have a minimum income or living standard without increasing unemployment we can use a *wage subsidy*. Unlike the minimum wage, wage subsidies reduce the cost of hiring and increase jobs. In principle, it is possible to bring wages up to the minimum level desired by giving *all* workers a uniform and sufficiently large wage subsidy (equal to X per cent of mean manufacturing wage), paid against hours worked up to some standard number of hours, for example 35 hours.[1] *If only the lowly paid workers are given the wage subsidy employers would be encouraged to reduce wages offered so as to "milk" the government.*[2]

It is useful to contrast such a *universal wage subsidy* (UWS) with the *negative income tax*. The negative income tax (NIT) was first suggested by Milton Friedman. The NIT is like providing a universal taxable "demogrant" to households.[3] This scheme has found favor among economists. However, whereas the universal wage subsidy is *conditional on the employment status of those assisted*, the negative income tax is totally unconditional. The negative income tax provides a net positive income to anyone so long as he is poor enough. Figure 1 illustrates how the universal wage subsidy works

Figure 1. How the Universal Wage Subsidy is Financed.

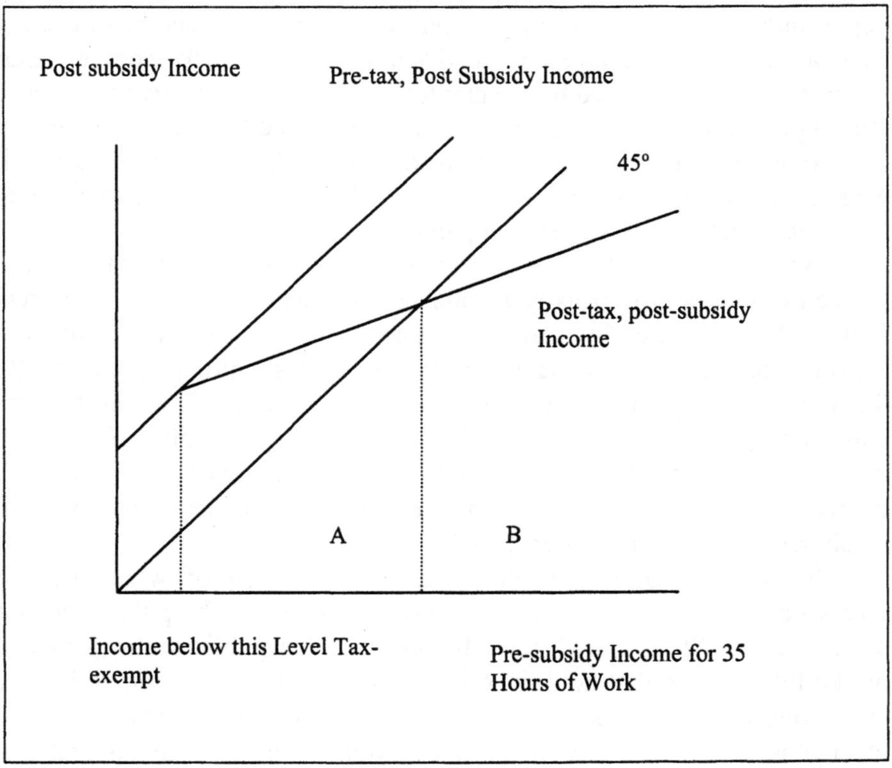

Note: Work hours are assumed fixed and same for everyone. High income workers (B) lose while low income workers (A) gain.
Source: Ho (2000, p.95)

Like the minimum wage the universal wage subsidy can ensure an effective minimum income for workers. Yet unlike the legal minimum wage the universal wage subsidy does not set a floor to market wages and will help create more job opportunities for workers. Unlike the Negative Income Tax, which redistributes income from income-earning people to non-income-earning people and has adverse incentive effects, the *universal wage subsidy* increases low income peoples' incentive to work. It should be recognized, however, that given the higher marginal tax rates imposed on higher income people *this increase in low income peoples' incentive to work is achieved at the expense of higher income peoples' working incentives.* Indeed, as a result of universal wage subsidy employers of high wage employees will need to pay *more* to hire workers (though workers receive *less* in net terms because of higher taxes), while employers of low wage employees will pay *less* (though workers receive *more* in net terms).

Some people may be concerned that a wage subsidy scheme opens up opportunities for fraud. To implement the scheme the government needs to have a record of the hours worked per month for each worker. Such information has to be filed by the employer with the government in order for the wage supplement to be paid. It may be objected that the employer may collaborate with individuals who pretend to be working in order to share the wage supplements. It may also be objected that the employer may reduce the wage offered in view of the supplement.

With regard to the first objection, occasional random checking by inspectors plus a stiff penalty should be sufficient to rule out large-scale fraud. In any case, by mandating that a worker can claim for wage subsidies only in one designated employment, we should be able to contain this kind of fraud. With regard to the second objection, it should be noted that employers have to compete for workers in the market place. The uniform wage supplement will not give any one employer an edge over the others. Competition will leave relative wages more or less intact, with the result that low-income workers benefit.

In addition to the private sector jobs creation of which may be increased by the universal wage subsidy it is wise for the public sector to directly create "*basic jobs*" for job-seekers. The public sector jobs need not be full time, so that holders of basic jobs will still have time to look for alternative work. Providing basic employment for, say, three days a week, to anyone who needs it will allow everyone to make a living and have options other than unlawful ways of making ends meet. Actually there are plenty of opportunities for productive work, particularly in environmental and community-related work. If money is paid to the unemployed in the form of welfare payments and to maintain prisons and crime fighting it is certainly more productive and worthwhile spending the same money on productive work. If jobs cannot be found you really cannot blame anyone for stealing, defrauding, or even robbing in order to survive. Availing job-seekers of a basic job will contribute to a safer and more just society for all.

3. THE PHYSICALLY AND MENTALLY HANDICAPPED AND THE OLD

It is recognized that many of the physically and mentally handicapped can also work, if given a chance. They may need additional support though. Subsidizing employers additionally for the hiring of handicapped people is worthwhile. Using the argument from the chapter on justice, anyone of us could be handicapped. The existence of a program in support of employers offering jobs to the handicapped will certainly increase the chances of obtaining work for these people. It will also alleviate the fear of all of us for not being wanted in the labor market in the event of an accident leading to a handicap.

Some of the physically and mentally handicapped may never be able to work. Again using the argument from the chapter on justice, it is in everybody's interest to offer them financial support and personal care. Such care and support should be at a level which most people consider adequate.

Many of the older workers also feel disadvantaged and experience great difficulty finding jobs. The wage subsidy program and the basic job program will help them find jobs, but some of the older people may not be able to work. If there is a sound public pension system these elderly people will have no worry about their daily living. In the absence of such a system some of the elderly who have not saved enough for their retirement will need an income transfer to meet their basic needs. In an affluent society their needs cannot be ignored. But giving them a generous transfer will create a moral hazard problem among the young, who may decide to enjoy life now and not to save, expecting that when they grow old they will be cared for by society. There is, therefore, a clear tradeoff between being humane to the poor old and holding people responsible for their own retirement needs. The society at large must decide for itself where it stands. Of course, to avoid the dilemma it is best to have a sound public pension plan in the first place.

4. UNEMPLOYMENT INSURANCE AS SAFETY NETS?

As Chapter 3 and Chapter 4 argue, all human beings are averse to big risks, so that insurance against big risks is welfare-enhancing. Unemployment insurance, in most cases, cannot be said to be an insurance against big risks. Indeed, for most people unemployment is a temporary phenomenon. The hardship would be over before too long and any financial difficulties are mostly temporary. For this reason there is no need for unemployment insurance as practiced in most western societies. What may be needed is the availability of unemployment loans that can be extended to the unemployed if needed. Such loans should be of a limited amount and are intended to allow the unemployed to meet the basic needs of food and lodging. They should be repayable as soon as the worker finds normal work. This way, the disincentive for work will be eliminated. The kind of unemployment insurance that we know requires a payroll tax on the employed, which clearly reduces the incentive to work. The stipend paid to the unemployed also tends to prolong the duration of unemployment.[4] While it is true that unemployment can be productive if the time is spent on trying to find the better job, requiring the unemployed to balance the potential benefits of the job search against the costs of job search is economically efficient and need not compromise basic premises of justice. The availability of a "basic job" on demand provides a further assurance that the unemployed will not face excessive hardship.

5. REDISTRIBUTION IN KIND OR IN CASH, IMPLICIT OR EXPLICIT

Clearly, safety nets have redistribution implications. However, they are not and should not be the only redistribution mechanisms. In general redistributive policies can be through the revenue side or the expenditure side of fiscal policy. On the revenue side, there can be a transfer through a tax-transfer system of income from the richer to the poorer. Most countries have a progressive income tax system which, together with basic exemptions and welfare payments, can have very significant redistribution effects. On the expenditure side, various expenditures on health, education, public transit, and particularly public housing, also redistribute real income in favor of the poor. There is no inherently right or inherently wrong with income redistribution, which can be Pareto-improving if socially desired (Hochman and Rodgers, 1969). It is important, however, that the redistribution is transparent and is deliberately executed through a public choice process, with people participating in the deliberation process alerted to the consequences of the redistributive measures.

It is well known that the American public pension system has redistributive features. While benefits are bigger for those who make bigger contributions on account of their incomes, benefits are not directly proportional to contributions. The implicit redistribution, however, is not transparent and cannot be easily calculated. On the other hand, the fully funded public pension plan that I proposed in Chapter 8 provides that people of the same cohort make the same contribution and receive the same benefits—with the exception that those who are classified as poor will have their contributions subsidized. This arrangement makes redistribution transparent.

Although it is highly desirable that a policy aimed at redistribution is best executed through the tax-transfer system, some redistribution will work through the expenditure side of the budget. This is because there are policies which are valued for purposes other than redistribution but which have redistribution implications. Education, health care, and housing are primary examples. Education, health care, and housing clearly have effects beyond those who enjoy the services. Expenditures on these items predominate in most government budgets all over the globe. Redistribution effects are significant but are incidental to the design of these policies. Because of the significant redistribution effects involved, however, redistributive policies must take full recognition of the effects of these policies. Otherwise there will be more redistribution than is warranted.

6. CONCLUSIONS

Distribution matters have always been given an important place in public economics and social policy analysts. Musgrave in his 1959 *Theory of Public Finance* treated distribution as one of three main responsibilities of the "Fiscal Department," along with allocation and stabilization. (Musgrave, 1959, p.5) Even today, social scientists regularly come up with fresh policy proposals addressed specifically to redistribution concerns. Following the Negative Income Tax Proposal (Friedman, 1962, 191-194), Phelps came up with alternative wage subsidy proposals to help the working poor (1994, 1997), Fitzpatrick (1999) gave a round-up of the debate on the idea of Basic Income Guarantee.

There is an obvious distinction between the Negative Income Tax and Basic Income Guarantee on the one hand, and targeted or universal wage subsidies on the other hand. The former are not conditional on work and will have adverse work incentives. The latter are conditional on employment and will have positive work incentives. Rather than a Basic

Income Guarantee, I propose a basic job guarantee and a universal wage subsidy. These measures will help reduce the unemployment rate, will provide alternatives to crime, and will make our streets and our homes safer. With expected declines in crimes and higher employment, savings generated from reduced prison and police costs, reduced welfare payments, and increased taxes will allow the government to finance the program. In addition, safety net provisions in the form of income transfers targeted at those hit by misfortunes such as physical or mental disabilities will make the society more humane, more just, and more efficient.

NOTES

1 The following material is largely drawn from Ho (1999). A similar proposal, unknown to the author at the time, was made by Jackman and Layard (1986).

2 Phelps (1997) discussed ingenious ways of overcoming this problem, but they may be bogged down by heavy administrative costs.

3 In some versions the demogrants can be means-tested. For an introduction see Fischer, Dornbusch, and Schmalensee (1988).

4 Ljungqvist (1999) concluded that reducing unemployment benefits or imposing work requirements would be necessary if unemployment in Europe was to be reduced. Christofides and McKenna (1996) found evidence, using Canadian longitudinal data, that a significant number of jobs terminate when the duration of employment have gone past the qualifying requirement for a unemployment insurance claim.

Part 5

PUBLIC POLICY AND ECONOMIC ECOLOGY

The two chapters in this section make the point that the economy is like an ecological system. It contains many different sectors and sub-sectors, and they all depend on one another and hang together in a delicate "ecological balance." In general we can say that the economy consists of a public sector, a business sector, a household sector, and an external sector. Of these four sectors the public sector figures dominantly. Public policy is not something to play with. It has big impact on the economic system. Chapter 17 shows that macroeconomic policy can cause serious problems. Indeed, the Great Depression of the 1930s was the direct result of misguided macroeconomic policy that sets out to curb the excesses of speculation and mishandling of events that unfolded. Chapter 18 shows that a misguided microeconomic policy, one that appears to impact only on a sub-sector within the economy, can also produce gigantic economic losses. The two chapters attest to the wisdom of the Chinese adage that when we do not know, we had better grope the stones underneath carefully as we wade across the river.

Chapter 17

ECONOMIC ECOLOGY: THE CASE OF THE GREAT DEPRESSION OF THE NINETEEN THIRTIES

Ours is a land rich in resources; stimulating in its glorious beauty; filled with millions of happy homes; blessed with comfort and opportunity. In no nation are the institutions of progress more advanced. In no nation are the fruits of accomplishment more secure. In no nation is the government more worthy of respect. No country is more loved by its people. I have an abiding faith in their capacity, integrity and high purpose. I have no fears for the future of our country. It is bright with hope.

President Hoover, Inaugural Address
March 4, 1929

There is a story we wanted to tell. It is the tale of powerful, well-intentioned people in several countries who committed an incredible sequence of policy errors that generated a cataclysmic event reaching around the entire globe. The disasters of the 1930s were not caused by some uncontrollable event such as the eruption of Mt. Vesuvius that buried Pompei. Instead the Depression was caused by people with good intentions carrying out misguided economic policies that they thought were proper, but that actually created an absolute disaster.

Hall and Ferguson (1998), from the Preface

1. INTRODUCTION

Many historians believe that the Great Depression of the nineteen thirties was a direct result of the excesses of the "roaring twenties." The Great Depression was routinely blamed on excessive speculation and greed, and increasing inequality in income distribution, as a result of which the masses did not have the necessary purchasing power to sustain the humming production machinery of the United States. As a matter of fact, however, the 1920s was a time of true prosperity and solid economic growth. The solid economic growth was achieved with almost no inflation, and was brought about by major breakthroughs in technology that raised productivity tremendously. The US Federal Government ran a budget surplus for every year from 1920 to 1930 inclusive. With support from Hoover as Secretary of Commerce and a healthy dose of export credit extended from overseas branches of US banks, American exports rose from $3.8 billion in 1922 to $5.2 billion in 1929, while imports lagged behind, resulting in trade surpluses which reached $800 million by 1929. The United States had already emerged as a creditor nation after the First World War, and had continued to accumulate net claims against the rest of the world through aggressive investment abroad. Indeed, the rest of the world had become so dependent on the loans from America that one standard American history text observed: "Should American loans abroad cease, disastrous consequences would be inevitable." (Barck Jr. and Blake, 1974, p.287)

It is certainly true that stock prices had soared to unprecedented levels. But does this necessarily imply excessive speculation? While some are convinced that the stock market on the eve of the crash was a bubble others find the case not closed. Sirkin (1975) and Bierman (1991) argued that the stock prices in 1929 were consistent with the economic fundamentals. Based on data on the 29 profitable firms out of the 30 used to compute the Dow Jones Industrial Average, Sirkin found that the mean price-earnings ratio in September 1929 was 21.6 while the median was 15.1. To maintain such ratios for another 5 years, earnings only needed to rise at the same pace as that between 1925 and 1929, which would not seem to be an unrealistic assumption at all.

Just as with any crisis, including in particular the Asian Financial Crisis of 1997-98, one could find many things wrong and could attribute the crisis all to all these factors. It is the purpose of this chapter to argue that the "excesses" notwithstanding, the Great Depression came not because it was "payback time," but because of silly policy mistakes. Policy mistakes cost over a decade of economic growth.

2. THE ROARING TWENTIES

Table 1. Annual Macroeconomic Data 1921-1941 (per cent)

	GDP Deflator Inflation	Real GDP Growth	Unemploy-ment Rate	M1% Change	Real M1 % Change	S&P Index %Change	Labor Productivity Growth
1921	-12.8	-3.5	11.7	-9.5	3.8	-13.3	7.0
1922	-7.0	7.2	6.7	1.0	8.5	20.8	0.0
1923	2.5	14.0	2.4	5.7	3.1	2.3	5.5
1924	0.0	2.7	5	3.6	3.6	5.6	4.9
1925	1.6	2.2	3.2	8.2	6.5	23.4	-1.2
1926	0.8	6.0	1.8	2.0	1.2	12.1	2.5
1927	-1.6	0.6	3.3	-0.4	1.2	17.7	1.2
1928	-0.8	1.8	4.2	1.2	2.0	26.8	0.9
1929	0.0	6.4	3.2	0.8	0.8	27.3	4.5
1930	-3.3	-9.4	8.9	-3.1	0.2	-21.5	-2.9
1931	-8.4	-8.5	16.3	-6.3	2.2	-37.1	-0.3
1932	-11.0	-13.4	24.1	-12.7	-1.9	-48.4	-2.1
1933	-3.1	-2.1	25.2	-5.8	-2.8	30.2	-1.2
1934	9.6	7.7	22	10.3	0.7	14.6	9.5
1935	2.9	8.1	20.3	18.2	14.9	8.5	2.5
1936	0.0	14.1	17	13.8	13.8	41.2	6.3
1937	3.8	5.0	14.3	4.9	1.0	0.0	-1.3
1938	-1.8	-4.5	19.1	-1.3	0.5	-25.0	4.7
1939	-0.9	7.9	17.2	12.1	13.1	7.4	2.5
1940	1.9	7.9	14.6	16.2	14.0	-6.9	3.4
1941	6.4	17.7	9.9	17.0	9.9	-9.3	8.0

Source: Robert Gordon: *Macroeconomics*, 6th Edition, Harper Collins, 1993.

Table 1 shows that starting from 1922, the US economy was on a healthy growth track. Except in 1925 when there was a slight decline, labor productivity was rising at a healthy pace. The real GDP grew rapidly in 1922 and 1923, took a breather in 1924 and 1925 before picking up again in 1926. In 1929 the economy was growing very rapidly, but only after two rather slow years in 1927 and 1928, when the unemployment rate rose to 4.2 per cent. There was no inflation and no sign of overheating. While the stock market was booming, annual rates of growth between 2 and 27 per cent during a time of expanding profits, productivity growth, and rapidly accumulating savings cannot be said to be grossly excessive. It should be noted that during this decade of economic boom the private sector was running a "surplus" which is reflected in a favorable trade balance and increasing net investment abroad.

At the same time the government had also been running a budget surplus for every year since 1920.

Many economic historians picked on the rising income inequality to be a key contributory factor to the Great Depression. Over the period from 1922 to 1929, the share of income accruing to the top 1 per cent of income earners rose from 12 per cent to 13.7 per cent. The share of wealth owned by the top 1 per cent of adults rose from 32 per cent to 38 per cent. Even more dramatic is the fact that, in 1929, the top 1 per cent of income recipients accounted for 80 per cent of total savings in the country, up from 49 per cent in 1922 (Hall and Ferguson, 1998, p.21). It was believed that such a concentration of wealth and income meant that total consumption would not be adequate to maintain full employment.

In point of fact, the roaring twenties generated jobs and higher living standards for the great majority of Americans, though some sectors, particularly agriculture and coal mining, were left in the limbo. But it was a time of great technological change, and the most gains were achieved by a small minority who could take advantage of the new opportunities. At the time, investing in common stock was rather uncommon. Galbraith (1954) estimated that only 1 per cent of the US population participated in stock market investment. This might lead us to think that the stock market crash of 1929 should not have caused excessive damage on the economy. It is important, however, to understand the dynamics involved in the stock market advance and set off in the stock market decline.

The economy revived rapidly in 1922-23 after the post World War I recession. New industries, particularly the chemical industry, the automobile industry, and the steel industry, developed rapidly. Because of a boom in construction, other industries like steel, cement, lumber, electrical appliances, plumbing, and heating equipment benefited. The profits generated in these industries benefited the stocks of the companies, and investing in stocks was the best investment. From 1922 to 1929, not a single year turned in a loss for stockowners. Stocks were the best collateral for loans. These loans financed real investment as well as more stock purchases. Margin loans were common, and banks were happy to extend loans to brokers who in turn were happy to extend to investors. Obviously, if the stock prices turned unfavorable, lenders would exercise their call for repayment to keep the loans in good standing against the shrunken collateral. The investors would get hurt but this would not be a big thing for the economy, because it was not a systemic problem. Brokers acquired a total of $7.63 billion in loans in 1924 from banks and non-financial corporations for re-lending to investors in the form of margin loans. This rose to $26.53 billion by 1929 (Hall and Ferguson, p.24). Galbraith (1954), who subscribed to the thesis that excessive speculation was at fault, pointed to the fact that the interest rate on margin loans was 8.56 per cent while the dividend yield on stocks in September 1929 was 2.92 per cent. But such interest rate spreads are quite common anywhere and should not in itself suggest any imminent disaster.

To put things in perspective, America's economic achievement during the roaring twenties was most remarkable. Office towers were erected, extensive roads and bridges were built, new industries took root. Annual production of motor cars rose from 1.9 million in 1920 to almost 4.8 million in 1929. Notwithstanding the big investments throughout the twenties, the United States accumulated claims against the rest of the world, as the following table, taken from Shannon (1974, p.90), shows:

	July 1 1914	December 31 1919	July 1 1929
Private Credits:			
Securities	862	2576	7839
Direct Investments	2652	3880	7553
Short-term Credits	...	500	1617
Private Debits:			
Securities	5440	1623	4304
Direct Investments	1310	900	1400
Seized Enemy Property	...	662	150
Short-term Credits	450	800	3077
Net Private Debit or Credit	-3686	2971	8078
Intergovernmental Debt:			
Owed to United States	...	9982	11685
Owed by United States	...	391	...
Total Net Debit or Credit	-3686	+12562	+19763

If the American economy was so strong and the savings so concentrated, those who participated in the stock market must be the richest few in the country. Galbraith (1954) estimated that only 1 per cent of the population participated in the stock market. These were the people with the best credit standing and were usually high income earners. They had been putting their savings, as well as borrowed money, into the stock market, in overseas debt instruments. On the surface, the stock market crash should hurt only a tiny minority of the American population. The story of the Great Depression tells us, however, that if the fortunes of these wealthy, powerful people are *systematically* ruined,[1] the whole economy may suffer, because so many things depend on them.

The magnitude of the crisis that ensued after the stock market crash of 1929 took many experts by surprise. Shannon (1974, p. 154) cited the inadequacy of economic insight among the supposedly best minds. "Even after the crash, the economists remained optimistically reassuring. In

November, 1929, the Harvard Economic Society declared that "a serious depression...is outside the range of probability." Even Irving Fisher in 1930 wrote that the "outlook is bright." The truth is that these "foggy prophets" erred not on their assessment of the economic fundamentals. Perhaps Fisher should have said, "The fundamentals of the economy are sound but are highly sensitive to policies. If the policy makers do the right things the outlook is bright. Otherwise the economy can go awry."

3. THE CRASH

As things turned out, the Federal Reserve began to worry about excessive speculation in 1928, and started to raise interest rates and tighten credit at a time that actually begs for looser money. Although money supply figures appeared to be rather neutral they were highly misleading. Statistics suggest that the money supply growth had provided the impetus for the stock market to rise to dangerous levels. Just as Adam Smith feared, high interest rates inhibited entrepreneurs but may not inhibit speculators (p.379). It was this tightening that resulted in a sudden reversal of economic fortunes for many private businesses, culminating in the stock market crash of October 1929 and the Great Depression.

Consumption spending had slipped badly in 1929 well before the Crash. Residential construction, which had been falling since 1925, declined markedly in 1928. Farmers had been hurting throughout the decade from falling world prices and heavy indebtedness (Walton and Rockoff, 1998, 518-519). There was deflation, not inflation. There was little sign that the economy was overheated. The economy should have needed some stimulation, certainly not contraction.

Yet, from the beginning of 1928 to May 1929 an unprecedented monetary tightening took place. The Federal Reserve sold $405 million worth of government securities, raised the discount rate three times from 3.5 per cent to 5.0 per cent, raised the buying rate on bankers' acceptances, and persuaded member banks from making loans to finance speculative activities. The restrictive effects of these measures on the money supply, however, were to a large extent offset by member bank borrowing from the Federal Reserve, because while the discount rate had been raised money market interest rates had gone up much more, making it profitable to borrow from the central bank and lend it out. From what we know, however, although the money supply did not fall noticeably *a significant fraction of the money supply facilitated stock market transactions rather than transactions in the real economy.* The stock market continued rising, with high volume, well through September 1929. At the same time, the higher interest rates hit home at the real economy and aggravated an ongoing economic slowing down that had already taken hold.

"The combination of tight credit conditions and the recession moved the New York Times Index of industrial stocks to 403 on October 24 (from a peak of 453 reached in September) (Black Thursday). The panic occurred on Monday and Tuesday, October 28 and 29, when prices fell by a total of 23 per cent." (Hall and Ferguson, p.66) By November 13, the trough for 1929, the index had fallen about 50 per cent from its peak in September.

Because of the high concentration of stocks in only 1 per cent of the American population, superficially the direct impact of the stock market crash on consumption should be relatively small. However, because of the high leverage usually associated with stock holdings, the balance sheets of the wealthiest few deteriorated dramatically. To the extent that many firms were holding part of their surpluses in the form of stocks and had loaned their surpluses to stockbrokers the balance sheets of these firms had an about-face. The urge to self-protect led to further "dumping" in the stock market. The resulting price declines generated more fear and further rounds of dumping. Bankruptcies fed into more bankruptcies, while bad inter-firm loans and bad credit snowballed. During these times despite interest rate hikes the actual level of nominal interest rates in 1930 were not particularly high,[2] but banks had reasons to worry about their own survival. So few would lend to businesses to help them through the hard times. Within the business sector, the *ability to invest,* as much as the confidence to invest, was hard hit. Investment in real terms fell 23.4 per cent, 31.7 per cent, and 42.0 per cent respectively in 1930, 1931, and 1932. Mirroring such dramatic declines in business fixed investment was the surge in unemployment, which jumped to 8.9 per cent in 1930 (from 3.2 per cent in 1929), jumped further to 16.3 per cent in 1931, and peaked at over 25 per cent in 1933.

Setbacks in the stock market and in the real economy led to waves of bank failures.[3] Particularly in October 1931, after a series of bank failures in the South and Midwest, there was widespread panic. More bank runs followed. While many of the banks besieged by depositors trying to get their money back were solvent but illiquid, the Federal Reserve failed to come to the aid of these banks, believing that allowing banks to fail would condone inefficiency. During a time of uncertainty, this was a serious mistake. According to Bernanke (1983), borrowers who used to borrow from a bank that had failed were completely new to other banks. It is difficult for these other banks to assess the credit standing of these new borrowers. To play safe they simply would not lend. As a result, many firms, particularly the smaller ones, could not get the credit needed to stay in operation.

Because of deflation, which intensified in 1931 and especially in 1932 debt-ridden companies had a rough time servicing and repaying their debt.

Here again we see the important value of indexing bonds against inflation. The borrower's real borrowing costs should not be at the mercy of price level changes. If businesses which had issued bonds could adjust their interest payments and repayments down with deflation, many of those firms that had failed would have survived. Unemployment and investment would have been higher, and with that consumption would also have been higher. The recession would not have been so serious.

4. THE BRITISH POUND WENT OFF THE GOLD STANDARD IN 1931: EXPANSIONARY MONETARY POLICY WORKED

During the twenties the United States had been running trade surpluses year in, year out. Under the gold standard, the United States' increased accumulation of gold reserves should have led to an expansion of the money supply and thus should have caused prices to increase. However, while American monetary reserves were rising on account of the trade surpluses, the Federal Reserve Board was selling US government bonds and thus reducing monetary reserves. Through such sterilization US incomes and prices would not rise as would under a classical specie-flow-price mechanism. With the British pound overvalued and the gold flows failing to cause a relative price adjustment between the US and the UK, the United Kingdom had to endure ongoing high unemployment rates of about 8 to 9 per cent during the period 1925-29. The problem was exacerbated in 1930-31, as the ongoing outflow of gold led to a selling of the British pound. Trying desperately to defend the pound without raising interest rates which would worsen the already very high unemployment rate further Britain tried to borrow money from the US and from France. But the borrowed amounts were far too small to stem the flight from the pound, which eventually went off the gold standard on September 21, 1931. By December the pound sterling lost 30 per cent of its value. While the Treasury wanted interest rate cuts, however, because of objection from the Bank of England this had to wait until February 1932. More cuts followed in the year, and the British economy rebounded quickly. According to Kindleberger (1986, p.240) the UK was the first economy to surpass the 1929 industrial production level. As early as the last quarter of 1934 the index of industrial production had reached 116, up from 114 in the last quarter of 1929.

5. CONCLUSIONS

There is still controversy over the cause of the Great Depression. People could debate over the role of the Smoot-Hawley Tariff Act of 1930, which by raising US imposition on imports to over 50 per cent started a tariff war against the US and ended up hurting US production. People could argue over whether the crash of 1929 was a natural outcome of the "excesses" of the earlier years, and whether it was largely a result of the Federal Reserve's engineering. Two things, however, are clear.

First is that tight money has a lot to do with the Great Depression. Tight money was intended to stem excessive speculation. In the end it succeeded, but the effects of the resulting Crash and the tight money were mostly in the real economy. Quite apart from the psychological effect of the Crash on investor confidence, the Crash hurt the ability to invest. Because stocks had served as collaterals for loans a large decline in stock prices means a *de facto* tightening of credit. Corporations with surplus cash lent to brokers suffered big losses as defaults mounted. Former net asset positions quickly turned into net liability positions. Personal and business bankruptcies followed. Other firms and persons were affected. Tight money in Germany in 1928, intended to stem a capital outflow, had caused in full-blown recession by mid 1929. Tight money in the U.S. in the same year when the economy was slowing down rapidly was badly timed.

The second is that when deflation set in all firms that had issued debt were in deep trouble. Deflation means falling incomes. Servicing cost and repayment costs, however, stay put when the debt instruments are not indexed against price movements. As deflation was a general phenomenon and debt issues were also common, the effects on the economy were very serious. The tragic note to this is that this problem could easily have been avoided, if the debt instruments issued had been indexed against price movements, as many economists from Keynes to Friedman have urged.

After the Crash had happened and the Great Depression had begun, it is easy for people to talk about the earlier "excesses." But on the eve of the Crash, American corporations had strong balance sheets, the federal government had a strong fiscal position, and most American households had enjoyed an unprecedented increase in earnings that was built on strong productivity growth and technological advance. Inflation was low. Unemployment was moderate. What kind of excesses are we talking about? Stock price increases of up to 30 per cent a year? Consumer credit and the "buy now, pay later" culture? Buying stocks and homes with margin or mortgage loans? The subtitle of Hall and Ferguson's book is apt: "an international disaster of perverse economic policies." Yes, leveraged investments are risky. Income and wealth distribution was highly skewed. Expectations were too high. But to argue on the basis of all this that the great crash was implicit in the stock price increases is not convincing. Irving Fisher was reputed to have remarked, shortly before the crash, that "stock prices have reached what looks like a permanently high plateau" and that "anything in the nature of a crash" was not in sight." (Walton and Rockoff, 1998, p. 512) From what we can gather, although the economy was slowing down, the economic fundamentals of the American economy in 1929 were basically sound. Instead of stimulation that was needed the Federal Reserve gave the economy a heavy dose of monetary restriction. It did not realize that the economic system is like an ecological system. Different elements hang together closely and depend on one another.

Policy makers may not like the leveraged purchase of stocks and homes. But if the leveraging is already a fact of life you cannot simply undo it overnight. Given the institutional framework and the economic conditions, even without intervention stock prices would come to an equilibrium (the kind of price plateau that Irving Fisher was talking about) and, if there was excessive speculation, would fall back to a level befitting the economic reality. The fact that the economy was already slowing down and that profits were already declining would have limited further increases even without central bank intervention. Raising interest rates would only accelerate and amplify stock price declines. Since investment in stocks were highly leveraged, such price declines quickly led to more declines, as brokers had to sell off the stocks of those investors who could not come up with the needed cash to meet margin requirements. Since many firms directly or indirectly had positions in the stock market, the crash hurt their balance sheets and prevented them from investing. Sharp declines in investment led to unemployment and reduced consumption. Well-intended policies that set out to stabilize things turned out causing the greatest instability of all time.

NOTES

1 This is in contrast to individual tycoons losing their fortunes, which should not have serious repercussions.

2 Real interest rates, however, had begun to be painfully high in 1930.

3 According to Hall and Ferguson (1998, p. 83), the failure of the Federal Reserve to come to the aid of banks hit by runs in October 1930 using the criterion of the real bills doctrine, sowed the seeds of disaster by shaking confidence in the U.S. banking system.

Chapter 18

ECONOMIC ECOLOGY: THE CASE OF HONG KONG

1. INTRODUCTION

This chapter seeks to find an explanation for the Hong Kong economy's unprecedented plunge into deep recession in the wake of the Asian Financial Crisis. Hong Kong had gone through so many ups and downs through its history, and until 1998 not a single year since 1961 was there recorded negative economic growth (See Table 1). Among the crises that Hong Kong had gone through are: the Great Proletariat Cultural Revolution in 1966 through 1968;[1] the two major oil crises of the seventies; the plunge of the Heng Seng Index from over 1700 in 1973 to less than 200 in 1975; the unprecedented interest rate hikes of 1981-82, when the prime rate momentarily shot up to 20 per cent; the Tiananmen incident of 1989, etc. Hong Kong had gone through true financial and banking crises, in the early 60s and from 1982 through 1986, with multiple bank failures, and it was in the context of widespread panic and currency depreciation that the current linked exchange rate system was set up in 1983. But Hong Kong's growth engine never failed, until 1998.

Table 1. Hong Kong's Economic Growth 1961-1999 (GDP % change)

1961	n.a.	1971	7.1	1981	9.2	1991	5.1
1962	14.2	1972	10.3	1982	2.7	1992	6.3
1963	15.7	1973	12.4	1983	5.7	1993	6.1
1964	8.6	1974	2.3	1984	10.0	1994	5.4
1965	14.5	1975	0.3	1985	0.4	1995	3.9
1966	1.7	1976	16.2	1986	10.8	1996	4.5
1967	1.7	1977	11.7	1987	13.0	1997	5.0
1968	3.3	1978	8.5	1988	8.0	1998	-5.3
1969	11.3	1979	11.5	1989	2.6	1999	3.1
1970	9.2	1980	10.1	1990	3.4		

Source: Gross Domestic Product 1961-1999, Government of HKSAR

It is true that the Asian Financial Crisis of 1997 was a serious one and had plunged many otherwise economies into deep recession. But given Hong Kong's tight links with China and the United States, both of which registered strong growth in 1998, and Singapore's tight links with the ASEAN countries, all of which had been directly or indirectly affected by the Asian Financial Crisis, Hong Kong should have fared better than Singapore. Yet Singapore's economy in 1998 registered a 1.3 per cent growth, as compared with Hong Kong's negative 5.3 per cent. Hong Kong should in any case be in much better shape than debt-ridden South Korea. But by the second half of 1999 South Korea had rebounded to well over the pre-crisis level. Having declined by 5.8 per cent in 1998, the South Korea economy bounced back by 10 per cent in 1999. In contrast, Hong Kong's economy shrank by 5.3 per cent in 1998, and grew by a mere 3.1 per cent in 1999.

Hong Kong's trade figures started to improve markedly in 1999 and by the first quarter of 2000 Hong Kong appears to be well on its way to recovery, with a 14 per cent year-on-year growth. But the strength of the external sector had scarcely benefited domestic consumption through late 1999. Most of Hong Kong people continued to feel the crunch of the recession.

To understand the predicament of Hong Kong people we have to understand the cause behind the unprecedented recession that hit Hong Kong so suddenly. What really caused such dramatic changes in the first quarter of 1998 when the economy lost 12.0 per cent of its GDP?[2] One could easily blame the currency turmoil in South East Asia spilling over to Hong Kong, but this is really not convincing. As a matter of fact, in the first quarter of 1998 there was one interest rate drop, and the currency turmoil had shown signs of stabilizing. There was even a brief period of property price increase in March, following the interest rate decline and the announcement of a stimulative budget. To put things in perspective, Hong Kong's economic performance in the first quarter of 1998 was worse than that of Malaysia, and much worse than that of Singapore or Taiwan. A *transmission mechanism* whereby major declines in the values of the Indonesian rupiah and the Thai baht caused the property bubble to burst and the Hong Kong economy to lose its characteristic vigor and legendary resilience is simply lacking.

My simple hypothesis is this. The economic decline was the direct and immediate result of misguided housing policy, particularly its drive to increase ownership in the property market. The Chief Executive in his first Policy Address of October 1997 explicitly called for increasing the homeownership ratio from 50 per cent to 70 per cent in ten years, and tried to achieve it through an ambitious yet flawed public housing privatization program. *The recession was a result of the working of "economic ecology," as a misguided microeconomic policy worked through the economic system to produce a gigantic macroeconomic disaster.*

2. THE BASIC AND NON-BASIC SECTORS AND THE RICHER-PAYS-MORE "HOUSING SUBSIDY POLICY" OF APRIL 1987

In the eighties the Hong Kong economy took advantage of the opening up of the Chinese economy and started moving the bulk of manufacturing processes into China, particularly the Pearl River Delta. Superficially there is a "hollowing out" of the economy. But despite the hollowing out the economy was marching along quite well, on the basis of what some commentators called the "virtual economy." Indeed, borrowing the terminology from regional economics, Hong Kong's external sector, the so-called "basic sector," has suffered only a temporary setback during the Asian Financial Crisis. This sector includes the export of goods and services, and earnings from investment overseas, and offshore trade. Hong Kong is the brain center directing so much happenings in the region and around the world. Yet not everyone works in the basic sector. For each individual who works in the basic sector, perhaps four or five people work in the non-basic sector. The non-basic sector, i.e., the sector that depends on the domestic market, draws its strength from the basic sector and depends on the basic sector for its survival.

In order for more people to share the material benefits achieved in the basic sector, the economy needs a mechanism to transmit the economic benefits to the rest of the economy. The property market provides such a mechanism. In particular, when people get richer, they tend to move to bigger houses, and in so doing benefiting real estate agents, banks, lawyers, retailers, decorators and interior designers, furniture makers, insurance agencies, restaurants, etc. It is on the basis of a very strong basic sector that Hong Kong had enjoyed its property market boom for decades.

The rather spectacular property market boom from 1987 to 1997 that Hong Kong enjoyed, however, is not only a result of strength in the basic sector. One key factor that is unique to Hong Kong is the implementation of a new public housing policy. The so-called "Housing Subsidy Policy," first introduced in April 1987, expressly sets out to reduce the implicit subsidy to the richer tenants in public housing estates by making them pay higher rent. Although the spirit of the policy was clear at the outset it had been refined a few times. In essence, the policy requires those tenants who have been accommodated for over ten years and who have a household income three times that of the maximum eligibility limit to pay double rent, while those who have breached stipulated income and asset thresholds are required to pay market rent.[3]

Such a policy alerted the complacent public housing tenants that they could not take low rent for granted. Given that they had enjoyed long periods of very low rent amidst high inflation, they had accumulated considerable savings, which were ready to be tapped on to buy properties. In a survey conducted by the Housing Authority in 1993, some 24 per cent of all home purchases in the market place were traceable to public housing tenants. Since public housing tenants are supposed to be poor people hardly able to pay market rent this figure is quite disturbing but at the same time it shows that the Housing Subsidy Policy is right.

The continual pouring of money from the richer public housing tenants into the market buoyed up home prices. First Home Ownership Scheme Housing (a low cost homeownership program administered by the Housing Authority) owners found that they could sell their homes at a handsome profit. Such handsome profit allowed them to place an attractive bid for the next higher category of homes. The owners of the latter, in turn, being able to sell at a high price, are also able to pay a higher price for better still housing. The effect goes on. Figure 1 shows that property prices rose spectacularly from 1987 through 1997.

3. TENANT PURCHASE SCHEME

As Figure 1 shows, a dramatic reversal of this chain of events appeared to have taken place in December 1997.

On 8 December 1997 the Government announced a Tenant Purchase Scheme (TPS) that would allow public housing tenants in designated blocks to buy their existing units at as low as 12 per cent of the estimated market value. Since public housing tenants were the primary source of buyers for HOS housing and the structure of the more recent vintages of public housing has become quite similar to HOS housing, the effect on HOS housing market was immediate. Both prices and turnover fell precipitously. Because HOS owners could not sell their units at good prices, they also could not pay good prices for higher-tier housing. The owners of the latter, without the HOS owners as their potential buyers, also had a hard time buying still higher-level homes. Even luxury homes are affected. As a result the entire housing market was paralyzed. Figure 2 shows that, excluding the TPS transactions which involved sitting tenants buying their own flats, second hand transactions dropped precipitously in the first quarter of 1998.

Figure 1. Price Index of Private Residential Property

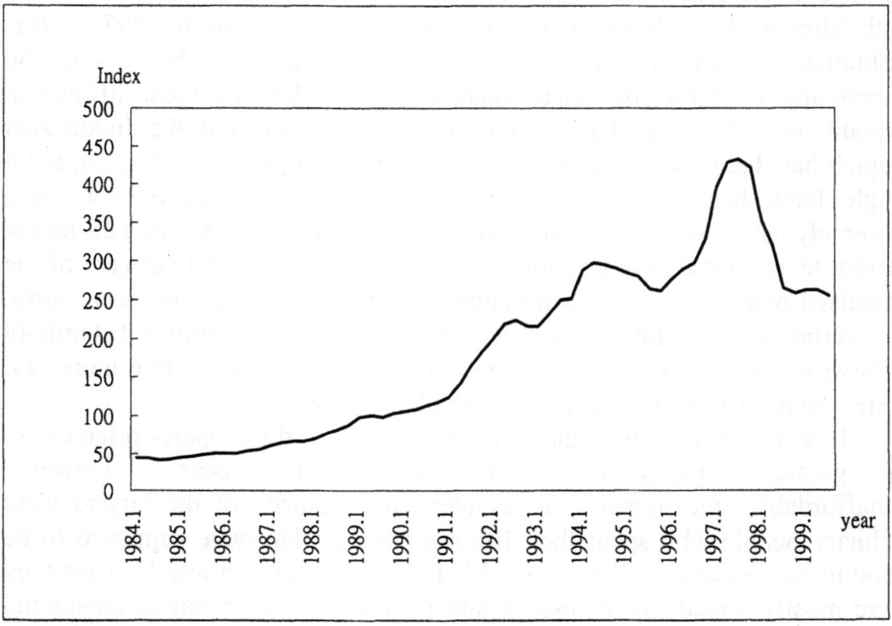

Source: Rating and Valuation Department.

Figure 2. Percentage of Second-hand Transaction in Total Transaction

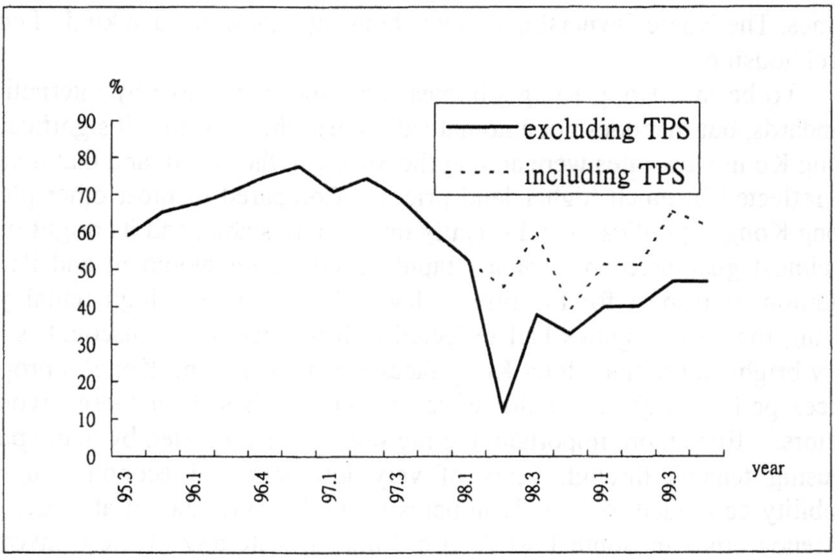

Source: Census and Statistics Department, Centaline Property Agency Ltd., Housing Authority

By the time the SAR Government announced the nine-point rescue package on June 23 1998 Hong Kong' s housing prices and stock prices had both fallen by some 40 to 50 per cent from their recent peak in 1997. It is fashionable to talk of this major asset price decline as the bursting of the bubble and trace it to the Asian Financial Crisis. Yet it is most difficult to explain why the deep depreciation of the Thai baht and the Indonesian Rupiah has that much effect on Hong Kong's home prices. After all, not a single bank had failed in the financial crisis. Our banks were also extremely cautious, not only in routinely valuing property prices well below market levels but also in providing loans at no more than 70 per cent of the appraised prices. There was, moreover, during the peak or the recent lows, no overbuilding. Although supply had indeed increased quite substantially relative to the immediate past, largely in response to sharp price increases, there was no overhanging excessive supply in 1998.

It is important to note that even at the peak of the property price cycle, the greater majority of buyers were genuine users. However "unaffordable" the property prices were, the majority of the buyers were ordinary people who spent their life savings on what were supposed to be good inflation hedges. They were able to pay such high prices because they were mostly already homeowners and thus were able to pay a substantial down-payment with the equity realized through selling their existing homes. It must be noted that in Hong Kong's market the average home had seldom been for the entry-level buyer. The entry-level buyers had always been paying much more modest and affordable prices for much more modest homes. The Home Ownership Scheme housing flats were such kind of entry-level housing.

To be fair, Hong Kong's homes were very expensive by international standards, but that does not automatically mean they had to fall significantly. Hong Kong's tax rates were among the lowest in the world, and that tends to be reflected in much higher land prices. Compared to most other places, Hong Kong is politically and socially much more stable, and its bright future is almost guaranteed by China's rapid economic development and its fine tradition of respect for the rule of law. Just as a very high rental yield during the early eighties had reflected a deep uncertainty discount, so the very bright future that Hong Kong faces means that Hong Kong' s property prices perhaps rightly should reflect a premium based on these favorable factors. Even more important, the big savings accumulated by many public housing tenants through years of very low rent and economic upward mobility continued to provide impetus to the housing market at large.[4] The currency crisis in South East Asia did not mitigate any of these favorable factors, and should not warrant the dramatic decline in property prices since July 1997.

To be fair, Hong Kong's home prices in the middle of 1997 were perhaps too high and could be due for a major correction. Hong Kong's home-buyers knew that prices could fall. While it is totally legitimate for market participants to form their own opinions about whether prices were too high, however, it is totally wrong for the government to imagine what is the right price and attempt to engineer a price decline to reach "more acceptable levels." If the government does this, it will have given up its role as the custodian of the free market and will have become anti-market and unnecessarily interventionist.

4. THE STATISTICAL EVIDENCE

Table 2 shows that the introduction of the Tenant Purchase Scheme has an additional and very significant dampening effect on second hand transactions in the housing market over and above the effect of the Asian Financial Crisis, which occurred in the third quarter of 1997. I use the volume of transactions in existing homes as the dependent variable, and I use the difference between the spot exchange rate and the one-year forward rate to proxy the financial crisis. This CRISISDUMMY variable is non-binary, but normalized to have a minimum value of zero and a maximum value of unity. PPIMR is a price appreciation variable. In general, if prices rise faster second hand transactions will also rise.

Table 2. Dependent Variable: Second hand transaction volume: TRANSACT2 (1996M3 to 2000M2)

Variable	Coefficient	T-ratio
Constant term	10261.0	12.067***
CRISISDUMMY	-2949.1	-1.7952*
TPSDUMMY	-3965.3	-2.8409***
PPIMR	33.289	1.5030

R-bar squared = 0.49601
DW-statistic = 2.0709 The Cochrane-Orcutt AR (1) procedure was used to correct for serial correlation.
*** means statistical significance at 1 per cent level
* means statistical significance at 10 per cent level

Table 3 shows the results of a regression exercise that seeks to explain changes in private sector domestic demand (NETDOMDER) in Hong Kong, which is simply the sum of private consumption and investment. The unit of the dependent variable is percentage change. S1 and S3 are seasonal dummies for the first and the third quarters. GOVE90R is the rate of change of real government expenditures on goods and services. Such expenditures should have a positive impact on private sector domestic demand through the multiplier effect. Similarly, EXPORT90R, and EXPORT90R (+1), which are the rates of change of real exports, current and leading one quarter, have an impact on private sector domestic demand through the multiplier effect. Because production precedes actual exports the lag structure is advanced one quarter relative to that of government expenditures. *A priori*, I expect that both exports and government expenditures have positive effects on domestic demand. Because GOVE90R (-1) does not have a statistically significant coefficient it was dropped. Finally, the real interest rate[5] and inflation have negative effects on domestic demand. We can see that all the estimated coefficients have the expected signs.

Table 3. Dependent Variable: NETDOMDER, 1984 Q2 to 1997 Q4

Variable	Coefficient	T-ratio
Constant term	7.0249	2.8052***
S1	-8.9173	-2.9421***
S3	-7.7852	-5.8722***
GOVE90R	0.26317	1.9948**
EXPORT90R	0.18427	1.6075
EXPORT90R (+1)	0.16797	2.4505**
REALIMRA (-1)	-0.31523	-1.4794
GDPDEFRA (-1)	-0.23405	-1.1353

R-bar squared = 0.61719
DW-statistic = 2.0674
*** means statistical significance at 1 per cent level
** means statistical significance at 5 per cent level

Based on the parameters thus estimated, using data from 1984 Q2 to 1997 Q4, I forecast the effects on the rate of change or domestic private demand. Along with the actual values of change, the forecast values are tabulated below:

Table 3a. Forecast for NETDOMDER for 1998 Q1 to 1999 Q3

Observation	Actual	Prediction	Error
1998 Q1	-9.4982	-4.1557	-5.3425
1998 Q2	5.1774	3.3680	1.8094
1998 Q3	-7.2065	-1.3093	-5.8972
1998 Q4	-3.9714	-0.6435	-3.3279
1999 Q1	-8.9805	-3.1268	-5.8537
1999 Q2	8.6339	5.8449	2.7890
1999 Q3	4.8060	0.4650	4.3410

Source: Based on regression results reported in Table 3

According to the forecast, which uses the realized values of the rates of change of government expenditures, real exports, the real interest rate, and the inflation rate, the actual decline in quarter 1 1998 was much larger than the predicted value. The difference can be attributed to the implementation of the TPS. Actually, the effect of the TPS may be even more serious than this, because the SAR government had adopted a very stimulative budget since 1998, giving generous tax rebates, an unprecedented mortgage interest deduction from taxable income, interest-free home purchasing loans, etc. Moreover, competition among the banks has driven mortgage-lending rates to unprecedented low levels relative to the prime rate. Not counting these positive effects on the economy, according to my estimates, by the end of the first quarter of 1999, TPS had resulted in a loss of 17.46 per cent of domestic demand. Largely as a result of various stimulative measures adopted starting to take effects the cumulative loss was reduced to 11.5 per cent by the end of quarter 3 in 1999.

Table 4 shows the results of a regression using a similar statistical model but adding an additional CRISISDUMMY to capture any independent effect of the financial crisis that may have effects other than through exports and real interest rates. The definition of CRISISDUMMY is as explained above. We can see that the variable carries the right, negative sign. It is not very significant, but we will use the equation to do a forecast, which is presented in Table 4a. We can see that adding the CRISISDUMMY does generally reduce the negative errors of the forecasts, but it also increases the positive errors. Thus it explains part of the economic declines. The slower predicted recovery after 1999Q1 compared to the previous model suggests that the stimulative measures taken by the government may be more effective than is implied by the model without including the crisis dummy variable.

Table 4. Dependent Variable: NETDOMDER, 1984 Q2 to 1997 Q4

Variable	Coefficient	T-ratio
Constant term	7.0875	2.8043***
S1	-8.7331	-2.8381***
S3	-7.6637	-5.6434***
GOVE90R	0.25724	1.9267*
EXPORT90R	0.18491	1.6002
EXPORT90R (+1)	0.15887	2.2242**
REALIMRA (-1)	-0.31721	-1.4765
GDPDEFRA (-1)	-0.24168	-1.1600
CRISISDUMMY	-1.4681	-0.50375

R-bar squared 0.61102
DW-statistic = 2.0539
*** means statistical significance at 1 per cent level
** means statistical significance at 5 per cent level
* means statistical significance at 10 per cent level

Table 4a. Forecast for NETDOMDER for 1998 Q1 to 1999 Q3

Observation	Actual	Predication	Error
1998 Q1	-9.4982	-5.0188	-4.4794
1998 Q2	5.1774	1.9839	3.1935
1998 Q3	-7.2065	-2.6994	-4.5071
1998 Q4	-3.9714	-0.9596	-3.0118
1999 Q1	-8.9805	-3.6761	-5.3044
1999 Q2	8.6339	5.5848	3.0491
1999 Q3	4.8060	0.2956	4.5104

Source: Based on regression results reported in Table 4

Many people blamed the Tung Administration for setting a yearly production target for housing units and called this central planning. Yet there is nothing intrinsically wrong with such a strategy. Given that the Government is *the* producer of buildable land and the largest supplier of such land in Hong Kong, there is a need to have a vision as to how much land is to be released each year. A land release strategy based on a production target that is set in the light of demographic trends and economic growth projections seems logical and should be superior to any other kind of strategy.

It is not clear how the Government came up with the annual production target of 85,000. What is clear, however, is that behind this annual production target is the intention to bring down home prices, and this would be wrong. A total of 85,000 units, with 50,000 units coming from the public sector and 35,000 units coming from the private sector, as proposed by the government,[6] would be a significant departure from the trend average of about 70,000 per year over the past ten years. It could be justified only if the population increase and income growth were both expected to be much faster than before. The maturing of the Hong Kong economy suggests that trend economic growth over the next ten years should be much more modest than that of the past. This immediately calls into question the wisdom of increasing the supply of housing to the extent proposed.

Although the effects of the TPS, neatly described as a disruption to the ecology of the housing market, are explained in sequential order, they actually took effect immediately. This is like a train engine pushing a series of linked carriages: even though the force comes from the engine at the end of the chain there is virtually no difference in the timing of the motion of the first carriage as compared with the last. Moreover, we have good reasons to believe that the prices of luxury homes, which corresponds to the theoretically last "carriage" affected, would fall even more than the entry-level homes do. Luxury homebuyers are almost always already homeowners and such owners depend entirely on their ability to sell their existing homes before they could buy better ones. On the other hand the entry-level homebuyers have never owned homes before and have all along depended on their cash savings for their buying power.

The injury from the collapse of home prices is deep and wide. Some homeowners have lost all their equity and have become net debtors. Some have actually lost both their homes and their jobs, and have been pushed to the brink of bankruptcy because their lenders will continue to chase after them for the balance of the amount loaned to them upon selling the collateral properties at very low prices. These impoverished homeowners, ironically, were among the most productive within Hong Kong's labor force and had more than their fair share of commitment and trust in Hong Kong's future. Many of them have never had the benefit of receiving subsidized housing from the Government. The great risk to Hong Kong is that they may be so disheartened that they dared not buy homes again in the future, even if they regained the ability to do so. Rather than putting money into their homes in Hong Kong, they may simply ship their savings out of Hong Kong. The result would be massive and continuing capital flight, while the dream of realizing the 70 per cent homeownership target becomes more and more remote.

The collapse in turnover in the housing market is particularly damaging for the Hong Kong economy. Because a number of key sectors depend on housing turnover for their business, the collapse in turnover virtually eroded the basis of their survival. Foremost among those taking the brunt of the shock is the property brokerage sector. Others also hit seriously include decorators, movers, lawyers, bankers, stockbrokers, retailers, sellers of construction materials, and of course real estate developers. As the values of properties fall, the banks had to curtail their lending activities--the worst thing to happen at a time of high interest rates. As a result other sectors are also hit. In a matter of four months, Hong Kong's unemployment zoomed, from an average of 2.5 per cent in the November 1997 to January 1998 period, to an average of 4.2 per cent in the March to May 1998 period. By February 1999-April 1999, the unemployment rate reached a high of 6.3 per cent. The rise in the unemployment rate was, however, not entirely due to a loss of jobs. Hong Kong's labor force was growing rather rapidly partly as a result of population growth and partly as a result of rising labor force participation, which is most noticeable among women.

The effects of the TPS on employment can be inferred from Table 5, which clearly shows that employment growth is positively and significantly related to changes in the volume of transactions in homes (HMDEEDSC). Given that the volume of home transactions had fallen after the introduction of the TPS, employment growth must have been significantly reduced by the TPS.

Table 5. Dependent Variable: Change in Employment in Millions (1984Q3 to 1997Q3)

Variable	Coefficient	T-ratio
Constant term	0.02631	4.2338***
S1	-0.04087	-3.9369***
S3	-0.03128	-2.5946***
EXPORT90C (-1)	0.35402E-06	1.5606
HMDEEDSC	0.12518E-05	2.0350**

R-bar squared = 0.28736
DW-statistic = 2.3706
*** means statistical significance at 1 per cent level
** means statistical significance at 5 per cent level

As the economy took a tailspin downturn, the SAR Government's fiscal revenue plummeted. Land sales of course turned in far less revenue than originally forecast. Appeals to sharply reduce land premiums to be paid for conversion of land use and for upzoning jumped, while any land premiums to be collected for similar purposes fell. Meanwhile, profits tax, stamp duty, even salaries tax, all declined sharply. As a result, the Government ran a fiscal deficit in 1998/99, and was able to avoid another deficit in 1999/2000 only because of the huge capital gains achieved subsequent to the incursion in the stock market in August 1998.[7]

5. RESCUE ACTIONS

The SAR Government's first budget, announced on February 18, 1998 was a significantly stimulative one and was designed as a rescue package. It gave a tax relief to everyone. The basic personal allowance was raised by 8 per cent. An unprecedented deduction for home mortgage interest payments up to $100,000 per year for five years is given to all owner-occupiers. The profit tax rate was reduced from 16.5 per cent to 16 per cent. The rate of stamp duty on stock transactions was cut from 0.3 per cent to 0.25 per cent. Rates chargeable on properties were reduced from 5 per cent to 4.5 per cent. These and other measures on the revenue side were expected to cost $13.6 billion in 1998-99 and nearly $100 billion up to 2001-02. These measures, together with a symbolic interest rate cut in February, prompted the property market into action, as both turnover and prices recovered noticeably. However, the revival was short-lived, largely because the fundamental problems, namely an excessively large housing production target and a disappearance of buyers of HOS housing as a result of the Tenant Purchase Scheme, remained.

The continual and sharp rise in unemployment prompted the government into rescue action again, as a high level committee was formed to deal with the situation. The 12-point rescue package announced on June 3, 1998 included stepping up the training programs, accelerating hiring procedures for civil servants, and bringing forward the infrastructure program. At about the same time, the Housing Authority announced it would allow tenants of retail premises in public housing estates, whose leases were due to expire in 6 to 31 months, to apply for a reassessment of rent.

Came June 22, 1998. The Government was about to auction two pieces of land the next day. The Financial Secretary and then the Chief Executive together with a panel of top government officials suddenly announced a further nine-point rescue package, the most controversial and striking component of which being a halt to all land sales through the end of the fiscal year in March 1999. Market reaction was positive, as the number of viewers for homes put on sale jumped. The stock market, though, reacted coolly. The atmosphere in the financial market was so pessimistic that people were skeptical about the effectiveness of the proposed measures and took a wait-and-see attitude rather than going on a buying spree.

6. WHAT SHOULD BE DONE?

Many people blame the linked exchange rate system of Hong Kong for the poor performance (see for example the numerous editorials in the Hong Kong Economic Journal). There is no doubt that the linked exchange rate system has something to do with the severity of the crisis. In this regard, Singapore's system of implicitly linking to a basket of currencies is much wiser. I have argued for a basket link and invented a mechanism for an easy and transparent system to produce just that back in 1990 (Ho, 1990). But another problem is that the Hong Kong Monetary Authority had kept Hong Kong's interest rates high—much higher than US interest rates--for too long. I have argued elsewhere, the damage of very high interest rates may not be salvaged even if interest rates fall steeply later on, because once a firm or an individual has gone bankrupt, lower interest rates would not help (Ho, 1998b). Singapore, on the other hand, aggressively reduced interest rates not long after the Asian Financial Crisis.[8]

A more serious policy error made by the SAR Government, as this chapter shows, is the way the Housing Authority privatized its public rental housing stock. As yet the SAR Government has not yet recognized its mistake. The Housing Authority continued to expand the Tenant Purchase Scheme. The Government, clearly in an attempt to revive the property market, had expanded the quotas for home purchase loans while converting some of the Home Ownership Scheme housing into rental units. Adding to the irony, many of those homeowners given interest-free loans to buy homes had become negative equity holders.

In order for the housing market to recover it is necessary for the Government to formally revise downward its long-term housing production target, and put forth a credible, revised land sale program that is consistent with the revised target. The Government has to rework its public housing sale program so as to push the better-off public housing tenants to the HOS or the private housing market. The public housing privatization scheme must exclude all households not meeting the prevailing criteria for eligibility for public housing. Privatized public housing units should also be subject to a resale restriction such that they can be resold only to buyers meeting the criteria for public housing.

Does this mean that I recommend going back to a so-called "high land price" policy? Not at all. As a matter of fact, I must point out that no government can successfully implement a "high land price" policy against economic fundamentals. Can Indonesia today implement a high land price policy and keep the economy humming along? Could Macau (formerly a small Portuguese colony an hour's hover ferry trip from Hong Kong) have implemented a high land price policy and actually attract real buyers who paid prices anywhere near Hong Kong's land prices? Hong Kong's land prices were high because people were willing and able to pay for those prices. Would making land available cheaply have transformed Hong Kong's economy into one that was stronger than it had been? Had Hong Kong done so, Hong Kong would have needed much higher tax rates to finance its government functions. If the Hong Kong Government had always supplied so much land that land prices never rose, Hong Kong belongers would have been deprived of the opportunity of using their homes as their primary store of value. Hong Kong people probably would have remitted their savings away to some offshore places that promised better returns. If Hong Kong's home prices had been stagnant, the drive to save more to buy better and more expensive homes would have been averted. The economy would have been much less vibrant.

Some people say that elsewhere people pay low housing prices and high taxes. In Hong Kong people pay low taxes and high housing prices. The total burden is no different. Some people also say that Hong Kong people actually pay high taxes because they pay so much for the land cost. Indeed land costs, land premiums, stamp duties on housing transactions, etc., boil down to a tax of another form. The crucial question is: which kind of tax provides better incentives for people to work hard and to create wealth? In the late 19th century, the American economist Henry George advocated a single tax on land as the least distorting of incentives. My conjecture is that he is right. According to him, as society progresses, land values increase, and it is right for the government to collect the increase in site values. This is exactly what the Hong Kong Government has been doing. When the developmental value of land has increased to a certain level, developers often want to redevelop their land at higher densities. In Hong Kong such requests are often entertained, subject to planning considerations, provided that they pay the necessary premiums. Is this a good system? Hong Kong's long history of economic success suggests yes.

Such a policy is not quite the same as a " high land price policy." A high land price policy may be defined as one that is designed with the intention of drawing the largest possible revenue from land sales and from land redevelopment levies. This is not what I would recommend. My recommendation is only that for any year land should be supplied as long as the marginal value to society of supplying it is larger than the full marginal cost. The full marginal cost includes the cost of preparing the site and providing the necessary infrastructure links to service it as well as the cost of possible instability added to the housing and the financial market. On June 22 1998, when the Government announced a moratorium to land sales for the rest of the fiscal year, the latter cost was likely to be extremely great. Given that the availability of credit in the banking system is already low, land sale would be badly timed because, like an open market operation made by a central bank, it would suck in liquidity from the market and thus would amplify the credit crunch. For this reason I applauded the halt to land sales. But over the long run something more fundamental has to take place. The government should abandon or amend the public housing privatization program.

7. CONCLUSIONS

Just as a misguided macroeconomic policy can cause crisis to an economic ecological system, as discussed in the last chapter, a misguided microeconomic policy can also bring havoc to an entire economy, as the example discussed in the chapter has shown. The economic system is a system under "general equilibrium." Different components hang together in a rather delicate fashion. Some components, in particular, are particularly important because other components may depend on them so much, directly and indirectly. The rapid development of information technology and the increased division of labor through trade are making the ecological system even more delicate. By learning to understand how the economic ecological system works, however, it is possible to harness this development and reduce instability. Public policy makers should exercise great care and caution when they ponder the introduction of highly leveraged, financial market derivatives which are very sensitive to financial news and interest rate movements, and when they introduce new policy initiatives, particularly in sensitive areas that have to do with peoples' savings. The example of Hong Kong demonstrates, loudly and clearly, that we have to be extremely cautious in dealing with peoples' life savings. Savings drive investment and future consumption. Housing is an important element in the economic ecological system in part because it is often the depository of life savings, and in part because it is often a highly leveraged product in the sense that people have to take out a large loan to acquire the asset. For this reason policies with regard to housing should be worked out carefully.

NOTES

1 The Cultural Revolution started on the Mainland but spread to Hong Kong quickly. People were killed in street riots. Bombs were set off. Property prices slumped.

2 Not seasonally adjusted. The largest decline in the first quarter on record was *9.3* per cent, in *1989*.

3 "Safeguarding Rational Allocation of Public Housing Resources: A Consultation Document" published by the Hong Kong Housing Authority in December 1995.

4 Watanabe (1998) presented figures showing that public housing tenants saved much more than HOS owners, private housing tenants, and private housing owners, in absolute and relative terms.

5 This is the standard mortgage rate, equal to the prime rate +1.75 up to February 1996, but declining smoothly to a weighted mortgage rate applicable at the start of 1999, minus the quarter-to-quarter GDP implicit deflator inflation rate annualized..

6 Mr. Tung Chee-wa, Chief Executive of the Hong Kong Speical Administrative Region, announced in July 2000 in passing while speaking to reporters that the policy of 85,000 units production target per year "was gone in 1998"—notwithstanding a member of the Executive Council maintaining the contrary just a week before he made those remarks.

7 The government bought over HK$100 billion worth of shares in August 1998 while the Hang Seng Index was around the 7000 level. In August 2000 the Hang Seng Index was around 17000.

8 From September 15, 1998 through December 10, 1998 Singapore reduced interest rates five times, bringing the prime rate from 7.5 per cent to 5.5 per cent. In contrast, Hong Kong's prime rate started to drop from 10 per cent on October 19 1998, but remained at 9.25 per cent on December 7.

Epilogue

Chapter 19

PUBLIC POLICY IN THE NEW MILLENNIUM

1. BACKGROUND

The new millennium is characterized by five major trends. Evidently, public policy making has to fully appreciate the impact of these trends on human society and respond accordingly.

These trends are:

- the trend of globalization and intensifying competition,
- major technological breakthroughs promising major increases in longevity and improvements in information processing and transmission,
- increasing inequality in income and wealth distribution, both globally across nations and domestically across the population,
- continuing unrest in Africa and transitional economies like Russia and some Latin American countries,
- increasing interdependencies underscoring the need to appreciate the ecology of economic systems.

These major trends are posing important public policy questions that policy makers around the world have to face. Policy makers cannot and must not deny these underlying trends. If policies are not set right, these trends could lead to a more turbulent and dangerous world. On the other hand, if policies are appropriate, globalization and technological breakthroughs will bring major advances in human welfare, while the unrest in transitional economies will be arrested.

2. PRINCIPLES OF PUBLIC POLICY THAT WORK WITH GLOBALIZATION AND COMPETITION AND RISING INCOME INEQUALITY

Principle of Information Cost Minimization, Principle of Availability of Alternatives, and Principle of Residual Risk Reduction

The proposal of a World Currency Unit is a workable proposal that will produce big benefits in a world of increasing globalization and competition (Chapter 11). This is because it is a standardized unit of account that can reduce information cost for savers and investors. Holders and issuers of bonds denominated in the WCU know what interest rate, in real terms, they are earning or paying. To the extent that savers and investors around the world use this standardized unit of account the information content of interest rates becomes clearer, competition becomes more effective, and the world capital market becomes more efficient. To the extent that savers have such global indexed bonds as an instrument to hold their savings, the need to put money in bubble-prone assets will be diminished. The availability of this alternative should reduce bubble formation, thus rendering our international financial markets more stable. Because the WCU is implicitly diversified among five major currencies, exchange risks are reduced for savers and investors.

Principle of Fair and Open Competition

Globalization is an ongoing world trend and the clock cannot be turned back. Despite the street riots in Seattle protesting against globalization at the WTO meeting in December 1999, no one can stop globalization. Globalization does mean that workers in North America will face the competition of low wage workers in emerging economies. They may decry the low wages and poor working conditions of these "sweatshops," but the availability of these jobs, however lowly paid, improve the welfare of the employed workers. If we are concerned about the welfare of these people, we will not condemn globalization. We would ensure that the workers have a reasonable working environment and safe working conditions rather than trying to undermine the principle of fair and open competition.

Redistribution and Safety Nets

Globalization does mean that income and wealth distribution may become more skewed than ever. Successful businesses will thrive. Unsuccessful ones will be wiped away. Skilled workers whose skills are wanted by a growing market will find their wages rise spectacularly. Other workers may find their wages stagnant or even decline, or worse still, their jobs may be eliminated. Globally productivity will rise. Products will become cheaper and better. But for the unemployed there are no cheers. There will therefore be greater need for safety nets and for redistribution. Governments ensuring the availability of basic jobs will see their societies not so vulnerable to crimes and will be attractive to investors. Redistribution through wage subsidies of the kind discussed in Chapter 16 will prove a stabilizing factor for society and will foster a greater sense of social justice.

3. PRINCIPLES OF PUBLIC POLICY THAT MAY ARREST SOCIAL UNRESTS

Fiscal Health and Public Policy

The kind of social and economic problems currently inflicting such socially turbulent countries as Russia and some of the African countries and other transitional economies is certainly highly complex. There is clearly no easy solution to such problems. However, it is also clear that the ineffectiveness of the government, which is in part due to the very poor fiscal positions of the governments concerned, is a key factor behind all the problems. If the government cannot afford to pay its employees and these employees wield power, there is little wonder that they would resort to corruption to boost their incomes. If the police, the army, and other government officials are all bribable, we will have an everything-goes society. No one will invest unless one is backed up by powerful people. Widespread unemployment and crimes are inevitable.

Shleifer and Vishny (1993)'s model suggests that a corrupt government whose departments work together to maximize joint profit is superior to one whose departments independently try to maximize their own profits. Obviously, it is in such a government's interest to maintain law and order to the extent that private enterprises can operate and can pay bribes. A thoroughly corrupt government still has to run like an enterprise. You cannot expect such a government to defend social justice in any sense, but if it can keep the economy going, some kind of stability can be achieved, and this would be a big improvement over what would happen if the government cannot function.

Principle of Availability of Alternatives and the Deterrence Principle

Once the government has achieved some degree of fiscal health it will be able to start paying its employees. Only when these employees earn sufficiently to maintain a living can we start to fight corruption. If government employees particularly the police and the judiciary enjoy a reasonable salary, and if the government makes available "*basic jobs*" to anyone who seeks jobs, then the government can apply the deterrence principle to deter people from committing crimes. Only then will people have the choice to lead a crime-free life.

The *deterrence principle* is to use punishments to prevent crimes. Traditionally people take prison terms as a humane form of punishment and corporal punishments to be inhumane. Chapter 5 shows that this need not be true. Deterrence is always achieved through pain of a physical or a psychological nature. Detaining someone for months and years produces a psychological pain on the culprit, and negative spillover effects on the taxpayers and the culprit's family members. There is no proof that psychological pain is more civilized or more humane than physical pain. Judicious use of physical pain as a deterrence can be fairer, more economical, more humane, and more effective than prison terms.

4. PRINCIPLES OF PUBLIC POLICY THAT FULLY CONSIDER BREAKTHROUGHS IN BIOTECHNOLOGY AND MEDICINE

The Fully Funded for the Cohort Principle

The next decade or two may see major breakthroughs in medicine that are made possible by genetic engineering and biotechnology, following the recent advances in knowledge about the human genome. It is no longer unthinkable that human life expectancies in socially and politically stable countries extend well beyond 100. Already recently there were reports that traditionally estimated life expectancies had been significantly underestimated. This means greater risks for public pension schemes that run on a pay-as-you-go principle.

The proposal for a fully funded pension plan for each cohort (Chapter 8) therefore deserves attention from policy makers. Although the general point that productivity advances and immigration could offset the effects of a rising dependency ratio that may be driven by demographic dynamics is well taken (Papadimitriou and Wray, 1999), no one can deny the fact that the sustainability of pay-as-you-go pension systems (unless they are very small-scale and pay tiny pensions) depends on chance. By making each cohort save for its own retirement and allowing members within the cohort to benefit from the pooling of longevity risks, members of a cohort are protected from the risks of not having saved enough for retirement. If the cohort discovers that its life expectancy has significantly improved the entire cohort may have to postpone its retirement age, but the financial burden of sustaining itself through a much longer retirement period will not be shifted onto the younger generation.

5. PRINCIPLES OF PUBLIC POLICY THAT UPHOLD SOCIAL AND ECONOMIC JUSTICE

The Principles of Universality, Excessive Burden Insurance, and *Ex Ante* Welfare Maximization

Advances in medicine and medical technology may also significantly increase the cost of caring for the sick. Are we prepared to pay for the cost of caring for the sick? Suppose it costs a million dollars to extend one's life for ten years, and it is a functionally healthy ten years, are we prepared to pay for it? Suppose we are behind a veil of ignorance and do not know which one of a hundred among us will be hit by such a health problem in our life-time. Are we willing to pay for it?

If we consider all of ourselves as equals, and we abhor the condition of helplessness caused by the prospect of not being able to pay for a surgical operation that can extend a functionally healthy life for ten years, we may well decide in favor of excessive burden health insurance. Excessive burden insurance requires that we pay for the cost, up to a point per year, of our own medical care. Beyond that point, however, taxpayers will come to our aid, and we will have the life-saving medical care regardless of how expensive it is (Chapter 5).

Do we all feel better off with such a system? If we feel better off living in a society that provides such excessive burden health insurance and so choose to pay heavier taxes for it, we are maximizing our *ex ante* welfare. Each of us does not know if he will actually benefit from it (as assumed, only one in a hundred will benefit from it). But it enhances our state of well being since we know that we will not fall into the state of helplessness which we so much abhor.

Should the system be available to all within the society? I believe yes. This principle of universality for benefits of an insurance nature has been unfairly criticized as allowing people with better means to enjoy benefits which are targeted at the poor. The fact is that universality is not only administratively simpler to implement than a system based on means-testing, but it is also fair in that even though better-off people also benefit, it is also the better-off people who pay taxes. From this perspective, the poor, non-tax-paying people never subsidize the better-off. It is only the better-off people who pay for the benefits enjoyed by the poor. The principle of universality only additionally allows the better-off people to "insure among themselves."

6. PRINCIPLES OF PUBLIC POLICY THAT PREVENTS OR MINIMIZES FINANCIAL CRISES AND CONTAGION EFFECTS OF FINANCIAL CRISES

Principle of Enlightened Monetary Policy that Keeps Monetary Conditions Close to What is Required for a Healthy Economy

The eve of the new millennium saw the introduction of many financial market innovations many of which work on the leverage principle. It also saw a big revolution in information technology. Against this background almost all financial markets have turned global in the sense that, although participation may not be global, the ups and downs of all markets are monitored around the clock all over the world.

These developments have made diversification on a global scale possible for the average investor, and this obviously helps reduce risks. At the same time, however, the influence of mass psychology and herd behavior have become greater than ever, as investors nervously watch what other investors are doing. Given the effects of leverage, big profits readily turn into big losses and vice versa. The kind of gyrations in stock market indices, interest rates, and exchange rates that have occurred in individual markets during the 1980s and 1990s dwarf the stock market crash of 1929.

While the financial markets have become more volatile, the real economy has become more stable, thanks to a much more enlightened approach to monetary policy by the Federal Reserve under the leadership of Alan Greenspan. The American economy has registered the longest economic expansion in history. Following the debacle of Long Term Capital Management in 1998, the Federal Reserve coordinated a bailout for the hedge fund—not in order to save one private company, but in order to contain the damage. The Federal Reserve these days does not make any assumption about the "natural rate of unemployment" and clearly weighs costs against benefits when it deliberates on the conduct of monetary policy. There is no doubt the continuing economic prosperity of the United States has served as a major stabilizing force for the world economy.

This is not to say that policy makers around the world have learnt to be flexible and enlightened. The Asian Financial Crisis of 1997-98 is a case in point. On the eve of the crisis, a number of Asian currencies were overvalued and were suffering from already high real interest rates. The problem had to be relieved through devaluation and reducing interest rates. Instead, although currencies were devalued, interest rates were raised to back-breaking levels. One enemy was chased away but an even worse enemy was brought back. In contrast, the "sterling crisis" of 1992 turned out to be a blessing for the UK economy. While the sterling was devalued UK interest rates were also reduced. The enlightened monetary policy jumpstarted the economy. This happy ending and the unhappy episode before the sterling delinked with the European Monetary System explain why the United Kingdom is still hesitant about joining the Euro.

International Lender of Last Resort

When a currency is under attack and is seen to require a devaluation, very often the devaluation is what is needed. The fundamentals of the economy will be improved by the devaluation, other things being equal. However, given human nature as it is and imperfect perception, speculative pressures if allowed to run their course could render the devaluation momentarily excessive. Excessive devaluations can be destabilizing because they can lead to serious inflation. To avoid this scenario some central banks may choose to raise interest rates but this could render the monetary conditions excessively contractionary again. Actually, however, this is not necessary. After the exchange rate has been allowed to come down to levels consistent with full employment and thus consistent with macroeconomic balance requirements, the new exchange rate can be said to be defendable. *At this point, the country should have access to lending facilities to defend the defendable exchange rate.* The country should borrow as much as needed and other countries should lend as much as needed, through some kind of international lender of last resort mechanism. This way the damage can be contained, and the contagion can be stopped.

7. DEMOCRACY AND THE NEW ENLIGHTENMENT

Principle of Pragmatism

The last century has seen a lot of attention devoted to the cause of democracy. The new millennium will see a new enlightenment marked by *pragmatism.* People will awake to the fact that democracy in the sense of multi-party politics and general elections is neither a necessary nor a sufficient condition for economic and social justice. Multi-party politics and general elections are neither a necessary nor a sufficient condition for a clean and effective government, a stable society, full employment, and protection against misfortunes. The success of the authoritarian China and the flop of the democratic Russia is the case in point. Of course it will be that much nicer if China is, in addition to being able to feed and house its people and giving them a realizable dream for a better future, also democratic. But what really counts is not whether the government derived its legitimacy from a general election, but rather whether the government can effectively contain crime and corruption and protect basic human rights, whether investors feel comfortable enough to invest in the country, and whether the government can maintain a stable currency and contain inflation.

Principle of Autonomy and Choice and Principle of Maximization of Ex Ante Welfare

The philosophy of democracy is founded on the assumption that people are different and need representation, so that the political process is needed to balance the interests of different groups. The theoretical basis of this book is that we should assume people in fact share similar aspirations and needs, even though they may each like to find different ways to manifest those aspirations and satisfy those needs. People need protection against excessive burden. People need food and clothing. People need the freedom to express themselves and exercise their creativity. People need a reliable instrument to hold their savings and a stable value currency. People need recognition and social acceptance. While governments should respect people's choice and autonomy, the purpose of public policy is not so much to play one group's interest against that of another, but rather to maximize *ex ante* welfare for everyone of us.

8. CONCLUSIONS

Jeremy Bentham believed that society should pursue the "greatest happiness of the greatest number." Modern economics developed the concept of "social welfare function," which is a mathematical function based on the welfares of all individuals constituting the society. Maximizing the greatest happiness of the greatest number, or maximizing the social welfare function, however, has serious conceptual problems, and is not very helpful for public policy. Bentham's approach requires knowing the *ex post* welfare of all individuals and adding them up. There is also the strange implication that increasing the population may enhance social welfare even though the welfare of the existing population declines. Other forms of the social welfare function is equally problematic, since there will never be a consensus over the form of the social welfare function.

The approach of this book is that starting from the assumption about the commonality of human nature, public policy should aim at maximizing the *ex ante* welfare of you and me, you and me being no different "under a veil of ignorance." We will not worry about A's and B's *ex post* welfares. We will not take $100 from A and give it to B on the ground that *ex post* A's loss is known to be smaller than B's gain. We will treat A the same as B, and ask ourselves whether it is socially desirable to take $100 from someone and give it to another against his will.

Maximizing *ex ante* welfare, we will protect A as well as B against arbitrary income redistribution. We will protect A as well as B against natural misfortune by setting up an insurance mechanism and we take solace at the fact that since both A and B opt for the insurance they must be better off *ex ante*. Rather than playing one person's *ex post* gain against another person's loss, public policy should aim at enhancing *ex ante* social welfare. By designing institutions that are socially just, conducive to mutual trust and respect, and allow the biggest room for each individual to live his own way, we will have a world that will allow us to realize the best within ourselves.

REFERENCES

"A Symposium on Education Reforms" (1999), *The World Bank Economic Review*, September.

Abel, Andrew B. (1986) "Capital Accumulation and Uncertain Lifetimes with Adverse Selection," *Econometrica*, September, 54:1079-1097.

Ainslie, George (1992) *Picoeconomics: The Strategic Interaction of Successive Motivational States within the Person*, Cambridge: Cambridge University Press.

Akerlof, George A., William Dickens, and George Perry (2000) "Near Rational Wage and Price Setting and the Long Run Phillips Curve," *Brookings Papers on Economic Activity*, 1:2000.

American Bankers' Association (1990) *Federal Deposit Insurance, A Program for Reform*, Washington, DC: ABA, March.

Appleton, Simon, John Hoddinott, and John Knight (1996) *Oxford Bulletin of Economics and Statistics*, 58:1, February, 211-219.

Arnett, Jerome C., Jr. (1996) "Ontario's Health Care: A Pox on Doctors and Patients," *The Asian Wall Street Journal*, October 3, 8.

Arrow, Kenneth (1950) "A Difficulty in the Concept of Social Welfare," *Journal of Political Economy*, 58:328-346, reprinted in *Social Choice and Justice*, Cambridge: The Belknap Press of Harvard University Press.

Arrow, Kenneth (1973) "Some Ordinalist-Utilitarian Notes on Rawls's Theory of Justice," *Journal of Philosophy*, 70:245-263.

Asher, Mukul G. (1994) *Social Security in Malaysia and Singapore: Practices, Issues, and Reform Directions*, Malaysia: Institute of Strategic and International Studies.

Auerbach, Alan J., Jagadeesh Gokhale, and Laurence J. Kotlikoff (1994) "Generational Accounting: A Meaningful Way to Evaluate Fiscal Policy," *Journal of Economic Perspectives*, 8:1, 73-94.

Barck, Oscar Theodore Jr. and Nelson Manfred Blake (1974) *A History of the United States in Our Times*, NY: Macmillan Publishing Co.

Barro, Robert (2000) "Democracy and the Rule of Law," *Fraser Forum*, June, 8-9.

Baumol, W.J. and A.S. Blinder (1991) *Economics: Principles and Policy*, 5th edition, NY: Harcourt Brace Jovanovich College Publishers.

Bernanke, Ben (1983) "Nonmonetary Effects of the Financial Crisis in the Propagation of the Great Depression," *American Economic Review*, 73:257-276.

Bierman, Harold, Jr. (1991) *The Great Myths of 1929 and the Lessons to be Learned.* New York: Greenwood Press.

Blundell, R., L. Dearden, A. Goodman, and H. Reed (1997) *Higher Education, Employment, and Earnings in Britain*, London: Institute for Fiscal Studies.

Card, D. and A.B. Krueger (1994) "Minimum Wages and Employment: A Case Study of the Fast-food Industry in New Jersey and Pennsylvania," *American Economic Review*, 84:4, 772-793.

Chaloupka, Frank (1991) "Rational Addictive Behaviour and Cigarette Smoking," *Journal of Political Economy*, 99:4, 722-742.

Chami, Ralph, and Jeffrey H. Fischer (1996) "Altruism, Matching, and Non-Market Insurance," *Economic Inquiry*, October, 630-648.

Christofides, Louis N. and C.J. McKenna (1996) "Unemployment Insurance and Job Duration in Canada," *Journal of Labor Economics*, 14:2, 286-312.

Clark, John and Jay Hein (1999) "The Political Economy of Welfare Reform in the United States" The Economics of Welfare Reform published in the London-based Institute for Economic Affairs upcoming book, Fall.

Coats, W.L. Jr. (1994) "In Search of a Monetary Anchor: A New Monetary Standard," San Francisco: Institute for Contemporary Studies Press.

Colton, Roger D. (1993) "Consumers Information and Workable Competition in Telecommunication Markets," *Journal of Economic Issues*, 27:3, September, 775-792.

Commissioner of Banking: *Annual Report,* various years.

Consultation Paper: Deposit Protection Scheme, (1992) Monetary Affairs Branch, Government Secretariat, February.

Cooper, Kerry and Donald R Fraser (1986) *Banking Deregulation and the New Competition in Financial Services,* Cambridge: Ballinger.

Davis, L.J. (1990) "Chronicle of a Debacle Foretold: How Deregulation Begat the S&L Scandal," *Harper's Magazine,* September.

Davis, L.J. (1991) "The Problem with Banks? Bankers" *Harper's Magazine,* June, 45-53.

De Palma, A., G.H. Myers, and Y.Y. Papageogiou (1994) "Rational Choice under an Imperfect Ability to Choose," *American Economic Review*, 84:3, June, 419-440.

Diamond, Peter (1993) "Privatization of Social Security: Lessons from Chile", *NBER Working Paper,* no. 4516, October.

Dietz, Thomas, and Paul C. Stern (1995) "Towards a Theory of Choice: Socially Embedded Preference Construction," *Journal of Socio-Economics*, 24:2, 261-279.

Dornbusch, Rudi (1995) "And You Thought Social Security was in Trouble," *Business Week*, August 28, p. 7.

Eckstein, Zvi, Martin Eichenbaum, and Dan Peled (1985) "Uncertain Lifetimes and the Welfare Enhancing Properties of Annuity Markets and Social Security," *Journal of Public Economics*, 26:3, 303-326.

Fischer, S., R. Dornbusch, and R. Schmalensee (1988) *Economics*, 2nd Edition, N.Y.: MaGraw Hill.

Fishburn, Peter C. (1988) "Expected Utility: An Anniversary and a New Era," *Journal of Risk and Uncertainty*, 1:267-283.

Fishkin, James S. (1983) *Justice, Equal Opportunity, and the Family*, New Haven: Yale University Press.

Fitzpatrick, Tony (1999) *Freedom and Security: An Introduction to the Basic Income Debate*, N.Y.:St. Martin's Press; London: Macmillan Press.

Freeman R.B. (1996) "The Minimum Wage as a Redistributive Tool," *Economic Journal*, May, 639-648.

Freeman, Katherine B. (1993) "The Images of Human Nature in Economics," *Rivista Internationale di Scienze Economiche e Commerciali*, 40:8, 625-639.

Friedman, Milton and L. Savage (1948) "The Utility Analysis of Choices Involving Risk," *Journal of Political Economy*, August.

Fromm, Erich (1957) *The Art of Loving*, London: George Allen & Unwin.

Galbraith, John Kenneth (1954) *The Great Crash 1929*, Boston: Houghton Mifflin.

Galbraith, John Kenneth (1969) *The Affluent Society*, 2nd Edition, Boston: Houghton Mifflin.

Garratt, Rod and John M. Marshall (1994) "Public Finance of Private Goods: The Case of College Education," *Journal of Political Economy*, 102:3, 566-582.

Gates, William (1996) "Achieve the Extraordinary, Not Wealth," *Hong Kong Economic Journal*, October 8.

George, Henry (1839-1897), *Progress and Poverty: An Inquiry into the Cause of Industrial Depression and of Increase of Want with Increase of Wealth*, NY: Robert Schalkenbach Foundation.1990.

Gonzales-Hermosillo, Brenda and Takotoshi Ito (1997) "The Bank of Canada's Monetary Policy Framework: Have Recent Chagnes Enhanced Central Bank Credibility?" *International Monetary Fund Working Paper* WP/97/171, December.

Gray, Alastair M. (1994) "The Reform of Legal Aid," *Oxford Review of Economic Policy*, 10:1, 51-67.

Gray, Alastair, M., N. Rickman and P.Fenn (1999) "Professional Autonomy and the Cost of Legal Aid," *Oxford Economic Papers*, 51:545-58.

Grenville, Stephen (1999) "Financial Crises and Globalization," *Economic and Labour Relations Review*, 10:2, 260-277.

Grube, G.M.A. (1974, Translator) *Plato's Republic*, Indianapolis: Hackett Publishing Co.

Hall, Thomas E. and J. David Ferguson (1998) *The Great Depression: An International Disaster of Perverse Economic Policies*, Ann Arbor: The University of Michigan Press.

Harsanyi, John C. (1953) "Cardinal Utility in Welfare Economics and in the Theory of Risk-taking," *Journal of Political Economy*, October, LXI:434-435.

Harsanyi, John C. (1955) "Cardinal Welfare, Individualistic Ethics, and Interpersonal Comparisons of Utility," *Journal of Political Economy*, August, LXIII:309-321.

Harsanyi, John C. (1997) "Utilities, Preferences, and Substantive Goods," *Social Choice and Welfare*, 14:129-145.

Havemen, Robert (1994) "Should Generational Accounts Replace Public Budgets and Deficits?" *Journal of Economic Perspectives*, 8:1, 95-111.

Hay, Joel (1992) *Health Care in Hong Kong*, HK: Chinese University Press for the HK Centre for Economic Research.

Hewitt Associates LLC and GML Consulting Ltd. (1995) *Report of the Consultancy on the Mandatory Provident Funds System.*

Hirshleifer, Jack (1977) "Shakespeare vs Becker on Altruism," *Journal of Economic Literature*, June, 500-502.

Ho, Lok Sang (1981) *Value Capture: An Analysis of Policy Alternatives*, University of Toronto Ph.D. dissertation.

Ho, Lok Sang (1988) "Towards an Optimal Public Housing Policy," *Urban Studies*, 25:204-211.

Ho, Lok Sang (1990) " A Proposal for an Adaptive Linked Exchange Rate System," *Hong Kong Economic Papers*, 20: 89-96.

Ho, Lok Sang (1991) *A Proposal for Deposit Insurance in Hong Kong,* CUHK: HK Institute of Asia-Pacific Studies, Occasional Paper No. 9, October.

Ho, Lok Sang (1993) "Regional Balance of Payments Problems: An Interpretation," *Regional Studies*, 27:5, 457-466.

Ho, Lok Sang (1994) "Democracy and Economic Development," *Hong Kong Economic Papers,* HK: HK Economic Association, 23:63-65.

Ho, Lok Sang (1995a) "Privatisation of Public Housing: An Analysis of Policy Alternatives," *Contemporary Economic Policy* (USA), 8:3, July, 53-63.

Ho, Lok Sang (1995b) "Inflation: New Risks for the Hong Kong Economy," *The Other Hong Kong Report*, 183-197.

Ho, Lok Sang (1997a) *Health Care Delivery and Financing: A Model for Reform*, HK: City University of Hong Kong Press for the HK Centre for Economic Research.

Ho, Lok Sang (1997b) "Institutional Foundations for a Just Society," *Journal of Socio-Economics,* 26:6, 627-643.

Ho, Lok Sang (1997c) "A Universal Public Pension Scheme," *Contemporary Economic Policy* (USA), XV, July.

Ho, Lok Sang (1997d) "Flaws in Housing Policy," *South China Morning Post*, December 30.
Ho, Lok Sang (1997e) "Hong Kong in the 21st Century," *New Asia*, 4:2, 88-98.
Ho, Lok Sang (1998a) "A Model of Human Nature and Personal Development," *Journal of Socio Economics*, 27:2, 271-287.
Ho, Lok Sang (1998b) "Credit Squeeze is Wrong," *South China Morning Post*, January 14.
Ho, Lok Sang (1998c) "Policy Blunder of the Century," *South China Morning Post*, March 24.
Ho, Lok Sang (2000) "Towards a New International Monetary Order: The World Currency Unit and the Global Indexed Bond," *The World Economy*, 23:7, July, 939-950.
Ho, Lok Sang, J.J. Lee, and J.P. Leung (1991) *Retirement Benefit Programs: Analysis and a Proposal for Hong Kong*, CUHK: HK Institute for Asia-Pacific Studies, Occasional Paper.
Hochman, Harold M., and James D. Rodgers (1969) "Pareto Optimal Redistribution" *American-Economic-Review*, 59:4, September, 542-557.
Hong Kong Housing Authority (1990) *Report of the Ad Hoc Committee to Review Domestic Rent Policy and Allocation Standards*, December.
International Social Security Association (1987) *Relationship between Pensions and Occupations*, Geneva, European Series no. 13.
Ito, Takatoshi and Tokuo Iwaisako (1995) "Explaining Asset Bubbles in Japan" *National Bureau of Economic Research Working Paper*, no. 5358, November, p. 32.
Ito, Takatoshi, Eiji Ogawa and Yuri Nagataki Sasaki (1998) "How did the Dollar Peg Fail in Asia," *NBER Working Paper*, no. 6729, September.
Jackman, R.A. and P.R.G. Layard (1986) "A Wage-tax, Worker-subsidy Policy for Reducing the Natural Rate of Unemployment," Chapter 7 in W.Beckerman (ed.) *Wage Rigidity and Unemployment*, London: Butterworth.
James, Estelle and Dimitri Vittas (1994) "Mandatory Saving Schemes: Are they an Answer to the Old Age Security Problem?" Working Paper Series, Wharton School, Pension Research Council, no. 94-14.
James, Estelle (1995) "Averting the Old-Age Crisis," *Finance and Development*, 32:2, June, 4-7.
James, Estelle and Robert Palacios (1995) "Costs of Administering Public and Private Pension Plans," *Finance and Development*, 32:2, June, 12-15.
Jao, Y.C. (1982) "Deposit Insurance for Hong Kong: A Tentative Proposal," *Asian Monetary Monitor,* September/October, 19-27.
Jao, Y.C. (1989) "Monetary System and Banking Structure", *The Economic System of Hong Kong,*in H.C.Y. Ho and L.C. Chau (ed.), HK: Asian Research Service.
Johansson, Per-Olov (1991) *An Introduction to Modern Welfare Economics*, Cambridge: Cambridge University Press.
Kane, E.J. (1987) "Dangers of Capital Forbearance: The Case of FSLIC and 'Zombie' S&Ls," *ContenTorary Policy Issues,* January, 71-83.
Kane, E.J. (1989) "The High Cost of Incompletely Funding the FSLIC's Shortage of Explicit Capital," *Journal of Economic Perspectives,* 3:4, 31-48.
Kaus, Mickey (1992) *The End of Equality*, NY: Basic Books.
Keynes, John Maynard (1936) *The General Theory of Employment, Interest, and Money,* London: Macmillan & Co. Ltd.
Kindleberger, Charles P. (1986) *The World in Depression, 1929-1939,* Berkeley: University of California Press.
Kohn, Alfie (1986) *The Brighter Side of Human Nature*, NY: Basic Books.
Kolm, Serge-Christophe (1994) "Rational Justice and Equality," in Wolfgang Eichhorn (ed.) *Models and Measurement of Welfare and Inequality*, Berlin: Springer-Verlag.
Kolm, Serge-Christophe (1996) "The Theory of Justice," *Social Choice and Welfare*, 13:151-182.

Kukathas, Chandran, and Philip Pettit (1990) *Rawls: A Theory of Justice and its Critics*, Polity Press in association with Blackwell Publishers (Oxford).

Kuttner, Robert (1997) "The American Health Care System—Health Insurance Coverage," *New England Journal of Medicine*, 340:2, 163-168.

Kuttner, Robert (1998) "A Dirty Little Secret: Managed Care is Bad for Business," Economic Viewpoint, *Businessweek*, December 21.

Lancaster, Kelvin (1966) "A New Approach to Consumer Theory," reprinted in Martin Ricketts (ed.) *Neoclassical Microeconomics*, Elgar: 1988, 19-44.

Lassey, M.L, W.R. Lassey, and M.J. Jinks (1997) (ed.) *Health Care Systems around the World*, NJ: Prentice Hall.

Lawrence, Emily C. (1991) "Poverty and the Rate of Time Preference: Evidence from Panel Data," *Journal of Political Economy*, 99:1, 54-77.

Lazear, Edward (1999) "Education Production." *Discussion Paper Series 287,* School of Economics and Finance, University of Hong Kong.

Le Grand, Julian (1999) "Competition, Cooperation, or Control? Tales from the British National Health Service," *Health Affairs*, May/June.

Ljungqvist, Lars (1999) "Squandering European Labour: Social Safety Nets in Times of Economic Turbulence," *Scottish Journal of Political Economy*, 46:4, 367-388.

Lucas, Robert E. Jr. (1976) "Econometric Policy Evaluation: A Critique," in *The Phillips' Curve and Labor Markets,* Carnegie-Rochester Conference Series on Public Policy, Amsterdam, North Holland.

Marx, K. (1867) reprinted 1962, *Capital*, Moscow.

Maslow, A.H. (1965) "Some Basic Propositions of a Growth and Self-actualization Psychology," in G. Lindzey and C. Hall (eds.), *Theories of Personality: Primary Sources and Research*, New York: Wiley, 307-316.

Mill, John Stuart (1969) *Essays on Ethics, Religion and Society*, in John M. Robson, F.E.L. Priestley and D.P. Dryer (eds), Vol. X.

Mill, John Stuart (1972) *Later Letters of John Stuart Mill*, in Francis E. Mineka and N.N. Lindley (eds), XV:761-764.

Miron, Jeffrey A. and Jeffrey Zwiebel (1995), "The Economic Case against Drug Prohibition ," *Journal of Economic Perspectives.* 9:4, Fall, 175-192.

Mitchell, Olivia S. (1993) "Retirement Systems in Developed and Developing Countries: Institutional Features, Economic Effects, and Lessons for Economies in Transition", *NBER Working Paper,* no. 4424, August.

Mitchell, Oivia S. and Stephen P. Zeldes (1996) "Social Security Privatisation: A Structural Analysis," *NBER Working Paper*, no. 5512, March.

Montgomery, John D. (1996) "Recent Turbulence in Emerging Capital Markets: Lessons for Financial Policy," *Social and Economic Studies*, 45 (2-3), 89-107.

Muellbauer, John (1987) "Prof. Sen on the Standard of Living," in G. Hawthorn (ed.) *The Standard of Living*, Cambridge: Cambridge University Press.

Mundell, Robert (1963) "Optimal Currency Areas," *American Economic Review*, 51, 657-664.

Musgrave, Richard A. (1959) *The Theory of Public Finance*, N.Y.: McGraw Hill.

National Committee of Inquiry into Higher Education (1997). Higher Education in the Learning Society: Report of the National Committee, HMSO, Norwich.

Naylor, C. David (1999) "Health Care In Canada: Incrementalism under Fiscal Duress," *Health Affairs*, May/June.

Neumann, Manfred J.M. (forthcoming) "The Euro: Major Policy Implications for Europe and the Global Economy," *Pacific Economic Review.*

Ng, Yew-kwang (1965) "Why Do People Buy Lottery Tickets? Choices Involving Risk and the Indivisibility of Expenditure," *Journal of Political Economy*, LXXIII:5, 530-535.

Ng, Yew-kwang (1984) "Expected Subjective Utility: Is the Neumann-Morgenstern Utility the Same as the Neoclassical's?" *Social Choice and Welfare*, 1:177-186.
Ng, Yew-kwang (1997) "A Case for Happiness, Cardinalism, and Interpersonal Comparability," *Economic Journal*, 107:445, November, 1848-1858.
Ng, Yew-kwang (1999) "On Estimating the Effects of Events Like the Asian Financial Crisis: A Mesoeconomic Approach," *Taiwan Economic Review*, 27:4, December, 393-412.
Niskanen, William A. (1971) *Bureaucracy and Representative Government,* Chicago: Aldine-Atherton.
Niskanen,William A. (1992) "Economists and Drug Policy," *Carnegie Rochester Conference Series on Public Policy*; 36:0, July, 223-248.
Noguchi, Yukio (1983) "Problems of Public Pensions in Japan," *Hitotsubashi Journal of Economics*, 24:43-68.
Nozick, Robert (1974) *Anarchy, State, and Utopia*, New York: Basic Books.
O'Sullivan, Arthur (1996) *Urban Economics*, Third Edition, Chicago: Irwin.
OECD (1985) *Trends in Banking in OECD Countries,* Paris.
OECD (1987) *Prudential Supervision in Banking,* Paris.
Oswald, A.J. (1983) "Altruism, Jealousy, and the Theory of Optimal Non-Linear Taxation," *Journal of Public Economics*, 20:77-87.
Paarlberg, Don (1993) *An Analysis and History of Inflation*, Westport: Praeger Publishers.
Papadimitriou, Dimitri B. and L. Randall Wray (1999) "Does Social Security Need Saving?" The Jerome Levy Economics Institute of Bard College Public Policy Brief, no. 55.
Phelps, Charles (1992) *Health Economics*, Harper Collins.
Phelps, Edmund (1997) "Wage Subsidy Programmes: Alternative Designs," in Dennis J. Snower and Guillermo de la Dehesa (ed.) *Unemployment Policy: Government Options for the Labour Market,* Cambridge: Cambridge University Press.
Phelps, Edmund S. (1994) "Economic Justice to the Working Poor through a Wage Subsidy," in Papadimitriou, Dimitri B. (ed.) *Aspects of Distribution of Wealth and Income.* Jerome Levy Economics Institute Series. N.Y.:St Martin's Press, 151-164.
Pingle, Mark (1995) "Imitation vs. Rationality: An Experimental Perspective on Decision Making," *Journal of Socio-Economics*, 24:2, 281-315.
Posner, Richard A. (1980) *The Economics of Justice*, Cambridge: Harvard University Press.
Psacharopoulos, G. (1994) "Returns to Education: A Global Update," *World Development*, 22:9, 1325-1343.
Rawls, John (1971) *A Theory of Justice*, Cambridge: Harvard University Press.
Report of the Consultancy on the Mandatory Provident Funds System (1995) prepared jointly by Hewitt Associates LLC and GML Consulting Ltd., April.
Rickman, Neil, Paul Fenn and Alastair Gray (1999) "The Reform of Legal Aid in England and Wales," *Fiscal Studies*, 20:3, 261-286.
Roberts, Paul C. (1995) "It's Time to Privatize Social Security," *Business Week*, February 27.
Rodrigo, G. Chris (1998) "Crises in East Asia: An Evolutionary Perspective," August, Social Scientists Association, Colombo, Sri Lanka.
Roemer, Milton (1993) *National Health Systems of the World Vol.2*, Oxford: Oxford University Press.
Russell, Bertrand (1968) *The Conquest of Happiness*, New York: Bantam Books.
Sah, Raaj (1991) "Social Osmosis and Patterns of Crime," *Journal of Political Economy*, 99:6, 1272-1295.
Scanlon, Tim (1991) "The Moral Basis of Interpersonal Comparisons," in Elster J. Roemer (ed.) *Interpersonal Comparison of Well-being*, Cambridge: Cambridge University Press, 17-44.
Schuler, K. (2000), Information on the Currency Board System, Dollarization, and Related Topics, *http://www.erols.com/kurrency.*

Schwarz, Anita M. (1995) "Pension Schemes: Trade-offs between Redistribution and Saving," *Finance and Development*, IMF, 32:2, June, 8-11.

Sen, Amartya K. (1985) *Commodities and Capabilities*, Amsterdam: North Holland.

Sen, Amartya K. (1992) *Inequality Rexamined*, Cambridge: Harvard University Press.

Sen, Amartya K. (1995a) "Rationality and Social Choice," *American Economic Review*, 85:1, 1-24.

Sen, Amartya K. (1995b) *Mortality as an Indicator of Economic Success and Failure*, Development Economics Research Programme, Suntory and Toyota International Centres for Economics and Related Disciplines, London School of Economics and Political Science, No. 66.

Sessions, William S. (1990) "The FBI's War on Bank Fraud: Facts and Figures," *Challenge*, July/August, 57-59.

Shannon, David A. (1974) *Twentieth Century America, Vol.2: The Twenties and Thirties*, Chicago: Rand McNally College Publishing Co., Third Edition.

Shleifer, Andrei and Robert W. Vishny (1993) "Corruption," *NBER* Working Paper no. 4372, May.

Sirkin, Gerald (1975) "The Stock Market of 1929 Revisited: A Note." *Business History Review*, Summer, 49:223-231.

Smith, Adam (1976/1961) *The Wealth of Nations*, reprint edited by E.Cannan, London: Methuen.

Stark, Oded (1989) "Altruism and the Quality of Life," *American Economic Review*, May, 86-90.

Stigler, G.J., and G.S. Becker (1977) "De Gustibus non est Disputandum," *American Economic Review*, 67.

Stiglitz, Joseph (2000) "The Insider: What I Learned at the World Economic Crisis," *The New Republic*, April 17.

Tisdell, Clement A. (1995) "Asian Development and Environmental Dilemmas," *Contemporary Economic Policy*, 13:1, 38-49.

Tittenbrun, Jacek (1996) *Private versus Public Enterprises: In Search of the Economic Rationale for Privatisation*, London: Janus Publishing Company.

Walton, Gary M. and Huge Rockoff (1998) *History of the American Economy*, 8th edition, NY: The Dryden Press.

Wasserman, David (1996) "Let Them East Chances: Probability and Distributive Justice," *Economics and Philosophy*, 12:29-49.

Watanabe, Mariko (1998) "The Impact of the Public Housing Policy on Household Behaviour in Hong Kong," M.Phil. thesis, University of Hong Kong.

Weimer, David (1992) "Claiming Races, Broiler Contracts, Heresthetics, and Habits: Ten Concepts for Institutional Design," *Policy Sciences*, 52:2, May, 135-159.

Weimer, David and Aidan R. Vining (1998) *Policy Analysis: Concepts and Practice*, 3rd ed. Prentice Hall.

West, Edwin G. (1997) "Education Vouchers in Principle and Practice: A Survey," *The World Bank Research Observer*, 12:1, 83-103.

White, L.J. (1989) "The Reform of Federal Deposit Insurance," *Journal of Economic Perspectives*, 3:4, 11-30

Wong, Richard Yue-chim (1998) *On Privatizing Public Housing*, Hong Kong: City University of Hong Kong Press for the Hong Kong Centre for Economic Research.

Yang, Xiao-kai and Yew-kwang Ng (1993) *Specialisation and Economic Organization: A New Classical Microeconomic Framework*, North Holland.

Young, Leslie, and Douglas Marcouiller (1995) "The Black Hole of Graft: The Predatory State and the Informal Economy," *American Economic Review*, 85:3, June, 630-646.

INDEX

addictive drugs, 23, 137, 138
adverse selection, 88, 91, 96
Ainslie, George, 26, 27, 211
Argentina, 113, 131
Arrow, Kenneth, 41, 42, 52, 54, 211
Asher, Mukul G., 89, 97, 211
Asian Financial Crisis, 99, 109, 112, 118, 124, 125, 130, 174, 183, 184, 185, 188, 189, 195, 207, 216
Auerbach, Alan J., 89, 211
autonomy, 17, 28, 34, 39, 41, 51, 53, 63, 67, 68, 144, 147, 148, 209
Bank of Canada, 15, 131, 213
Bank of England, 106, 110, 180
Basic Income Guarantee, 169
basic job, 133, 163, 166, 167, 168, 170, 203, 204
Basic Law of the Hong Kong Special Administrative Region, 136
Baumol, W.J., 164, 211
benefit-cost analysis, 15, 30, 151
bequest, 48, 55, 89
Bernanke, Ben, 179, 211
Bernoulli-Morgenstern-von Neumann theory, 32
Bierman, Harold, Jr., 174, 211
Blinder, A.S., 164, 211
bubble, 99, 112, 117, 118, 120, 123, 124, 126, 141, 174, 184, 188, 202
capitation, 61
Card, David, 164, 211
Central Provident Fund, 14, 66, 89, 97, 155, 156
Chaloupka, Frank, 31, 211
charter schools, 148, 151
Clinton, Bill, 69, 87, 148, 151
Coats, W.L. Jr., 122, 212
coinsurance, 84
competition, 51, 53, 62, 63, 86, 103, 140, 144, 147, 148, 149, 191, 201, 202
conditional bidding, 157, 159
conditional fee agreements, 75, 76
conditional market, 157
corporate governance, 129, 132
corruption, 1, 4, 46, 141, 203, 204, 208
cost-push inflation, 104, 106
crime and punishment, 6, 13, 37, 49
currency area, 113
currency board, 104, 107, 113, 114, 131, 132
curriculum design, 143, 144
Davis, L.J., 83, 86, 212
defendable, 109, 110, 115, 208
defendable exchange rate, 110, 208
deflation, 113, 178, 179, 181
degree of justness, 40
demand management, 111
demand-side moral hazard, 65, 72, 74, 76
dependency ratio, 92, 96, 205
deterrence principle, 204
Diagnosis-Related Group, 74
Diamond, Peter, 87, 88, 93, 212
Dietz, Thomas, 35, 212
discount rate, 31, 32, 89, 90, 178
dollarization, 114
drug legalization, 137
economic fundamental, 109, 110, 115, 124, 125, 174, 178, 182, 196
education, 6, 16, 34, 47, 48, 54, 55, 133, 137, 143-151, 168
education vouchers, 148, 150
effective demand, 111
effective exchange rate index, 131
efficient pricing principle, 161, 162
efficient pricing structure principle, 162
emerging economies, 202
equal opportunities, 44, 47, 48, 55
euro, 114
European Central Bank, 114
European Monetary System, 110, 112, 207
euthanasia, 137
ex ante perceived utility function, 20, 24, 29
ex ante welfare maximization, 17, 35, 41, 52, 54, 205

excess capacity, 65, 124, 126
excessive burden insurance, 60, 66, 68, 72, 74, 76, 205
exchange rate, ix, 99, 107, 109, 110, 111, 113, 114, 118, 119, 120, 122, 125, 126, 131, 183, 189, 195, 207
exchange risk, 114, 117, 122, 123, 124, 202
exchange risk premiums, 114
exploitation, 37, 47
Federal Reserve Board, 107, 180
Federal Savings and Loans Insurance Corporation, 83
fee-for-service model, 59
Ferguson, J. David, 173, 176, 179, 181, 182, 213
filtering down, 153
financial intermediation function of banks, 126
fiscal deficit, 15, 18, 112, 115, 136, 194
fiscal deficits, 15, 112, 115
Fisher, Irving, 178, 182
floating exchange rate, 110, 125
flow in the housing market, 153, 156, 158
Fogel, Robert, 97
fraud, 83, 91, 166, 167
Freeman, Katherine B., 36, 212
Freeman, R.B., 164, 212
Friedman, Milton, 39, 54, 105, 165, 169, 181, 212
Fulfillment attributes, 21
fully funded for the cohort principle, 204
fully funded social security, 88, 89
fundamental justice, 39
Galbraith, John Kenneth, 36, 176, 177, 212
gate-keeping, 72, 73
generational accounting, 89, 97
George, Henry, 141, 196
German hyperinflation, 102
globalization, 201, 202
Gokhale, Jagadeesh, 89, 211
gold standard, 111, 180
Great Depression, 99, 111, 171, 173, 174, 176, 177, 178, 181, 211, 213
Great Proletariat Cultural Revolution, 183
Greenspan, Alan, 15, 125, 207
Grenville, Stephen, 130, 213
Hall, Thomas E., 173, 176, 179, 181, 182, 213
happiness, 19, 20, 21, 22, 23, 24, 26, 27, 38, 40, 54, 144, 145, 150, 209
Harsanyi, John C., xii, 27, 35, 36, 37, 38, 41, 42, 43, 51, 53, 213
Haveman, Robert, 97
health policy, 6, 16
hierarchy of policy goals, 7, 10, 12
high land price policy, 196, 197
Home Ownership Scheme, 154, 158, 186, 188, 195
Hong Kong, 3, 4, 12, 14, 35, 55, 59, 62, 65, 71-86, 88-97, 101-115, 121-160, 183-198, 212-217
Hong Kong and Shanghai Banking Corporation, 129
Hospital Authority, 62, 65
housing, 6, 12, 13, 121, 127, 132, 133, 153-159, 168, 169, 184-198
Housing and Development Board, 154, 159
Housing Subsidy Policy, 127, 157, 185, 186
human genome, 204
human nature, xi, 5, 7, 9, 10, 34, 35, 39, 104, 105, 130, 143, 145, 209
human right, 163
Hungary, 102, 108
hyperinflation, 102
IMF, 115, 117, 118, 217
income elasticity of demand for housing, 158
income-based safety net, 133
incremental justice, 37, 39, 43, 51, 52, 53
indexed bond, 108, 202
indexed global bonds, 122
indexing, 103, 108, 180
inflation, 12, 15, 18, 99, 101-106, 108, 111, 115, 117, 121-126, 131, 132, 174, 175, 178, 180, 186, 188, 190, 191, 198, 207, 208
information cost, 79, 202
inheritance tax, 47
initial conditions, 47
inner reserve, 129
institutional choice, 40
international lender of last resort, 115, 207, 208
International Social Security Association, 95, 214
interpersonal comparison of utility, 21, 30
Ito, Takatoshi, 120, 125, 131, 213, 214

Iwaisako, Tokuo, 120, 214
James, Estelle, 87, 91, 94, 95, 214
Jao, Y.C., 77, 82, 214
Japan, 95, 99, 110, 112, 118, 119, 120, 121, 122, 123, 124, 125, 214, 216
jury, 13, 193
just society, 7, 11, 37, 38, 40, 41, 43, 44, 45, 46, 49, 53, 55, 167
justice, 12, 13, 15, 37-54, 71, 72, 74, 76, 95, 149, 156, 167, 168, 203, 204, 208
Kane, E.J., 83, 214
Keynes, John Maynard, 47, 48, 106, 111, 181, 214
Kindleberger, Charles P., 180, 214
Kotlikoff, Laurence J., 89, 211
Krueger, Alan, 164, 211
land-based revenues, 140
law and order, 4, 135, 141, 203
Law Society, 72, 73, 75
Lawrence, Emily C., 31, 215
learning, 20, 22, 24, 25, 26, 30, 35, 145, 148, 197
legal aid, 60, 71, 72, 73, 74, 75, 76
Legal Aid Board, 73, 75
leverage, 118, 179, 181, 182, 197, 206
life entrepreneurship, 26
life skills, 24, 25, 30, 33, 144
Long Term Capital Management, 207
longevity risks, 87, 88, 92, 94, 205
Lucas critique, 10
Maastricht Treaty, 136
Malaysia, 14, 89, 97, 184, 211
managed care, 59, 61
managed care model, 59
mandatory private provident fund, 14, 92, 94, 97
marginal cost pricing, 139, 161
market model, 59, 60, 61, 68
mass transit systems, 139
means test, 71, 72, 75, 91
Medicaid, 61, 69
Medicare, 61, 69
Medisave, 66, 69
mental bad, xii, 28, 33, 143, 145
mental capital, 24
mental good, 28, 29, 33, 34, 143, 145
merit test, 72, 75
Mexican peso crisis, 130
minimum wage, 12, 97, 164, 166
Miron, Jeffrey A., 137, 215
monetary policy, 15, 104, 106, 107, 108, 112, 113, 114, 126, 131, 207
Montgomery, John D., 130, 215
Musgrave, Richard A., 169, 215
National Committee of Inquiry into Higher Education, 143, 215
National Health Service, 59, 62, 68, 69, 215
natural rate of inflation, 104
natural rate of unemployment, 104, 207
negative income tax, 165
net creditor nation, 119
Nikkei Index, 119
Niskanen, William A., 59, 60, 68, 137, 216
Noguchi, Yukio, 95, 216
non-arbitrariness, 38, 45, 49
Office of Management of the Budget, 89
open market operation, 131, 197
opportunity cycle, 23
optimal degree of decentralization, 17
optimal size of government, 135
Papadimitriou, Dimitri B., 205, 216
Parieto risk efficiency, 54
pay-as-you-go, 87, 89, 90, 95, 97, 205
pegged exchange rate, 110, 125
perceived fulfillment attributes, 24
perceived household production functions, 24
Peregrine Investment Holdings, 123
personal development, x, 20, 25, 34
picoeconomics, 26
Pingle, Mark, 29, 35, 216
policy-by-discretion, 131
policy-by-rule, 131
possibility theorem, 41
pragmatism, 208
principle of availability of alternatives, 202, 204
principle of equal opportunity, 53
principle of fair and open competition, 202
principle of information cost minimization, 202
principle of insurance, 44
principle of residual risk reduction, 44
privatization, 87, 132, 139, 184, 196, 197
professional model, 59, 60, 62, 63, 68
Psacharopoulos, G., 143, 216
public housing, 121, 154, 155, 157, 158, 159, 184, 185, 186, 196, 197

racism, 33
rationality, xi, xii, 19, 28, 30, 32, 34, 37, 51, 52, 126
Rawls, John, xii, 37, 38, 39, 41, 42, 43, 47, 50, 51, 53, 55, 95, 97, 211, 215, 216
Rawlsian utility function, 54
real interest rate targeting, 107
real value unit of account, 99, 122
recession, 15, 18, 101, 104, 110, 111, 112, 115, 132, 176, 179, 180, 181, 183, 184, 185
redistribution, 2, 3, 12, 39, 44, 45, 53, 55, 74, 91, 92, 94, 96, 97, 133, 140, 163, 168, 169, 203, 209
representative individual, 7, 17, 23
residual risks, 43, 44, 49
Rickman, Neil, 73, 75, 213, 216
risk-related premiums, 81
risks, 2, 7, 17, 30, 34, 37, 39, 41, 43, 44, 49, 52, 53, 54, 57, 61, 75, 78, 81, 84, 88, 92-96, 99, 108, 114, 117, 123, 130, 168, 205, 206
Rockoff, Huge, 178, 182, 217
Rodrigo, G. Chris, 130, 216
rules of the game, 47
rules of thumb constraint to public spending, 141
Sachs, Jeffrey, 117, 118
Sah, Raaj, 29, 216
satiation fluctuation cycle, 23
satiation/attribute cycle, 31
Savings and Loans (S&L) crisis, 83
Scanlon, Tim, 27, 216
school curriculum, 144, 145
Schuler, Kurt, 131, 216
Seamless health care, 67
self-protection, 78, 79, 80, 82, 84, 130
Sen, Amartya K., 35, 41, 52, 54, 68, 215, 217
Shannon, David A., 177, 217
Shleifer, Andrei, 203, 217
Singapore, 4, 14, 66, 69, 89, 97, 154, 155, 156, 159, 184, 195, 198, 211
Sirkin, Gerald, 174, 217
size of the government, 135, 136, 138, 142
Smith, Adam, 19, 125, 178, 217
Smoot-Hawley Tariff Act, 181
social safety net, 54, 163
social security, ix, 6, 37, 51, 53, 87, 88, 135
social welfare function, xii, 11, 41, 42, 209
socially embedded preference, 35
Soros, George, 110, 112
South Korea, 184
sovereign risks, 123, 126
specie-flow-price mechanism, 180
speculation, 13, 107, 113, 130, 131, 171, 173, 174, 176, 178, 181, 182
Steady Safe, 123
sterling crisis, 207
Stern, Paul C., 35, 212
Stiglitz, Joseph, 115, 129, 132, 217
stock market crash, 99, 119, 126, 176, 177, 178, 179, 207
substantive democracy, 2, 135
substantive goods, 19, 21, 25, 27, 34
success, 4, 12, 22, 25, 46, 51, 54, 72, 75, 99, 109, 112, 114, 119, 121, 141, 145, 146, 156, 196, 197, 203, 208
Summers, Lawrence, 118
supply-side moral hazard, 62, 64, 72, 73
sweatshops, 202
Sweden, 65, 68, 95
systems perspective, 15, 144
Tenant Purchase Scheme, 132, 155, 186, 189, 194, 195
Thatcher, Margaret, 139
theory of surplus value, 46
Tittenbrun, Jacek, 139, 140, 217
transparency, 99, 107, 129, 130, 131, 132
true utility function, 20, 22, 24, 25, 26, 27, 29, 30, 35
unemployment insurance, 10, 168, 170
unemployment loans, 168
universal access principle, 66
universal fully funded pension, 89, 90, 91, 92, 93, 96
universal wage subsidy, 165, 166, 170
universality, 66, 75, 76, 205, 206
user pays principle, 80, 139
utilitarian utility, 22, 23, 26, 27
valorization accounts, 103
valun, 122
vicious circle, 30, 112
Vishny, Robert W., 203, 217
Volcker, Paul, 15, 112
von Neumann-Morgenstern, 28
wage subsidy, 164, 166, 167, 169

Walton, Gary M., 178, 182, 217
World Currency Unit (WCU), x, 122, 124, 132, 202, 214
Wray, L. Randall, 205, 216
Yugoslavia, 102
Zwiebel, Jeffrey, 137, 215

MIX
Papier aus verantwortungsvollen Quellen
Paper from responsible sources
FSC® C105338
FSC
www.fsc.org

If you have any concerns about our products,
you can contact us on
ProductSafety@springernature.com

In case Publisher is established outside the EU,
the EU authorized representative is:
Springer Nature Customer Service Center GmbH
Europaplatz 3, 69115 Heidelberg, Germany

Printed by Libri Plureos GmbH
in Hamburg, Germany